A SOCIAL HISTORY OF
ENGLISH MUSIC

STUDIES IN SOCIAL HISTORY

edited by

HAROLD PERKIN

Lecturer in Social History, University of Manchester

A SOCIAL HISTORY

OF

ENGLISH MUSIC

by

E. D. Mackerness

LONDON: Routledge and Kegan Paul
TORONTO: University of Toronto Press

First published 1964
in Great Britain by
Routledge and Kegan Paul Limited
and in Canada by
University of Toronto Press

Printed in Great Britain by
W. & J. Mackay & Co. Ltd., Chatham

© E. D. Mackerness 1964

Contents

Plates

vii

Preface

In this volume I have tried, without going over too much
familiar ground, to present a view of English musical history
which is supported by the evidence available to me. I do not
claim that my treatment of the subject is in any sense exhaustive,
or that it could not be handled in other ways. I have attempted
to see English music and musical customs in relation to significant social tendencies, my aim being to follow up the musical
consequences of the trends and movements I discuss. That something of this kind has already been done by more capable scholars
I should be the first to admit: nor do I deny that a good many
of the topics I have merely touched on in passing could, given a
few more years' research on my part, be fully and definitively
documented. But my aspirations have been comparatively
modest; I have simply hoped that here and there I may have
added something to what earlier writers have said: or at any
rate, that I may have placed certain things in a perspective which
will be of interest to the reader who is not primarily a musicologist.

Of the many friends who have assisted me in the composition
of this book I must mention two in particular—Charles Cudworth
and Reginald Nettel. Their encouragement and interest have
always been a source of pleasure to me: I only hope that what I
have written shows an adequate appreciation of their abundant
generosity over the years. From Harold Perkin, the editor of
this series, I have learned a great deal about the scope of social
history, and I must thank him for putting his expert knowledge
at my disposal. In different ways I have received valuable
counsel from Professor W. H. G. Armytage and Professor Sidney
Pollard, and at one stage Dr. Macdonald Emslie gave me
pertinent advice. The staffs of the Sheffield Central Reference
Library and the Sheffield University Library were unusually

PREFACE

considerate in meeting my demands: in the sphere of reference and bibliography I received essential help from J. A. B. Townsend of the Brotherton Library, University of Leeds, and from Leonard Duck, Librarian of the Henry Watson Library, Manchester. Several other librarians in different parts of the country responded promptly to my requests for specific information: I am glad to acknowledge such collaboration, particularly as it frequently involved quite detailed researches by people unknown to me.

Our Department Secretary, Mrs. I. W. Fawcett, came to my aid when I was preparing the manuscript for the press. I am, of course, solely responsible for the book in its final form. But in this connection I owe a considerable debt to my colleague W. E. Yuill, Senior Lecturer in German at the University of Sheffield. His wide experience of scholarship, research and publication has saved me from embarrassment on more than one occasion, and I record with gratitude the many hours we spent—mainly in the vicinity of Great Russell Street and Gordon Square—discussing this project in the various phases of its evolution.

E. D. MACKERNESS

Department of English,
The University,
Sheffield.

Introductory

THE social history of music first makes an appearance—even if only sporadically—in treatises which during the seventeenth and eighteenth centuries gave some account of the manners and morals of specific periods, and of these socio-historical writings one of the most comprehensive is Voltaire's *Siècle de Louis XIV* (1751). In the thirty-third chapter of that work the author writes: 'The arts which do not depend solely upon the intellect had made but little progress in France before the period which is known as the age of Louis XIV. Music was in its infancy; a few languishing songs, some airs for the violin, the guitar and the lute, composed for the most part in Spain, were all that we possessed. Lulli's style and technique were astonishing. He was the first in France to write bass counterpoint, middle parts and figures. At first some difficulty was experienced in playing his compositions, which now seem so easy and simple. At the present day there are a thousand people who know music, for one who knew it in the time of Louis XIII; and the art has been perfected by this spread of knowledge. Today, there is no great town which has not its public concerts: yet at that time Paris itself had none; the king's twenty-four violins comprised the sum total of French music.'

The key word in that passage is, of course, 'progress', and Voltaire's attitude is akin to that of Dryden when, in an address to the author of *The Double-Dealer* (1694), he hails William Congreve as a master dramatist sent into the world to rectify the tasteless errors of earlier playwrights. From a purely factual standpoint Voltaire's observations may fail to satisfy the

1

scholarly critic, but he has devoted at least one sentence of this cursory account to the specifically *social* history of music: 'At the present day there are a thousand people who know music, for one who knew it in the time of Louis XIII.' It would obviously be rash to draw significant conclusions from a single item such as this. All the same, Voltaire's very choice of topics points to the fact that he does not think of seventeenth-century music solely with reference to the outstanding performance of leading composers, and he is aware that musical expression is not entirely unrelated to social behaviour.

Voltaire's habit of uttering large generalizations in a tone of optimism with cynical undercurrents had some effect on the formal musical histories of the second half of the eighteenth century. In England two major works of this kind appeared almost simultaneously: Sir John Hawkins's *History of Music*, which was issued complete in 1776, and Charles Burney's *General History*, of which the first volume appeared in the same year. For a long time these writings were unsurpassed. Indeed, a recent critic has declared that at the opening of the nineteenth century 'Burney and Hawkins loomed so large that the history of music seemed to be a subject that had been exhausted.'[1] Both writers have their own peculiar virtues and shortcomings, but their interest for us lies in the fact that they paid a considerable amount of homage to the purely social history of music.

A careful selection of materials drawn from these two great source-books would yield a valuable social history of music up to the middle of the eighteenth century. But it is clear from Dr. Burney's working definition of music that his general point of view would not be altogether acceptable to the modern reader. 'Music', Burney writes, 'is an innocent luxury, unnecessary, indeed, to our existence, but a great improvement and gratification of the sense of hearing.' This definition could only have been drawn up in a society which had come to a tacit agreement that 'the arts' are to be regarded as an ornament to life, and are to a large extent the acquired property of suitably enlightened *cognoscenti*. On the face of it, Burney's description seems perfectly sane and reasonable. Yet a careful examination reveals its inadequacies. If man were an entirely rational creature, devoid of passions and unaccountable predilections, the notion of music as

---

[1] Warren Dwight Allen, *Philosophies of Music History* (1939), p. 85.

simply a 'great improvement and gratification of the sense of hearing' might be acceptable, but in ordinary conditions it is not. In the present state of existence, indeed, it is not too much to claim that music is very much a necessity of life in both civilized and uncivilized communities. Even the simplest social groups evolve—whether deliberately or not—distinctive musical traditions, and all sophisticated societies seem to have a strong inclination to establish their own characteristic preferences among possible patterns of sound. And though it may be argued that men can exist without music, just as they can exist without drama, poetry, or formalized recreation, experience has shown that a balanced and integrated social life inevitably produces its appropriate form of musical expression.

This, perhaps, is a truism, and most people would agree that there is a whole range of human experiences which seems incomplete without some kind of musical accompaniment. To Europeans, for instance, dancing without music—as performed by some primitive tribes—is quite unthinkable; and although café and restaurant orchestras are now less numerous than they were thirty years ago, the dissemination of canned music in many public eating-houses would argue that *Tafelmusik* still has an important part in our national life. The great majority of religious denominations make elaborate provision for music in worship, and many of the better-known hymns enjoy great popularity in purely secular contexts. Brass bands are always in demand at garden fêtes and other outdoor functions, and music is essential for the creation of certain types of 'atmosphere' as at weddings, funerals, Remembrance Day and during Christmas festivities. The social functions of music, in fact, are numerous and varied, and the main difficulty about Dr. Burney's definition is that it would seem to place a disproportionate value on what for want of a better name we must call 'art-music'—music composed with the intention of giving pleasure solely by virtue of its formal beauties. For art-music is, after all, only one branch of music as a whole, and we have no right to assume that it is necessarily superior in status to occasional or *Gebrauchsmusik*.

Throughout the ages the social value of music has been generally recognized. So much so that at certain periods historical writers have simply not considered it necessary to place on record the customs and attitudes which, as they thought, were too commonplace to mention. A case in point is that of the twelfth-century topographer Giraldus Cambrensis, whose *Description of Wales* is often quoted in histories of early English music. Giraldus's observations on part music (in his thirteenth chapter) are of the first importance, but they tell us rather less than they appear to do because Giraldus has not felt it necessary to supply the background information to illuminate his account 'Of their Symphonies and Songs'. Other writings are similarly inconclusive, and it has been left to the archaeologist and the musical palaeographer to piece together whatever is now known about the instruments and vocal ensembles of early times. Admittedly, savants like Burney and Jean-Jacques Rousseau have produced learned dissertations on the music of the pre-Christian and mediaeval epochs, but for the most part they drew their material from literary sources dating from the periods in question, and then engaged in speculation upon these. But they did not suppose that ancient Greek melodies or the 'mediaeval church modes' would be acceptable to the ears of their more enlightened contemporaries. Burney's distaste for most of the music written before the fifteenth century is, indeed, well known: from passages quoted by Franchinus and Thomas Morley he concluded that John Dunstable's melodies were 'very uncouth and unmeaning'. For Burney, in fact, mediaeval music (like mediaeval theory) had an existence on paper, but its habitual use of unpolished themes and inaccurate harmonies rendered it unsuitable for performance along with the masterpieces of Haydn and Pergolesi. Needless to say, more recent scholars have taken a different point of view. Thanks to the labours of men like Barclay Squire and Arnold Dolmetsch it is now possible for us to adopt a less strictly antiquarian attitude towards the remoter periods than was inevitable a hundred and fifty years ago.

It is only fair, however, to acknowledge that from the social historian's standpoint some parts of Burney's *General History* are unusually generous in their treatment of the subject (the same is true, to a less extent, of Hawkins's *History*). His account of minstrelsy, for instance, is extremely full: and when treating of the sixteenth and seventeenth centuries he gives a great deal of attention to the musical profession. In the later sections of his work we find Burney displaying one or two traits which subsequent writers on music developed more exhaustively than he did. Like his friend Samuel Johnson, Burney was a biographer of some distinction. This aspect of his writings has not hitherto received much recognition, though many of the short bio-graphical sketches which he contributed to Abraham Rees's *Cyclopedia* would have done no discredit to Johnson himself. It was after Burney's time that the private lives of the great composers came to have a particular fascination for those interested in music. Handel, as we know, was the subject of many pane-gyrics both before and after his death in 1759, but Edward Holmes's *Life of Mozart* (1845) was perhaps the first fully documented character-study in English of a universally cele-brated foreign master. Of Beethoven and Schubert it might almost be said that too many personal details are known, and in the case of Wagner and Tschaikovski there is an overwhelming mass of private records. Since the early days of the romantic movement we can observe an increasing tendency on the part of the 'musical public' to idolize composers and to set them apart from the rest of mankind. One consequence of this has been the habit of conceiving musical history largely in terms of dominant personalities.

Like drama, music has a tendency to give rise to ephemeral chatter and trivial anecdotes. During the nineteenth century a whole literature sprang up for the purpose of satisfying the curiosity of a rather special kind of reader. The type of thing represented by, say, William Bingley's *Musical Biography* (1814) and Thomas Busby's *Concert-Room Anecdotes* (1825) is not likely to have more than a marginal interest for the social historian. Fortunately, in musicological matters there are other ways of communicating a sense of historical relationship; and one of the commonest ways of doing this is through the study of musical form. In this case, the personal inclinations of the com-poser carry less weight than do the particular innovations he may have inaugurated. It is not our business to trace the stages by which, shall we say, simple dance measures such as the passa-caille and the minuet developed into movements which could be incorporated in symphonic compositions: nor need we dwell on the functions of expositions, *stretti*, canonic variations and fugal development. The laboured investigation of form as an end in itself may easily become as tedious as the discussion of 'temperamental' peculiarities. All the same, it must be conceded that some knowledge of the principles on which musical compositions are designed is a prerequisite to sensitive discrimination. Form, it can be argued, has its value as exercising (within an historical context) the comparative faculty. For a person who is capable of perceiving aurally the difference between a fugue by Sweelinck and one by Bach will have arrived at a kind of musical knowledge which no amount of factual information about the composer's personal idiosyncrasies can supply. Or, to put it another way: there is some point in stressing that a familiarity with one or two characteristic overtures by Lulli may very well enhance our appreciation of Handel's instrumental sinfonias.

Related to the subject of musical form is that of interpretation. Ideally, a full and detailed musical score contains explicit directions as to how the music itself must sound: it represents the composer's intentions in their totality. But the composer, however skilful he may be in the craft of composition, can do very little through the agency of mere notation to offset the limitations imposed by conditions of performance. 'Klemperer's Beethoven', as is well known, differs from 'Beecham's Beethoven', though in what ways we will not enquire. Instead we will note the significance of a situation in which it is possible for a number of different 'readings' to have gained currency. This consideration may perhaps appear to have little connection with the social history of music. Yet it would be wrong to claim that there is such a thing as an entirely *right* performance of any known composition: for every performer or group of performers imposes at some stage nuances and stylistic variants which the composer himself did not envisage. Only a wholly mechanical rendering could entirely eliminate this uncertainty, and it may be that electronic composition has moved in this direction. Most people, however, would agree that a large part of the enjoyment of music arises from the very existence of the discrepancies we have just mentioned; and the possibility of an exact correspondence between what was *intended* and what is actually realized in sound would probably rule out the existence of a specifically musical taste. This in turn would have its effect on the social relationships which music calls into being.

On the other hand, in order to guard against reckless improvisation in the concert room it is necessary to discover as much as possible about the conventions which governed the performance of music at the time when it was composed. In the days of Corelli, for instance, music for a solo violin was elaborately decorated with ornaments which the player added (usually from memory) to the printed notation. The score served as a simple indication of the composition's main melodic features, and it was left to the violinist to apply to the melody itself figures which would enhance its original beauty. But this practice of 'gracing' was by no means arbitrary: for it was essential that its harmonic tendencies should not run counter to those of the movement as a whole. A twentieth-century violinist, trained to respect other conventions of performance than those which prevailed in the seventeenth century, might well regard Corelli's Opus 5 (1700) as a comparatively unsubtle collection of sonatas; but when it is borne in mind that during Corelli's lifetime an executant would be judged on his ability not merely to play the notes in front of him but also to produce tasteful ornaments, the importance of interpretative knowledge becomes clear. And this is also applicable to developments in the sphere of keyboard writing, solo song, and orchestral scoring.

II

What we have called interpretation is frequently influenced by conditions which are not, in the first place, of a musical nature. Turning from instrumental to vocal virtuosity we may mention the case of the *castrati*, since they figure in most musical histories. It was the intervention of humanitarian sentiment which put an end to the barbarous practice of emasculating young boys so as to produce adult male treble voices; but their absence from the European musical scene since the early part of the nineteenth century explains why some of the music which was popular in the time of Domenico Scarlatti and J. C. Bach has never been revived. The *castrati* are perhaps a somewhat exceptional phenomenon, and less drastic changes than those which brought about their disappearance can occasionally be seen to have an effect on other aspects of interpretation. There are fashions in music just as in other things. One of the most interesting was the craze for flute-playing which arose in the eighteenth century. Yet why, we may ask, did the recorder and the flageolet fall into disuse after their considerable popularity in the seventeenth century? Partly because the German flute, which superseded them, has a more self-assertive tone-quality which, together with its wider range of notes (particularly in chromatic scale passages), could hardly fail to appeal to performers and composers. Apart from this, though, the keyed flute would never have reached the standard of development it had attained by 1800 if mechanical craftsmanship had not made it possible for delicate adjustments to be applied to the fittings used on flute barrels. The same thing, of course, is true in respect of other wood-wind instruments.

Yet we must not conclude that mechanical inventions are necessarily an unqualified advantage to the musician. Most modern string players would agree that the violin bow fitted with an adjustable 'frog' is a far less clumsy object to handle than the bow which was commonly in use in the time of Vivaldi and Geminiani. It need hardly be said that the older type of bow, with its high arched stick and loose hairs, is out of place in the performance of contemporary music. Yet there exists a school of thought which maintains that 'contrapuntal' violin music, such as the unaccompanied Sonatas of Bach, can only be properly played with the less delicately fashioned 'Bach' bow, the hairs of which are tightened or relaxed at the will of the player. It is now generally agreed that Baroque keyboard music is not heard to best advantage on the modern pianoforte, despite the fact that subtle gradations of tone can be obtained from it. The reaction in favour of the clavichord and harpsichord is now accomplished. But when performing music of the pre-classical era many concert pianists are put to the necessity of imitating harpsichord tone on an instrument which invites a different kind of touch.

These, then, are a few of the considerations which writers on musical history are obliged to take into account. They have been discussed so as to suggest the extent to which questions of 'technique' occupy the attention of musicologists. There are, of course, some perfectly good reasons for this. In music it is comparatively easy for a tolerable creative talent to produce work that is competently derivative, but it is very difficult indeed for a composer to evolve a personal idiom. Because of this, critics are inclined to give a good deal of serious attention to the manner in which a composer confronts his particular 'problems'. Consequently—since the Renaissance especially—the stylistic peculiarities of the different composers (and schools of composers) have assumed a great significance. The temptation to idolize the composer himself is a fairly recent development; but it has been such as to prevent some critics and historians from visualizing a situation in which the claims of the composer, and to a lesser degree those of the performer, may be secondary to those of the listener. Even now, some people whose capacity for musical 'appreciation' is beyond dispute have difficulty in realizing that the presence of a well-known composer's name on a piece of music does not guarantee greatness; or, conversely, that a wholly anonymous composition, produced under circumstances where authorship was considered immaterial, may well have some of the attributes of genius.

III

To pursue this question further would involve us in a discussion of aesthetics; at this stage, however, some consideration must be given to the scope of music in its larger relationship with social history. Music, as has been said, has virtually no existence until it has become a shared experience between the composer-performer and the audience. There may, indeed, be composers who write music solely for their own private satisfaction: but they are few in number. The great majority normally have some kind of performance in mind when embarking on the labour of composition, and in most cases a definite demand prompts their designs. Before the nineteenth century nearly all music was produced in response to a request from some kind of patron, private or public. But the nature of the composer's contract is only partly the concern of the social historian. He is more interested in the steps taken by the various classes of society in order to satisfy the taste for music, which seems to be fairly widespread at all times. For though the capacity to assimilate the more highly developed forms of musical invention is necessarily limited by the opportunities of education and environment, the power to enjoy some kind of musical experience appears to be present in all men and women who are not afflicted with a total insensitivity to tonal stimuli. (What is commonly called 'tone-deafness' is, incidentally, a phenomenon of a different kind.)

Unfortunately for the social historian, a great deal of all music-making is quite informal, and this may mean that it leaves behind little palpable evidence. For this reason deductions have to be made from extraneous sources such as diaries, letters, journals and public records. Samuel Pepys's tastes in music are well known, as are the observations of his friend John Evelyn. Other writers are in the habit of making helpful disclosures. Thus Daniel Defoe, in his account of Bath, tells us that 'the musick plays (the visitor) into the bath',[1] indicating that as early as 1726 a form of 'utility' music was well established at a centre afterwards renowned for its concert enterprises. Occasionally pictorial representations provide us with useful information we might otherwise be unable to come by: painters like Zoffany, Gainsborough and some of the Pre-Raphaelites have left portraits of players, singers and their audiences. In churches and cathedrals, again, there are many wood and stone carvings of mediaeval instruments. These enable us to derive a very good idea of the different classes of instruments actually in use at various periods. What they do not help us to decide, however, is the exact manner in which such instruments were tuned—or what it felt like to play them in the manner depicted. How, for instance, did a woman of ordinary physique manage the twenty-string lute such as Arabella Hunt is shown holding in Kneller's famous picture? And how in any case did the performer keep such a huge instrument in tune? Then again, how did players of an earlier period endure the uncomfortable postures adopted by string players when violins were held below the shoulders and 'cellos were balanced (without any support) between the knees?

Instruction books are of considerable help as historical evidence. But it sometimes happens that accounts of musical activities are not available for periods when we would most like to have them. True, we are able to turn to writings like the *Memoirs* of Roger North, the letters of Thomas Twining and the private papers of Edward Fitzgerald. But it does not follow that the reminiscences and diaries of amateur musicians are always of the highest relevance. This is not, of course, to deny the great importance of the amateur; but the social history of music involves much more than a study of the cults which arise from the pursuit of specialized pleasures. The tastes of the inarticulate

[1] D. Defoe, *A Tour Through England and Wales* (Everyman ed.), II.34.

masses also have a claim on our attention, and to satisfy our-
selves on this head we need to consult material of a more public
nature than some of the specifically literary items just mentioned.

IV

It remains for us now to indicate a few of the topics which
seem to call for particular attention in a social history of music.
These will not necessarily be of equal importance in all periods;
but whatever approach we adopt, we shall find that some considerations naturally take precedence over others. First of all we
must keep constantly in mind the great number of activities—
religious services, the drama, dancing and civic celebration—
with which music is commonly associated. Music takes its place
in Christian observance as a consequence of direct Biblical injunction: but it soon came to have much more than a strictly
devotional significance. Songs and instrumental pieces are not,
indeed, essential to drama; yet the incidental importance of
music in the theatre is generally acknowledged, even when it
does not have a 'textural' relevance, as in many of Shakespeare's
plays. As for dancing, there can be no question but that music has
very subtle psychological associations with the dance, quite apart
from its purely rhythmical function. And much the same thing
applies in respect of corporate festivities: music has for centuries
been an effective agent for inducing 'group solidarity'—
whether the occasion be the Peace of Aix-la-Chapelle, the opening of the Manchester Ship Canal, or the Cup Final at Wembley.

We must not forget that the great majority of people regard
music as a form of entertainment—and indeed as only one form
of entertainment among many. This affects our outlook materially when we come to investigate the way in which musical taste
is manifested in different periods. For it is evident that the desire
for entertainment and the capacity to obtain it are greatly
affected by various social movements, great and small. In this
connection it is fairly obvious that English music has been
greatly influenced by the results of such phenomena as the
Reformation, the Industrial Revolution and the development of
popular education. Such topics as these are too momentous for
summary treatment. But of the Industrial Revolution it may be
said that the 'increasing accumulation of men in cities' of which

Wordsworth spoke in 1798 induced a craving for other kinds of distraction than the literary diversions the poet censures in the Preface to the *Lyrical Ballads*. On the purely technological side we may perhaps point out that without the application of mechanical inventions to the manufacture of instruments, a good many of the tone colours we now take for granted (those, for instance, of the modern organ, the concert grand piano and the brass ensemble) could not have been produced. Nor, incidentally, would a number of the well-established institutions which collectively help to make up our current musical life. The importance of music in mass education was given recognition long before 1870, but it is instructive to find a generally unmusical observer such as Matthew Arnold commenting, in his capacity as a Government Inspector of Schools, on the virtues of music as a trustworthy discipline of intelligence.[1]

There are other branches of English life with which music maintains a connection: of these we may perhaps mention philanthropy, sport and advertising. As Constant Lambert remarked in *Music Ho!* (1934), music has 'an odd way of reflecting not only the emotional background of an age but also its physical conditions'.[2] It is the social historian's business to ascertain the nature of this reflection, and to interpret it in terms which are acceptable to both the musicologist and the student of society itself. If he can do this with any degree of completeness he stands a chance of being in a position to make 'the spirit of the age' something more than a mere abstraction.

[1] See F. S. Marvin, ed., *Reports on Elementary Schools, 1852–1882, By Matthew Arnold* (1908), p. 148.

[2] Constant Lambert, *Music Ho! A Study of Music in Decline* (1942 ed.), p. 163.

I

Music and Society in the Middle Ages

THE music of the mediaeval period was dominated by one important characteristic: it was closely linked to specific non-musical social functions. The notion of music as an 'absolute' form of art is a comparatively recent one. To the mediaeval mind such a thing as a concert, at which large numbers of people collect together for the purpose of listening attentively to the singing and playing of others, would have seemed strange. For up to the seventeenth century music had its value in so far as it served activities other than itself. From woodcuts and pictorial records we do, indeed, occasionally derive the impression that informal recitals were not entirely unknown before the later Renaissance, and no doubt there were in the Middle Ages, as now, performers who prided themselves on their virtuosity. But generally speaking such considerations were subordinated to ends over which the individual was not called upon to exercise much discretion. In considering the music of the pre-Reformation era, therefore, we must examine its association with religion, communal festivity and the dance.

I

The early Christian missionaries to Britain disseminated in this country some knowledge of the liturgical music which for centuries before the time of St. Augustine had been cultivated among Christian communities owing allegiance to Rome. The Anglo-Saxons were certainly not an unmusical people; at the time of their 'migration' they brought with them choral hymns, death lays, bridal songs and battle chants, and they had developed many different kinds of instruments.[1] But it was appropriate, from our point of view, that St. Augustine should be the man chosen to attempt a general conversion of Britain to Christianity, since he had worked directly under the supervision of Pope Gregory and had been trained to revere the Gregorian chant. The litany 'for the eternal salvation both of themselves and those for whose sake they had come' which St. Augustine and his followers sang before King Ethelbert in April 597 may not have been an exact rehearsal of the music commonly heard in St. Peter's, Rome, for St. Augustine adopted elements of the Gallic liturgy when this suited his purpose. But the music of the Roman rite was gradually accepted by those who embraced the Christian faith in England, and teachers of plainsong were sent out to various parts of the country. Bede, in his *Ecclesiastical History*, makes particular mention of James the Deacon, Paulinus's disciple at York, who 'began to teach many people to sing the music of the Church after the Uses of Rome and Canterbury'.[2] He also speaks of John, the Arch-Cantor of the Apostolic See, who visited England in 680 primarily for the purpose of giving instruction in liturgical chant after the Roman fashion. Near-contemporaries noted for their musical gifts included Bishop Wilfrid (634–709), who developed Gregorian chant at Ripon, and Bishop Putta, who after being deprived of his see at Rochester when that city was sacked by Aethilred, King of Mercia, in 676 acted as a peripatetic teacher of music. From Canterbury itself, the first great centre of Christian culture in the south, came Maban, whose work as a cantor at Hexham Abbey is also spoken of by Bede.

The importance of music in day-to-day worship was given widespread recognition during the centuries which followed the Northumbrian supremacy in 613. Its place in church affairs was frequently discussed at the various synods held from time to time. The second council of Clovesho (747), for example, issued a proclamation 'De Sanctae Psalmodiae Utilitate'[3] which can be

[1] See F. M. Padelford, *Old English Musical Terms* (Bonn, 1899), *passim*.

[2] Bede, *History of the English Church and People* (trans. Leo Sherley-Price, 1955), p. 137.

[3] Translated in H. Gee and W. J. Hardy, *Documents Illustrative of English Church History* (1896), pp. 28–30.

paralleled in earlier pontifical utterances, and similar statements were forthcoming on later occasions. As Gregorian settings became more widely known the office of cantor in religious establishments assumed a great significance, and instruction on the *schola cantorum* principle spread a knowledge of liturgical tradition among the novices who proposed to enter upon a religious life. The musical medium used for the Catholic ritual was plainsong.

As the name implies, plainsong (*cantus planus*) is an arrangement of simple sounds intended to give vocal expression to the accepted phraseology of the Roman service. It is entirely monodic and does not stand in need of an accompaniment. This is not to deny that now and then it may have been supported by instruments; organs are found in this country as early as the ninth and tenth centuries, and they were probably used to keep the singers in tune. In a sense, plainsong may be regarded as a kind of 'heightened speech'; but although it follows to some extent the rhythm of spoken Latin, it clearly uses musical intervals and an appropriate alternation of long and short note values in order to give the words themselves an evocative quality which *recited* words alone cannot create. Plainsong melodies do not follow the patterns with which the music of the classical and romantic periods has made us familiar. But this does not mean that their structure is in any way *ad hoc*. On the contrary, at its best plainsong is characterized by a judicious unfolding of musical phrases which rise and fall, halt or progress according to the dictates of the liturgical text.

Some modern scholars claim for plainsong a kind of unearthly beauty which harmonized music does not attain. Cecil Gray, for instance, speaks of the 'remote, magical, and disembodied quality' of the simple unisonal chants;[1] and Dom David Knowles sees in plainsong a form of utterance 'wide in its range of emotional expression, majestic, spiritual and austere beyond all other forms of the art'.[2] Plainsong is, it must be confessed, a form of musical language which seems peculiarly pure and self-contained. Yet it is questionable whether many congregations in the early Middle Ages heard it in anything like the perfection it has achieved when performed under the direction of the monks of Solesmes.

[1] Cecil Gray, *The History of Music* (1928), p. 24.
[2] David Knowles, *The Monastic Order in England* (1940), p. 546.

The disturbed state of the English Church before the twelfth century makes it improbable that full musical settings of the Mass were very common outside the walls of the monasteries and larger churches. Until the time of St. Dunstan (925–88) attempts to establish monasticism at all widely in Britain were again and again defeated. Consequently the Benedictine revival of the tenth century itself was an occurrence which had important consequences for the social history of music.

The establishment of secure and well-organized monastic establishments all subscribing to an accepted *rule* of life meant that the divine Office of the Church was given perpetual observance in many different localities. The Mass alone provides ample scope for musical performance, consisting as it does of an invariable framework (the 'Ordinary') to which other segments are added as occasion demands. But under the Rule of St. Benedict, the Office—which has extensive musical requirements—dominated the whole of monastic existence and ensured that musical offerings to the Deity would be made every day of the year. The importance of this particular Rule in the cultural history of Europe can hardly be overestimated, since, in the words of J. M. Ure, 'it contains the liturgical service, the *opus Dei*, which was enjoined upon the monks as a duty over which nothing was to take precedence'.[1] In its completest form the Office grew from the desire, shared by many of the early Christians, that the Psalms and other scriptural matter should be given regular vocal expression. There have been many accounts of the asceticism to which the Benedictine discipline gave rise in its devotion to this ideal; but some notion of its demands in the specifically musical sphere can be gathered from the *Regularis Concordia*, a manual compiled during the reign of King Edgar (959–75).

The *Regularis Concordia* sets out the way of life which the Benedictine monks of certain religious houses in the south of England were expected to follow; it describes also the customs they were to observe in respect of dress, food and personal behaviour. Full instructions are given as to how the Canonical hours are to be celebrated, and the special arrangements for the major festivals of the Christian year are detailed. Thus on Ash Wednesday, after the office of *None* has been performed, the Abbot blesses the ashes and then lays them on each brother's

[1] J. M. Ure, *The Benedictine Office* (1957), p. 58.

16

head; the brethren immediately commence the antiphon *Exaudi nos Domine* 'with the Psalm *Salvum me fac Deus* . . . the *Gloria*, *Kyrie eleison*, *Pater Noster*, the psalm *Deus misereatur nostri, preces* and collect. They shall then proceed whithersoever they should (i.e. to other churches), singing the antiphons which are in the Antiphonar. When they have reached the church to which they are bound, they shall again pray awhile and then, after the antiphon of the saint, the psalm *Ad te levavi oculos*, the *preces* and the collect, they shall there begin the Litany and return to the Mother church where the Mass shall be celebrated as usual.'[1] Similar stipulations are laid down for Christmas Day and Easter Day, the latter being distinguished by very elaborate chanting. No doubt the Rule was not strictly adhered to in all places where it was professed, but a rigid observance of the liturgical requirements as outlined in the *Regularis Concordia* obliged all the brothers to memorize the entire psalter as well as a great deal more musical material such as hymns, introits, antiphons and so forth. This exposition of the Benedictine Rule enables us to form an adequate idea of the considerable quantity of music performed in monastic houses which adopted this particular mode of existence. Other rules, of course, exhibit variations on this scheme of life. A particularly interesting example is that followed by the sisters of St. Clare (Clarisses or Franciscan 'Minoresses'), as detailed in the fifteenth-century Bodleian MS. 585, composed for a convent near Aldgate, just outside the City of London wall.

Only a fraction of the population, naturally, spent their lives in monasteries; and, in any case, not all monastic houses were open for general worship. According to Sir Frank Stenton, the influence of the Benedictine revival on the parochial clergy was 'direct and strong'.[2] Yet it is difficult to trace this into parish life itself and to determine the part played by the laity in early mediaeval church services. They were free to join in parts of the Mass; and in theory the principle of responsorial chanting gave them an established position in the celebration as a whole. Yet the fact that the Mass—when sung at all—was celebrated exclusively in Latin must have made active participation impossible for most of the congregation. However this may have been, a knowledge of the Gregorian idiom was assimilated by countless

---

[1] Thomas Symons, ed., *Regularis Concordia* . . . (1953), pp. 32, 33.
[2] F. M. Stenton, *Anglo-Saxon England* (1943), p. 450.

generations of worshippers who could not conceive of devotional music in any other form. It has been persuasively maintained that scraps of plainsong were incorporated in some English folk songs, and there is a strong possibility that lay brethren may have helped to bring this about by dissociating the plainsong melodies from their sacred context. A good many of the un-attached minstrels in the pre-Conquest period were probably younger men who had become dissatisfied with a religious life and taken to a nomadic existence.[1]

Although due respect was paid to the hallowed corpus of Gregorian themes, it must not be supposed that church music was entirely bound down by the contents of the original rubrics. Means were, in fact, devised quite early in the Middle Ages whereby plainsong melodies came to be distended and variegated in a very ingenious way. One method was to draw out the last syllable of the word 'alleluia' in order to insert extra notes which collectively made up what was termed a sequence. Another practice was, in the words of Daniel Rock, 'that of weaving certain pious sentences, called by the Romans "festive praises", by the Franks "tropes", between the words of the psalm in the introit at mass, as well as all through the *Gloria in excelsis*, the *Sanctus*, and the *Agnus Dei*'.[2] For example, to the concluding words of the Mass ('*Ite, missa est*', pronounced by the celebrant and followed by the response '*Deo Gratias*' from the congregation) a monk at the Abbey of St. Gall added the following inter-polation:

ITE nunc in pace, spiritus sanctus super vos sit, iam MISSA EST.
DEO semper laudes agite, in corde gloriam et GRATIAS.

On this particular trope Karl Young comments: 'This meagre example . . . discloses sufficiently well the central intention of all these liturgical embellishments. Their purpose is to adorn the liturgical text, to enforce its meaning, and to enlarge its emotional appeal.'[3] The existence of fully-written-out tropers containing these additions to the basic Gregorian foundation confirms that such accretions were countenanced by authority— until such time, that is, as the Papacy was forced to prohibit some

---

[1] See E. K. Chambers, *The Mediaeval Stage* (1903), I. 42 *et seq.*
[2] Daniel Rock, *The Church of our Fathers* (1849–53), III. (Part 2, 1853), p. 21.
[3] Karl Young, *The Drama of the Mediaeval Church* (1933), I. 178.

of the irrelevancies introduced. And the presence of tropers among the service books is evidence of a desire on the part of church musicians to break away from the bonds of custom and to adopt—especially in the case of the dialogue tropes, which will be referred to later—a rudimentary form of self-expression within the framework of an otherwise stylized mode of worship.

II

'Hardly ever before or since', writes A. W. Clapham, 'has a national culture been so easily, so rapidly, or so completely submerged as was the Anglo-Saxon in the last thirty years of the eleventh century.'[1] During its early stages, indeed, the Norman invasion was as ferocious as the Danish incursions of an earlier period. Historians tend to dwell on the constructive energies of the Norman settlers and to neglect their arrogance and rapacity. 'Assimilated they were in time,' says H. R. Loyn, 'but the process did not approach completion till the age of the Plantagenet Edwards.'[2] The gradual imposition of Gallic culture which transformed Anglo-Saxon England had important musical consequences. The great secular cathedrals and collegiate churches founded in the period after the Conquest made provision for a full musical rendering of the liturgy and this was subjected to many foreign influences. At Salisbury, for instance, which was closely modelled on the Cathedral of Bayeux, St. Osmund in his Customary of 1091 (revised by Bishop Poore in the early thirteenth century) laid down the duties of a Chancellor and Chanter in a manner which emphasized their responsibilities as tutors to the novices and as custodians of cathedral documents—including, of course, the service books in daily use. St. Osmund's predecessor, Thurstan, had attempted to introduce a style of liturgical chanting which the monks themselves did not approve of; for this he was eventually relieved of his post and sent back to Normandy. St. Osmund doubtless had this incident in mind when drawing up his Customary.

Well before the Norman Conquest the Church had made itself responsible for the education of adolescents in grammar, writing

[1] A. W. Clapham, *English Romanesque Architecture After the Conquest* (1934), p. 1.
[2] H. R. Loyn, *Anglo-Saxon England and the Norman Conquest* (1962), p. 315.

and music. But up to the time of the Reformation the Song Schools maintained an independent existence; they were training establishments at which children were taught 'the elements of their faith, the *Ave Maria*, the Lord's Prayer, and the Creed, a few anthems and psalms, singing and spelling'.[1] After the Conquest the importance of the Song Schools increased, for great skill in reading music was now necessary to ensure adequate performance of the polyphonic settings which came to be used in the larger monastic and secular establishments. How and when polyphony first arose will always be a matter for conjecture. But it should be borne in mind that conditions in mediaeval religious houses were favourable to a certain amount of musical innovation. Not only does constant repetition invite determined deviation from the habitual melodic lines, but when individuals with different voice ranges are singing together there is bound to be a fair degree of 'natural' harmonization. Plainsong is unisonal; but unless special care is taken in the performance of vocal music, some voices will feel the necessity of coming to rest at, say, a third or a sixth below or above the concluding tone. Admittedly, plainsong itself moves within a fairly narrow compass. All the same, before a male voice has actually 'settled', there are occasions on which it seeks relief in unpremeditated consonances. For this reason some elementary types of harmonization must always have been known among church musicians such as we have been discussing. 'Organized' plainsong was heard at Ramsay Abbey as early as 991.[2]

The deliberate exploitation of harmonic effects is, of course, a different matter from casual and accidental harmonization. The practice known as parallel organum—doubling of melodic lines at the interval of the fourth or fifth—presupposes a fairly accurate means of setting the pitch of notes and also of indicating sound and note values accurately. This subject formed part of the study of *musica practica*, which early mediaeval scholars distinguished from *musica specualativa*, a branch of learning drawn from the writings of Martianus Capella, Cassiodorus and, in particular, Boethius (481–525), whose *De institutione musica*

---

[1] G. R. Potter, 'Education in the Fourteenth and Fifteenth Centuries' in *The Cambridge Mediaeval History*, VIII. 689. See also Nan Cooke Carpenter, *Music in the Mediaeval and Renaissance Universities* (Norman, Oklahoma, 1958), pp. 337–48.

[2] Knowles, *The Monastic Order in England*, p. 559, n.

served as a valuable source book for mediaeval theorists in many parts of Europe. English musicians studied practical music at various seminaries abroad and consequently took over the systems of notation in use there; by such agencies foreign methods of performance were introduced into this country. In France there arose schools of composers attached to the more famous churches and cathedrals; their work merged with that of English musicians, with the result that there was a continuous traffic in musical ideas between the two countries. By 1400 this interchange was such as to confuse later musicologists: for in the great mass of documents which still survive from the tenth century onwards it is no uncommon thing to find a fragment of a *Kyrie* trope composed for, say, Worcester Cathedral forming part of the service music used in an abbey in Brittany; or an introit from Notre Dame being sung at one of the cathedrals in southern England. So many religious houses stood in filial relationship with conventual establishments in northern France that this sort of overlapping is not to be wondered at.

Here mention must be made of an institution which eventually influenced the work of English composers considerably—the Chapel Royal. In creating a body of vocalists whose main duty was to sing Mass in the royal presence, English kings were emulating foreign court practice. 'It seems certain', writes Frank Harrison, 'that the development of the music of the Royal Household Chapel under the early Lancastrian kings owed much to the French idea of the manner in which a great Christian ruler should order his daily and festal observances.'[1] But though the Chapel Royal flourished brilliantly in the fourteenth and fifteenth centuries, its origins go back as far as the reign of Henry I (1100–35). The *Red Book of the Exchequer* gives details of the Royal Chapel about the year 1135 itself,[2] and there are several references in the following reigns.[3] Edward III, as is well known, was a liberal patron of musicians: Letters Patent confirm that he gave his consent to the continued existence of a Royal Chapel in 1351.

The later records of the Chapel Royal are very full, especially

---

[1] Frank Ll. Harrison, *Music in Mediaeval Britain* (1958), p. 223.
[2] Hubert Hall, ed., *The Red Book of the Exchequer* (1896), Part III, p. 807.
[3] See W. H. Grattan Flood, 'The Beginnings of the Chapel Royal' in *Music and Letters*, V. (1924), p. 85.

after about 1450. But before dealing with the later Middle Ages we must give further consideration to some features of religious music from the eleventh to the fourteenth century. For one thing, the practice of troping as mentioned above was not the only device by which musicians strove to embellish plainsong. The advent of rudimentary counterpoint suggested other means of treating the underlying melodic material of the liturgy. For instance, the different sections of a single item could be set to more than one voice; the principle of antiphony might be subjected to various forms of development, the soloist alternating with the choir more frequently than was usual in traditional responsorial chanting. 'Free' organum introduced the habit of contrary motion, while the rhythmical schemes of the Office hymns followed a more regular outline than is usually found in plainsong itself. In accordance with the tendency to elaborate the ceremonial aspects of worship, church musicians were called upon to provide short pieces of music for special events such as an ordination, a funeral or the visit of a bishop. A simple example of this is the *conductus*. From its earliest days the Church attached great importance to processions; these in time produced their own musical repertoire. When, at Mass, the priests were proceeding from the choir steps to the altar, the choir sang a composition intended to 'conduct' them on their way. This, obviously, had to be in a fairly simple rhythm; it was usually in triple time and was distinguished from the Mass music as a whole in that it was not necessarily within the Gregorian tradition. Another type of composition which came into favour under French influence was the Motet. The history of musical forms is not really our concern, but since the Motet is, in a sense, a kind of 'concert' music, it may be noted here. It was, in fact, a superaddition to the Mass (usually sung instead of or immediately after the Offertorium) which developed from the 'clausulae' or short harmonized passages based on plainsong melodies. In the later Middle Ages a distinguishing feature of the Motet was that it frequently made use of secular—not to say profane—words.

In the exclusively religious sphere, mediaeval belief and custom gave rise to a great deal of musical activity. The 'Middle Ages' covers a long period, and no account can really do justice to the meticulous care with which, in hundreds of churches, cathedrals and monastic foundations, the liturgy was given regular performance. We must not, of course, romanticize this aspect of mediaeval life, for not every worshipper was as single-minded in rendering the *Alma redemptoris* as was Chaucer's 'litel clergeon' who is the subject of the Prioress's Tale. Between the tenth and the fourteenth century, indeed, there are indications that although a good many church musicians continued their work in a spirit of sobriety, there were others who took the opportunity of making alterations in the service music and of adding improvisations designed to show off their talents. The testimony of two twelfth-century writers, John of Salisbury and Aelred of Rievaulx, has frequently been quoted in this connection ever since they were mentioned together in William Prynne's *Histriomastix* (1633). Both writers raised objections to the over-elaborate nature of church music, John of Salisbury in his *Polycraticus* and Aelred in the *Speculum Caritatis*.[1] Speaking of the singers' facility in running up and down the scale, John of Salisbury mentions the custom of clashing the voices together, 'while, in all this, the high or even the highest notes of the scale are so mingled with the lower or lowest, that the ears are almost deprived of their power to distinguish'. This comment reveals a certain amount of astonishment that such an effect can be obtained. Aelred's more rhetorical criticisms also are aimed at the manner of performance rather than at the substance of the music heard. But the gestures and contortions which he finds so objectionable imply the use of cross-rhythms as well as an ambitious accompaniment; he deplores the fact that the common people are drawn to admire 'the sound of the Organs, the noyse of the Cymballs and Musicall instruments, the harmony of the Pipes and Cornets'. To Aelred all this seems inconsistent with pure devotion. As Dr. Harman observes, allowances have to be made for the Puritanical fervour of Aelred's seventeenth-century translator; yet the tenor of the original is what one might expect from a member of the austere Cistercian order. The passage in the *Speculum Caritatis* is interesting on several counts. In the first place, Aelred is concerned because church music as he knows

---

[1] Quoted in Alec Harman, *Mediaeval and Early Renaissance Music* (1958), p. 69; for a more recent version of Aelred's 'The Pleasures of Hearing' see *The Mirror of Charity: The Speculum Caritatis of St. Aelred of Rievaulx*, translated and arranged by Geoffrey Webb and Adrian Walker (1962), p. 72.

it seems to have departed from its primitive simplicity; secondly, he is disturbed by those who 'under the shew of religion do obpalliate the business of pleasure' by introducing into the house of God strains which are more appropriate to the theatre and other public exhibitions. 'Thus,' he writes, anticipating many later purists, '[this church-singing] which the holy fathers have ordained that the weake may be stirred up to piety, is perverted to the use of unlawfull pleasure.'

Too much must not, of course, be made of these well-known passages, but it would seem that at the time they were written church musicians were coming to welcome the complexity of polyphonic composition because the performance of such music gave them a certain amount of pleasure. Moreover, it is clear that their treatment of the music was not intended to accommodate the tastes of the populace, who, in Aelred's words, 'stand by, trembling and astonished . . . but yet look upon the lascivious gesticulations of the singers, the meretricious alternations, interchanges, and infractions of the voices, not without derision and laughter'. This last observation is perhaps the most revealing part of Aelred's fulminations. In the thirteenth century Roger Bacon complained about the debased kind of singing heard in churches, with its lapses into irreverent softness, its desire for new harmonies and a multiplicity of *cantilenas*: 'I could quote instances from the very greatest cathedrals and other noteworthy establishments, in which the whole Office is ruined on account of the faults which I have enumerated.'[1] At a later stage it became a common criticism of the Church that the choir was actually allowed to impede worship by its maltreatment of language and division of notes into fragments. The Wycliffite tract *Of Prelates* (*c.* 1380) is particularly bitter on this subject; and the fifteenth-century tract *Dives and Pauper* refers to 'this curyous knackynge songe of the vycyouse mynystres in the churche/& specially in grete and riche chirches'.

III

It was through the medium of the drama rather than music that the mediaeval Church made its strongest appeal to the common people. It is often said that the Mass itself is dramatic;

[1] J. S. Brewer, ed., *Fr. Rogeri Bacon Opera* . . . (Rolls Series, 1859), I. 297–8.

in this connection the dialogue tropes mentioned above were especially important, for out of them evolved the liturgical dramas which once formed part of corporate Catholic worship. More is known of the liturgical dramas acted on the Continent than of those performed in this country, but it is established that the custom of giving such representations was fairly widespread throughout the Middle Ages.

In its earliest form liturgical drama was simply an intoned addition to the ceremonial which characterized the major festivals of the Christian year, such as Easter, Christmas, Ascensiontide and so on. The tropes used on these occasions commonly took the form of a brief colloquy accompanied by appropriate actions. An Easter drama embodied in the famous 'Quem Quaeritis' trope is the subject of a detailed passage in the *Regularis Concordia*; but this is only one of many such dramatizations. In this case it was acted after the office of *Nocturns* had concluded on Easter Day. Other versions make use of a slightly different wording, but the sequence of events—the visit to the sepulchre followed by a short conversation between the visitors and those guarding the place—is common to all 'Quem Quaeritis' dramas. The interesting point about the version as given in the *Regularis Concordia* is that it makes clear how completely the whole episode was intended to be vocalized and not merely spoken.

Among other liturgical plays performed in England were the *Officium Perigrinorum* (recounting the journey to Emmaus) and the *Officium Pastorum*, of which mention is made in a twelfth-century statute of Lichfield Cathedral. Liturgical dramas in which music played a great part were common throughout Europe in the Middle Ages. Unfortunately there is little concrete evidence as to their manner of presentation in this country: but it is known that on the Continent they made use of Biblical subjects from both the Old and the New Testaments. Paul Henry Lang has referred to 'the entirely musical character of the liturgical plays', and it is tempting to imagine them as operas in embryo. They bore some resemblance, certainly, to the simpler music dramas of a later date, but it would be unwise to represent the music as more impressive than it actually was, since spectacle, costume and gesture were also important. Music was essential, obviously, or it would not have been noted down in the texts of liturgical dramas, but it is unlikely that impersonation in song was seriously attempted. A more significant point to notice, however, is that these plays were given inside the churches by actors accustomed to performing music there and familiar with the musical material of the liturgy itself.

Our knowledge of how the music of the liturgical drama sounded is derived from what we know of the antiphons, hymns and other items incorporated in their musical framework. The mystery plays, which developed out of the liturgical dramas, also had recourse to music drawn from the office chants and the Mass. But they differ from their predecessors in that they employed a great deal more spoken dialogue, and were performed almost entirely in the vernacular. At what particular time the transition from musical to non-musical declamation was completed it is difficult to decide. But there is at least one English manuscript which denotes that the two languages, Latin and English, were used in conjunction in religious drama over a long period. The Shrewsbury fragments, as they are called in *Non-Cycle Mystery Plays*[1] follow in outline (as far as can be judged from a single actor's part) the liturgical scheme of the *Officium Pastorum,* the *Peregrini* and the *Officium Resurrectionis.* Some of the directions to the actors and the vocalized parts are in Latin (the latter with musical notation), but the dialogue is in English. It has been suggested that the Shrewsbury fragments belong not to Shrewsbury itself but to some more northern locality, possibly Beverley or York, though Lichfield is also suggested. A Resurrection play is said to have been performed at Beverley in 1220; it may be that the Shrewsbury *Officium Resurrectionis* is modelled on this.

From this transitional document we can now pass on to the English mystery plays themselves at a period when they were performed almost wholly outside the precincts of religious buildings. There is no need to dwell in detail on the great social significance which these pageant dramas held in English life, or to indicate the manner in which their organization came to be bound up with the activities of the craft gilds. 'The annual performance was, it would seem,' writes John Spiers, 'nothing less than the great occasion of the year in the town-community life of

[1] Osborn Waterhouse, ed., *The Non-Cycle Mystery Plays* (Early English Text Society: Extra Series, CIV, 1909), pp. 1–7.

the Middle Ages.'[1] The mystery plays are, of course, dramatizations of Biblical stories intended in part to promote in the populace a vivid interest in the characters and situations frequently spoken of in church. But the instructional aspect can be overstressed. It was indeed borne in mind by William Newhall in his famous 'Proclamation for the Plaies' as acted at Chester in 1544, yet he also added that these dramas were put on 'for the co'men Welth and prosperitie of this Citie'.[2] From a literary point of view these dramas are important because of the rude vigour with which their anonymous authors introduced extraneous characters and occasional lyrics. Some account of the way they utilized music, however, will reveal the extent to which they drew on available local talent and enabled it to make an effective contribution to the whole. In the mystery plays music is decidedly of an incidental nature, but that does not mean that its position is in any way negligible.

The major English craft cycles came into prominence soon after the inauguration of the Corpus Christi festival in 1311. Although 'we are not to infer that the very existence of long religious plays in England during the fourteenth and fifteenth centuries was due primarily to the institution of a new festival',[3] it is a fact that in this period such dramas were performed in most towns above a certain size; and their annual presentation continued until they were virtually suppressed at the time of the Reformation. Even as late as 1586 the inhabitants of Kendal were clamouring for 'the having of Corpus Christi play yearly as in former time'.[4] The mystery plays were not confined to the cathedral cities or to towns which boasted large religious establishments. As is evident from the table drawn up by E. K. Chambers, they were to be found in places which, like King's Lynn and Lydd (Kent), have declined in importance since the Middle Ages.[5] The surviving texts are of various dates; but it is important to recognize that so far as their music is concerned the stage directions are scanty. With one or two exceptions these plays as we have them simply *refer* to the music which is to

---

[1] John Spiers, 'A Survey of Mediaeval Verse' in Boris Ford, ed., *The Pelican Guide to English Literature* I ('The Age of Chaucer', 1954), p. 47.

[2] See Chambers, *Mediaeval Stage*, II. 349.

[3] Young, *op. cit.*, II. 425.

[4] J. T. Murray, *English Dramatic Companies* (1910), II. 295.

[5] Chambers, *Mediaeval Stage*, II. 328–406.

accompany them, and it is assumed that detailed instructions of what is to be sung and played will not really be necessary.

Of the various cycles, that from Chester is generally regarded as having been among the earliest to achieve its complete form. Consisting of twenty-four dramas stretching from the Fall of Lucifer to the Last Judgement, it allows scope for the introduction of music in a number of places. In the five Old Testament plays music does not figure very largely, except in the 'Fall of Lucifer' itself and 'The Deluge', where (in one manuscript) a drinking song is given to the gossips and a psalm, 'Save me, O God', is sung by Noah and his family. The New Testament dramas, however, make considerably more use of musical settings, and this is the case in other cycles. In 'The Nativity', for instance, angelic voices are heard singing 'Hec est ara Dei celi' as the Emperor Octavian censes the Roman temple; and in 'The Adoration of the Shepherds' there is a passage in which the shepherds comment on the *Gloria in excelsis* which is heard from above. They try to make out what the words are, and eventually decide that 'Terra' and 'Pax' occur in the phrases they have been listening to. This causes a sense of well-being to arise in the mind of the *secundus pastor* ('for never in this world so well I was'), and his friend Garth proposes a jubilation. So before proceeding to Bethlehem they join together in song ('omnes pastores cum aliis adjuvantibus cantabunt hilare carmen'). Indeed, much of the music brought into the mystery plays is intended to create a sense of gladness at the conclusion of especially joyful scenes. An interesting example of this occurs in the play of 'Christ's descent into Hell', acted by the Cooks and Innkeepers. Jesus takes Adam firmly by the hand, and intimating that the righteous will find their way to Paradise, addresses the attendant angel:

> Michael, lead these men singinge
> to joy that lasteth ever.

In his own final words Adam calls upon his associates to 'singe/ with great solemnity' the words *Te Deum laudamus, te Dominum confitemur*. In the Coventry pageant of the Shearmen and Taylors, Joseph finds that the shepherds' song 'Ase I owt rodde' greatly 'amends' his 'chere' or spirits.

The Coventry plays bring in a great deal of music. But apart from the light-heartedness which they lend to the scenes in which they appear, the shepherds have a further importance. Their presence seems to have given rise to a convention which is better exemplified in the Towneley plays than in the Chester cycle, the convention, namely, that earthly musicians should make some comment on the nature of heavenly music. In the first Shepherd's Play from the Towneley group, for instance, the *primus pastor*, after hearing the angels' song (line 306) is struck by the fact that it 'was wonder curiose/with small notes emang'. Later he goes on to point out that the melody introduced 'foure and twenty to a long' (line 414); that is to say the music was subjected to what afterwards became known as divisions. This has the effect of emphasizing the shepherds' sense of wonder. But in the second Shepherd's Play there is another discussion of the angels' performance; here the second and third shepherds agree that the angels' singing is more ambitious than their own modest efforts. What these characters have in mind in both the pastoral scenes is that the music which the dramatist has given to the angels is more studied and more highly 'organized' than that expected from such lowly creatures as themselves. To suggest, as N. C. Carpenter does, that 'the shepherds are over-whelmed by the angels' music because it represents a type of artistic, learned music more recherché than the simple poly-phony in discant style which probably constituted their own performances',[1] is surely to give the shepherds more credit than is due to them, since there is no certain evidence that they sang in parts at all. Nevertheless, the critical observations put into their mouths is indicative of the way in which two classes of musicians —roughly classifiable as amateurs and professionals—worked together to make possible the musical background of the mystery plays. The shepherds are, in fact, advancing a point of view that might be expressed by untrained singers, and they are drawing attention to the more highly developed kind of musical skill required by those who sang the *Gloria in excelsis Deo*.

In the presentation of the mystery plays, church musicians were called upon to assist the laity. In the 'Hegge' plays (for-merly known as the *Ludus Coventriae*, but now thought to belong to north-east England rather than to the Coventry area) there is

---

[1] N. C. Carpenter, 'Music in the *Secunda Pastorum*' in *Speculum*, XXVI (1951), p. 698.

a 'Conception of Mary' scene in which the sequence *Benedicta sit beata trinitas* is sung while Ysakar and his ministers cense the altar in the Temple. The subsequent scenes draw freely on liturgical music, the 'Assumption of the Virgin' towards the end of the cycle demanding a wealth of vocal and instrumental accompaniment. At one point, for instance, an angel comes down playing a cither, and further on the direction 'hic canatbunt organa' is the prelude to some serious and elaborate choral singing, including contributions from a 'Chorus martyrum' and on 'Ordo Angelorum'. Here the music becomes part of the dramatic texture and enjoys something more than the incidental status it is given elsewhere. The same holds true for those plays in the York cycle which deal with the Assumption of the Virgin. After the death of Mary, Jesus calls upon His Angels to bring her to the place she is to occupy in Heaven; having done this, they begin an appropriate valedictory song. It is perhaps in the Weavers' drama on the subject of 'The Appearance of our Lady to Thomas' that the most ambitious music in the York cycle is found. The strains of *Surge proxima mea* are heard as a background to Thomas's vision of Mary; this is followed by *Veni de libano* and, at the end of the vision, *Veni electa mea*. The part-music for these items has survived in the Ashburnham MS. 137, and it was edited by W. H. Cummings for Lucy Toulmin Smith's edition of the York plays. In style it would seem to belong to the early fifteenth century, and though it draws on liturgical phraseology it appears to have been specially composed for these plays. The playwright, according to Lucy Toulmin Smith, 'did not quote textually from any office, but wished to remind his audience in a general way of words with which they were familiar enough in church. The plays, themselves religious in origin, were being secularized; the music partook of the same character.'[1] Indeed, the employment of lay musicians ensured that the entertainment value of these plays was preserved. So much so that in the late fifteenth century we find a 'Prologus' speaking as follows just before the entrance of Herod in the 'Massacre of the Innocents' from the Digby cycle:

> And ye menstrallis, doth your diligens,
> & ye virgynes, shew summe sport & plesure,

[1] L. T. Smith, *York Plays* (Oxford, 1885), p. 525.

These people to solas, & to do god reverens,
As ye be appoynted . . . (line 56)

This, admittedly, is from a late period, but it affords some idea—
especially in the concluding lines of the play, where the minstrels
are requested to 'give us a daunce'—of the miscellaneous histrionic and musical material which is found in most of the craft
cycles. The range is wide, from the 'Old Musick, triplex, Tenor,
Medius, Bass' of the Norwich 'Creation and Fall' to the dance
interludes in the Digby plays. This, no doubt, was what the
author of the fourteenth-century 'Treatise against Miracle Plays'
had in mind when he admitted, scornfully, that 'summe recre-
acioun men moten han . . .'[1]

IV

Although most of the English mystery plays have been exhaustively edited by modern scholars, it is doubtful whether they
were ever intended to be regarded as works of literature. The
written texts simply served as a contribution towards an annual
public occasion on which spectacle, action and music were of
roughly equal importance. It would certainly be wrong to
suggest that these dramas were given an irreverent performance; yet it would also be a mistake to create the impression
that they were entirely solemn and lacking in vigour. In the Old
Testament plays especially, the dramatists introduce humorous
elements, and Hardin Craig even speaks of 'that forgetfulness of
religious purpose that appears so frequently in the mystery plays
of the fifteenth and sixteenth centuries'.[2] This is to look forward
in time. But even in the thirteenth and fourteenth centuries it is
unlikely that these dramas were very different in spirit from the
processions and ceremonial displays which were so common
throughout the Middle Ages.

Mention has already been made of processions. They were, of
course, an integral part of pre-Reformation worship, and were
held on innumerable occasions throughout the year. In his work
on the drama of the mediaeval church, Karl Young has shown
how intimately processional ceremonies were bound up with the

---

[1] Quoted in Rolf Kaiser, ed., *Mediaeval English* (Berlin, 1958), p. 258.
[2] Craig, *English Religious Drama* (1955), p. 319.

31

earlier forms of sacred drama.[1] The customaries and other books relating to religious institutions make frequent reference to processional procedures, and numerous hymns—apart, that is, from the hymns normally found in the breviaries—were written for such occasions. The musical and dramatic character of a religious procession may be gathered from a manuscript quoted in J. P. Neale's *Views of the Most Interesting Collegiate and Parochial Churches* (1825). This document, written by one Robert Martin who died in 1580, comes, admittedly, from a late part of the 'pre-Reformation' era, but it clearly describes a custom that dates back into the distant past. Martin is speaking of Melford in Suffolk. He writes:

> Upon palm Sunday, the Blessed Sacrament was carryed in Procession about the Church-yard, under a fair Canopy, borne by four Yeomen; the Procession coming to the Church Gate, went westward, and they with the Blessed Sacrament went eastward; and when the Procession came against the door of Mr. Clopton's Ile, they, with the Blessed Sacrament, and with a little bell and singing, approached at the east end of our Ladie's Chappel, at which time a Boy, with a thing in his hand, pointed to it, signifying a Prophet, as I think, sang, standing upon a Tyrret that is on the said Mr. Clopton's Ile doore, *Ecce Rex tuus venit*, &c.; and then all did kneel down, and then, rising up, went and met the Sacrament, and so then, went, singing together, into the church, and coming near the Porch, a boy, or one of the Clerks, did cast over among the Boys flowers, and singing cakes, &c.[2]

This refers to an Easter custom in a small East Anglian township. In larger places there were greater degrees of elaboration and more splendid music. At Beverley, for instance, the members of the Gild of St. Elene were in the fourteenth century accustomed to process 'with much music' to the church of the Friars Minors on their feast day, after which Mass was celebrated.[3]

Here it may be appropriate to notice the great part played by the music of bells during the Middle Ages. Bell-ringing accompanied a wide variety of activities in church, such as christenings, burials, installations and weddings; bells summoned the people to worship, and also marked the commencement and conclusion

---

[1] Young, *op. cit.*, I. 90 *et seq.*
[2] Neale, *Views* . . . , II. 13 (of Holy Trinity, Melford, section).
[3] J. Toulmin Smith, *English Gilds* (E.E.T.S., 40, 1870), p. 148.

of Mass. Large bells mounted in towers performed these functions, but smaller ones were in constant use in monastic houses and elsewhere to signify the regular intervals of time. Handbells similar to those illustrated in the York Psalter (1170) were very common in secular life, and sets of bells were used for decorative purposes on personal clothing. It was fashionable to fasten bells to the harness of horses, and another specialized use occurred in falconry, bells being attached to the jesses or leg-straps of hawks. The sounding of bells invariably took place whenever occasions of public rejoicing arose and when the more formal events in corporate life—gild meetings, coronations and so forth —took place. When processions were held there was usually an impressive chiming of bells.

Processions were an essential feature of civic celebrations. They were arranged to form part of triumphal entries, state visits and royal progresses, as when in 1432 King Henry VI approached London on his return from Paris. A chronicler reports that on this occasion the royal party made its way up from South London to St. Paul's, where hosts of 'angels' greeted the king with 'divers melodies and songs . . . And when he was come to St. Paul's, there he alighted down from his horse. And there came the Archbishop of Canterbury [and others together with] the Dean of St. Paul's with his convent, in procession in their best attire of holy church, and met with him, and did him observance . . . and so brought the king to the high altar, with royal song.'[1] Such ostentatious occasions as this served, among other things, to reassert the distinctions of social class which in times of unrest were likely to be ignored. Yet the 'minstrels', whose services were called upon at such times, were frequently rebuked for spreading discontent among the masses. The surviving records of civic functions and of mystery play performances make constant references to minstrels. And since there were large numbers of musicians answering to this description it is necessary to say something about their history and status.

Informal entertainers of one sort or another have existed in most human societies. Among the Romans, for example, there were various kinds of actors, jugglers, mimics, contortionists and dancers; but not all of them were necessarily musicians as well. When, as E. K. Chambers puts it, 'the conversion of

[1] Quoted in Kaiser, op. cit., p. 539 (spelling modernized).

England opened the remote islands to Latin civilization in general', it is not surprising that 'the *mimi*, no less than the priests, flocked into the new fields of enterprise'.[1] From an early period the practice of minstrelsy was closely associated with the performance of narrative poetry. 'The Minstrels', wrote Bishop Percy in his famous essay, 'were an order of men in the middle ages who subsisted by the arts of poetry and music, and sang to the harp verses composed by themselves, or others.'[2] This association of minstrelsy with harping has long persisted, though the harp of earlier periods was very much simpler than that used in the eighteenth-century drawing-room. A reconstruction of the instruments found at Taplow in 1883 and at Sutton Hoo in 1939 shows that these harps of the seventh century consisted of a slender frame about sixteen inches in height mounted on a pierced sounding-box which supported six strings. No one knows just how Anglo-Saxon harps were tuned, but Professor Wrenn conjectures that their apparently slender tone was increased in volume by placing them on a flat surface, as is done with the Finnish *kantele*.[3] It has been suggested, incidentally, that the instruments included in the Sutton Hoo and Taplow hoards are miniature replicas of those actually used; and pictorial representations of David and other figures in early English art seem to indicate that larger harps were customary. All the same, they would have to be small enough to be carried about from place to place. The music which accompanied such poems as *Widsith* and the Hymns of Caedmon was mainly rhythmical in character and was to some extent a mnemonic aid to the performer: it had, in all probability, very little melodic interest.[4]

Before the Norman Conquest the minstrel—scop or gleeman —was distinguished by his ability to utilize music for the purpose of imparting legends or scraps of historical information. Just as in religious services chanting was able to 'lull the mind to a waking trance', so in secular connections musical intonation had its own peculiar allurements. Among social groups in which literacy was rare, the minstrel performed a variety of functions which were afterwards taken over by the 'mass media'. By the

[1] Chambers, *Mediaeval Stage*, I. 33.

[2] Percy, *Reliques of Ancient English Poetry* (Everyman ed.), I. 9.

[3] C. L. Wrenn, *Anglo-Saxon Poetry and the Amateur Archaeologist* (Chambers Memorial Lecture, 1962), p. 8.

[4] See J. C. Pope, *The Rhythm of Beowulf* (1942), p. 92.

end of the fourteenth century the necessity for oral transmission
of romances and historical poems was not so great. Yet even
Chaucer, in the end of his *Troilus and Criseyde* (1385), envisaged
the possibility that the poem might be 'red . . . or elles songe'
(Book V, line 1797).

Bishop Percy described the Norman Conquest as 'rather likely
to favour the establishment of the Minstrel profession in this
kingdom than to suppress it'.[1] Its suppression was never in
question; for though the Church condemned minstrelsy in theory
(on the ground that it encouraged depravity), in practice the
clergy enjoyed the performances of 'menestrallis et wafferariis'
just as much as did the laity. The *Roll of the Household Expenses
of Richard de Swinfield*, Bishop of Hereford, records the payments made by him in 1289 to a viol-player, a harper and various
other minstrels. Thomas Cabham, Archbishop of Canterbury,
distinguished between those minstrels who might and those who
might not be given encouragement. The account books of
Durham priory and other establishments from the thirteenth
century onwards reveal payments to minstrels as a matter of
course. After the Conquest, as H. J. Chaytor explains, the term
'scop' was replaced by descriptive words of French origin such
as 'harpour', 'sautreour' and 'rymour': 'The mere variety artist
(of the time) was a *japer, jangler, juglour* or *tregetour. Goliadeis*
was in the first instance a special kind of clerical satirist. Of
these, *minstrel* becomes the most general term.'[2]

Minstrel songs were of many kinds: they were frequently
satirical and parodistic, and many of them contained social comments and complaints of abuses in Church and State. This is well
brought out in the political songs which have survived in the
Harleian manuscripts and elsewhere. A typical example is a
'Song against the King of Almaigne'. This is directed at Richard
Earl of Cornwall (Henry III's brother), who was known to
favour unpromising foreign alliances. A 'Song on the Times',
placed by Thomas Wright in 'the beginning of the reign of
Edward I', voices in a mixture of Latin and Anglo-Norman the
sorrows of a land in which sympathy and friendship seem to have
gone by the board. The 'Song on the Execution of Sir Simon
Fraser' is a stanzaic report of the early fourteenth-century

[1] Percy, *Reliques . . .* , I. 13.
[2] H. J. Chaytor, *The Troubadours and England* (1923), p. 7.

Scottish 'war of independence', weighted—as so many of these early political songs are—against the crime of treachery. Other songs from this period illustrate the manner in which minstrels frequently lent their musical gifts to the cause of socio-political propaganda. A good instance of this is the 'Song against the Retinues of the Great People', dating from the time of Edward II. This piece—which, incidentally, makes no mention of the musicians maintained by great people—though called a 'song' by Thomas Wright, may not have been actually sung, though its tone and alliterative nonchalance place it within the minstrel *ethos*.[1]

By the fourteenth century the distinction between free-lance and 'professional' minstrels had been accentuated by the fact that kings, queens and noblemen chose to enhance their prestige by including numbers of minstrels among their personal retainers. These musicians were expected to perform specific duties, and it is at this stage that the purely instrumental performers assumed an added significance. It is something of an exaggeration to say that 'Support was withdrawn from the practitioners of lyric song and given to professional performers on *veille*, lute, guitar, bagpipe, rebec, psaltery, and shalm';[2] yet there is plenty of evidence that social custom among the upper ranks did provide a great deal of employment for minstrels who played on the trumpet, tabor or drum. They were engaged to provide music at mealtimes, on ceremonial occasions and at receptions. In the more detailed household books their rates of payment are set out, and it is clear that they enjoyed a high position in the estimation of those they served. In the Household Ordinance for 1318, provision is made 'Pur toutz les ministraux', and many other documents, royal and otherwise, give a fair indication of their position.[3] Perhaps the completest available account of royal minstrels is to be found in the 'Black Book' which gives full particulars of the Household of Edward IV. From this it appears that the king employed thirteen minstrels, some as permanent servants, others on a temporary basis. They had strict instructions as to how they were to behave, and were specially

[1] Thomas Wright, ed., *The Political Songs of England* (Camden Society, 1839), pp. 69, 133, 212, 237.

[2] Arthur K. Moore, *The Secular Lyric in Middle English* (1951), p. 12.

[3] See T. F. Tout, *The Place of the Reign of Edward II in English History* (1914), p. 312; and Edith Rickert, *Chaucer's World* (New York, 1948), p. 232.

requested not to ask for gratuities.[1] Occasionally minstrels rose to be men of substance. The case of the fifteenth-century musician John Clyff is perhaps outstanding, but it illustrates the professional opportunities open to those who were fortunate enough to secure suitable patronage. Clyff had accompanied Henry V in his voyages abroad along with seventeen other minstrels. As a result of this there was due to him the sum of thirty-three pounds six shillings for the security of which he had received a considerable quantity of jewels and other valuable articles.[2]

The minstrels who came outside the scope of such munificence as John Clyff enjoyed had to pick up a living as best they could. They occasionally formed themselves into troupes, but in any case they had difficulty in overcoming the prejudices which were entertained against them. In the forty-sixth Statute of Roger de Mortival, Bishop of Salisbury (1319), for instance, there is a stern warning against these 'upholders of sloth' who are not to be given money or anything that will enable them to make money. The clergy under this Bishop's jurisdiction were admonished not to lend a willing ear to the tales minstrels relate, 'which are made up of back-biting, evil-speaking and scurrility', nor must they disclose any partiality for the kind of 'yelpings' such wandering players engage in.[3] It is clear from the B text of *Piers Plowman* (XIII. 228) and other sources that the life of an unattached minstrel was a hazardous one. The profession may, as some of the Chester records suggest, have attracted undesirable characters.[4] It was to protect themselves from the bad faith of such persons that the more respectable minstrels eventually decided to form themselves into recognized corporate bodies. In the larger towns they sought to bestow on their 'mystery' a certain dignity by establishing gilds of minstrels. One such gild was set up in London during the reign of Edward III (1350). In the Returns made to Richard II in 1399 on the subject of gilds, a 'Gild of the Minstrels and Players' is mentioned as flourishing in Lincoln. York was another provincial town which maintained a gild of minstrels, but one of the most interesting of such fraternities was that of Beverley, in the East Riding of Yorkshire.

In some ways, Beverley and its neighbourhood may be said to

[1] See A. R. Myers, ed., *The Household of Edward IV* (1959), pp. 47–48, 131–2.
[2] F. Devon, tr., *Issues of the Exchequer . . .* (1837), p. 423.
[3] Quoted in D. H. Robertson, *Sarum Close* (1938), p. 55.
[4] R. H. Morris, *Chester in the Plantagenet and Tudor Times* (n.d.), p. 346.

have contained an epitome of mediaeval music. In the Middle Ages it was a place of some consequence. It had escaped devastation at the time of the Norman Conquest and had managed to survive incursions from the Scots; the Charter granted to the town by Archbishop Thurstan gave its inhabitants power to make their own by-laws and also to hold fairs at various times of the year. Its proximity to Leckonfield, one of the seats of the Percy family, meant that important people were frequently in the locality. Its religious establishments were ancient and imposing. The minstrel fraternity at Beverley is said by tradition to date back to Athelstan, who is named as its founder in an 'Order of the Ancient Company or Fraternity of Minstrells in Beverley' dated 1555. The ordinances to which the minstrels were bound aimed at maintaining standards of performance and conduct among the musicians, and also at consolidating allegiance to the town of Beverley itself. Under the gild rules, for example, members were to be answerable to the aldermen and were to pay fines for breaches of discipline: they were expected to keep up the status of their craft by taking on apprentices, though at the same time they were to refrain from giving tuition to their own children. It was their business to see that no minstrel from outside Beverley came to perform within the town; they were responsible for enforcing the regulation that no shepherd or husbandman 'playing upon pipe or other instrument shall sue any wedding' except in his own parish; and no musician without the proper qualifications was to be allowed to usurp the offices of a Beverley minstrel. How serious this question of infringement was generally can be seen from a proclamation of 1496 made by Henry VII to confirm Edward IV's grant to the minstrels in 1469. 'We do perceyve', it runs, 'that many rude persons and artificers of dyvers places within this our Realme of englond do name them selffis to be mynstrellis Wherof many of them do take oure libertie To them never geven and doth name them to be oure propre mynstrellis By reason and collour of which libertie and by the said Crafte of mynstrelles they do gather and receive frawdelently grete Sommes of money of our leege people in dyverse places of this oure Realme aforesaid . . .'[1] In this particular, of course, the royal minstrels were

[1] E. W. W. Veale, ed., *The Great Red Book of Bristol* (Bristol Record Society Publications XVIII, 1953), Text, Part IV, p. 5.

being granted a form of protection which the members of craft gilds normally expected to obtain.

A typical fifteenth-century extract from the records and accounts of the Smiths' Company of Coventry reads: '1451, it. payed to the mynstrells viijs, it. spend on mynstrells dinner and their soper on Corpus Xristi day xxd; 1471, it. paid to the waytes for mynstrelship vjs . . .'[1] The waits are frequently mentioned along with the minstrels, and they were often the same musicians. But waits were distinguished from minstrels in general by the fact that they were assigned a more immediately practical function in the life of the community. As the etymology of the word 'wait' implies, waits were employed in the first place as watchmen equipped with horns and other instruments upon which they could sound notes of warning or mark the appropriate intervals of time. Thus in the 'Black Book' provision is made for 'A WAYTE, that nyghtly, from Mighelmasse til Shere Thursday, pipeth the wache within this court iiij tymes, and in the somer nyghtes iij tymes; and he to make bon gayte, and every chambre dore and office, as well for fyre as for other pikers or perelliz'.[2] In castles, palaces and walled towns the waits utilized their musical skill for the public good. They received recognition from the corporations of many towns, and are the subject of countless enactments at places like Chester, Durham, York, Liverpool and Leicester. In time their routine duties became less and less essential, so they were employed in other ways: they were called upon to perform before prominent visitors, to entertain civic gatherings and to assist in church when necessary.

Although some of the waits were 'strengmen', the majority of them performed on shawms, wooden cornets, oxhorns and sackbuts; their duties made it necessary that the instruments they played should have a reasonably strident tone. In a manuscript *Description of the Cittie of Exeter* (late sixteenth century) John Hooker reports that the Exeter waits had in their possession one double curtall (bassoon), a lyserden (possibly a tenor cornet), two tenor oboes, a treble oboe, a cornet and a 'sett or case of ffowre Recorders'. The waits, like the more wide-ranging minstrels, had occasional trouble with 'foreigners' who tried to

[1] Hardin Craig, ed., *Two Coventry Corpus Christi Plays* (E.E.T.S., 1957), p. 88.
[2] Myers, *op. cit.*, p. 132.

poach on their preserve. But they held their place in civic life, and in fact formed one mediaeval institution which the Reformation and English puritanism did not succeed in eradicating. Indeed, during the late sixteenth and seventeenth centuries most of the larger towns still retained bands of waits whose salaries were provided from specially levied taxes. The records of Northampton, Durham and Manchester are particularly detailed in respect of the services rendered by them. At Leicester their number was increased from three to five in 1688. Elsewhere the waits survived as corporate ensembles right up to the middle of the eighteenth century. Their final demise is attributable to the Municipal Reform Act of 1835. The true dignity of the mayoralty, it was held, did not consist with antiquated pageantry—and so this simple anachronism was at last dispensed with.

V

We know that dancing was an extremely popular pastime throughout the Middle Ages, but precise details of the dance steps used are not readily available. Systems of notation have, it is true, been devised for dancing, but these are of recent date. The earliest instruction books belong to the sixteenth century, and though they are informative enough once the formulas they employ are understood, they are written in a manner which assumes that the reader is perfectly familiar with the music. Some mediaeval dance music has been handed down to us. But since our knowledge of mediaeval dance as a whole is still largely conjectural, it may be best to discuss the matter retrospectively.

Puritan writers of the sixteenth century such as Gosson, Stubbes and Christopher Fetherstone (author of *A Dialogue Agaynst Light, Lewde and Lascivious Dauncing*, 1582) regarded dancing as reprehensible. In this they had been anticipated by mediaeval moralists who pointed out the vanity of an activity which diverted attention from more praiseworthy pursuits. But these fulminations against communal dancing and dance customs serve to remind us that in the Middle Ages the dance was looked upon as an essential accompaniment to weddings, feasts and other public occasions. The older 'folk' dances have their origin in the communal desire to perpetuate existence and to render homage to vaguely conceived beliefs. The dances changed from one century to another and were now and then given local variations, but certain basic patterns are traceable in nearly all those which began as folk amusements. We may, for instance, distinguish between *invitatory* and *imitative* dances: in the former, the dancers' impulse is to bring others to their way of feeling by means of sympathetic movement (as in courtship dances, etc.); in the latter, a life-process is mimed for the purpose of informing the tutelary spirits of some communal need. The dance known as 'Bean-setting' is a case in point.

But of the more general dances from the mediaeval period two features may be mentioned. One is that over several centuries there was a tendency for dancers from the courtly classes to imitate and incorporate the 'folk' traditions of dance. The other is that up till comparatively recent times the dancers themselves provided the music for the dance while they were actually dancing. Nowadays, sung dance music is so rare that we have difficulty in imagining what it can be like. But in the Middle Ages it was extremely common. The best-known form of sung dance was the Carole which as danced in Provence had two main forms, the Farandole and the Branle or Round Dance. English contact with Provence was close in the twelfth and thirteenth centuries; dance melodies were no doubt heard and repeated by English merchants and political emissaries returning from the Provençal region. The act of vocalization was a means of keeping the music in people's minds, even if the words were not properly understood. The true rhythm of most caroles is probably lost, but by studying the words of the 'carols' which derived from them we can determine something of their musical shape.

The most usual form was that which distributed the music between a soloist singing a strophe of three or four lines, and the group itself contributing a final couplet or burden (which might be simply one line). As an instance we may take the following passage from the fourteenth-century poem *Handlyng Synne*, by Robert of Brunne. In this work we are told the story of the sacrilegious inhabitants of Kolbeck, who one Christmas-time refused to discontinue their dance when it was time to go to Mass. For this they were duly punished and were held in a spell which caused them to go on dancing for a whole twelve months.

Robert of Brunne gives the words of their carole in Latin, which he translates immediately afterwards:

> By the leved wode rode Bevolyne,
> Wyth hym he ledde feyre Merswyne;
> Why stond we? why go we noght?

Although these lines have been discussed by R. L. Greene in his exhaustive study of the caroles,[1] they are worthy of further comment. The rhythm of the English version is strikingly different from that of the Latin ('Equitabat Bevo per silvam frondosam/Ducebat secum Merswyndam formosam. /Quid stamus, cur non imus?'). The same music could not have been used for both versions, as it can in the case of, say, a good many hymns. So it is probable that Robert of Brunne is fitting his translation to an English tune. A musical setting of the translated lines as they stand would be obliged to follow a rhythmical pattern of much the same kind as that found in 'Sumer is icumen in', which if not actually a dance song is admitted to show dance rhythms. A suggested notation, therefore, might run as follows:

That, perhaps, is the nearest we can approach to the musical outline of this particular dance fragment. The first two lines would be sung by the leader, the final one by the throng of dancers (twelve, according to Robert of Brunne), perhaps as they were in the process of changing to the next measure of the dance.

The dances contained in the Harleian MS. 978 (originally dated 1240–70, but now thought to be later) conform to the musical pattern demanded by Thoinot Arbeau for the *bransle*.[2] But the bransle, or brawle, which was defined by Randle Cotgrave in his *Dictionarie of the French and English Tongues* (1611) as a dance 'wherein many (men, and women) holding by the hands sometimes in a ring, and otherwhiles at length, move all together', is not usually spoken of much before the sixteenth

---

[1] R. L. Greene, *The Early English Carols* (1935), p. xxxii.
[2] Arbeau, *Orchesographie* (1589).

century. Yet the *Complaint of Scotland* (1549) mentions 'base dancis, pavvans, galyardis, turdions, braulis and branglis' along with ballads and dance tunes of a considerably older date. The base dances were the subject of a short treatise by Robert Copland which is appended to Alexander Barclay's *Introductory to wryte and to pronounce Frenche* (1521). Copland's explanation contains one significant phrase. After explaining that these dances begin by singles (or 'reverence') and end with a 'braule' (a particular type of movement, not the dance just referred to), he goes on: 'Also it behoveth to know the nombre of notes of every bace daunce & the pace after the measure of the notes.' By this time, it would seem, dances were becoming so complicated that very close attention to the music was a *sine qua non*. Hence the need for exclusively instrumental accompaniment. This, perhaps, is hinted at in John Rastell's *Interlude of the Four Elements* (1519), where Sensual Appetite calls for a dance, which is provided by himself and a group of dancers. To Ignorance's suggestion that they need a minstrel, Sensual Appetite replies that this 'maketh no force'; but after the dance has been gone through 'without a pipe', Humanity gives it as his opinion that

> This dance would do mich better yet,
> If we had a kit or taberet . . .

During the sixteenth century there were important developments in the art of dancing, but by Queen Elizabeth's time the sung dance—in the higher ranks of society, at any rate—was largely an anachronism.

VI

At the present time, when radio performances and gramophone recordings are making available to us a great deal of unfamiliar music, we are perhaps in danger of accepting uncritically the judgements of specialists who are inclined to substitute Matthew Arnold's 'historic' estimate of a piece of music for the 'real' estimate. Those who have heard a reasonable amount of English music composed before, say, 1500 must surely admit that very little of it is living art in the sense that the madrigals of Weelkes or the operas of Purcell are. It is not simply that our ears have become accustomed to different idioms and melodic shapes from those which were current in the Middle Ages. Much more important is the fact that the occasions which brought so much mediaeval music into existence are never likely to be repeated. This is not to deny that much music which is strictly functional in character does transcend place and time; yet it is a fact of social history that changes in the structure of society may render even hallowed customs obsolescent.

Nothing marks off the Middle Ages from the modern world more sharply than the mediaeval preoccupation with matters of an elemental nature. Chaucer and his contemporaries, for example, were conscious of the difference between the seasons of the year in a way that we are not: this is made clear by the Host's readiness, in the Introduction to the Man of Law's Tale, at telling the time of day by the length of a tree's shadow on the ground. In such a community as that to which the Canterbury pilgrims belonged, songs which welcomed spring or rejoiced at the passing of winter had a significance we do not readily appreciate. It is no exaggeration to say that there is only one part of the year which does—in a musical connection—exert much the same kind of appeal now as it did in the Middle Ages, namely Christmas. A few of our Christmas carols retain features by which they were distinguished in the mediaeval period. But the fact that carols have come to be associated almost wholly with Christmas alone indicates that this type of song has now, for various reasons, to be placed in a narrower context than it originally occupied.

The history of the carol has been traced many times. Briefly, carols derived from the carole dance song, retaining as an essential element the burden which was so important in the earlier dance form. Carols were written on several kinds of subject, but in the early Middle Ages they came into existence as part of a campaign by which clerical authorities undertook informally to woo the populace away from the last remnants of paganism. In order to do this they adopted the now familiar practice of stealing the devil's tunes and setting pious and uplifting words to them. 'Secular song,' writes R. L. Greene, 'whether associated with the dance or not, offered a far more promising field for the activities of the moralizing clergy [than the dance itself]. From the earliest period of Christianity vocal music had occupied an important place in divine worship, reaching its highest development in the Gregorian chant of the Mass. The hymns of the Office . . . were not far removed from the stanzaic form of popular song. Certainly there was nothing vicious in singing of itself. But the character of the pieces which were current among the people in the Middle Ages was often such as to cause grave concern to the guardians of their morals.'[1] The importance of moralizing must not be taken too seriously. Often it was enough if the people could be given the opportunity to sing innocuous convivial songs to which they themselves might make a contribution. The carol answered this purpose: it was a rhyming song in the vernacular with a burden repeated after each stanza. Professor Greene has argued that the development of the carol-type poem in England is bound up with the appearance in this country from the thirteenth century onwards of Franciscan friars. 'The tempering of the austerity of Christianity by the appeal to tender emotion and personal love for Christ,' he writes, 'the invocation of pity for His sorrow in the cradle and suffering on the cross, which is particularly to be noted in the lullaby and Crucifixion carols, are part of the legacy of St. Francis to the centuries which followed his ministry.'[2] In the Middle Ages the custom of singing carols was not necessarily confined to Christmastide. There are certainly upwards of a hundred Carols for the Nativity in Professor Greene's major collection; but there are also Carols for Epiphany, for the Virgin, for various saints and on several points of Catholic doctrine. The carol was, in fact, a means whereby the lay intelligence could be directed to religious topics without the intervention of formal homiletic guidance.

The carol, however, was only one of many vocal forms current in the Middle Ages. Among these the ballad holds an important place. The tunes to which ballads were sung are largely modal in character, and some writers have traced them to plainsong sources. But not all secular music was monodic. The date 1240 may or may not be the right one for the 'Reading Rota', but a fair amount of secular polyphonic composition went on in the thirteenth and fourteenth centuries. Stainer's *Early Bodleian Music* offers many examples of three-part settings to carol texts; and a piece like 'I have set my heart so hye' (*c.* 1425) shows that the principle of supplying 'instrumental symphonies' to short

[1] Greene, *op. cit.*, p. cxv.
[2] *Ibid.*, p. cxxvii.

songs was adopted even at this early stage. Some of these compositions are, by modern standards, quite unadventurous. Yet the first dozen items of R. H. Robbins's *Secular Lyrics of the Fourteenth and Fifteenth Centuries* gives a fair enough idea of the *ethos* to which the mediaeval carol belonged. Nor, on the whole, was the range of instrumental music in this period quite so circumscribed as the comparatively simple nature of the instruments themselves might suggest. What these lacked in mechanical subtlety they made up for in variety of types. Among the 'chordophones' alone Gustave Reese has listed the harp, rote, guitar (gitterne, gythorne, etc.), citole, dulcimer, symphony, echiquier, lute, rebec and rubebe.[1] Wind and percussive instruments were also quite numerous; so that it will not do to imagine that the mediaeval instrumental ensemble was confined to 'the pipe, the tabor and the trembling croud'. This is proved not only from the instruments that have survived but also from pictorial representations, and the fondness for combinations of instruments (not always, to our way of thinking, in the most desirable sort of balance) is shown by innumerable carvings in stone or wood and in stained-glass windows. There are musical sculptures at St. Mary's Church, Beverley, at Worcester and Ely Cathedrals, and at St. John's Church, Cirencester—to mention only a few.[2] One of the most perfect of all is a frieze in the church at the remote Buckinghamshire hamlet of Hillesden, near Aylesbury. Placed high up on the north and south walls of the choir, this group of exquisitely fashioned instrumentalists has somehow escaped the slightest trace of alteration or disfigurement.

VII

The greater part of mediaeval music was composed by men whose names are completely unknown to us. From the fifteenth century, indeed, composers did begin to place signatures to their work, but we are completely in the dark as to who composed the Reading Rota or the Agincourt Carol. Occasionally, as in the

[1] Gustave Reese, *Music in the Middle Ages* (1941), p. 407 (the author is speaking only of the British Isles). See also Clair C. Olson, 'Chaucer and the Music of the Fourteenth Century' in *Speculum*, XVI (1941), pp. 64–91.

[2] See Charles and Harriet Nicewonger, 'Mediaeval Musical Instruments Sculptured in the Decorations of English Churches' in *Music Libraries and Instruments* (Hinrichsen's Eleventh Music Book, 1961), pp. 253–6.

case of John Dunstable, a musical genius might be honoured by his fellow practitioners, but generally speaking the personal identity of the composer mattered very little. Music was regarded as a craft or 'mystery' and those who practised it were judged by the suitability of what they wrote, not by the intensity of their inspiration. Conditions did not favour the emergence of highly idiosyncratic styles; these were to arise later when, as a result of social and intellectual changes, the aspirations of the composer had ceased to be subservient to the communal will.

II

Renaissance, Reformation and the Musical Public

AFTER the close of the Middle Ages the social history of English music was affected by three related phenomena: the diffusion of humanistic teachings, the Protestant Reformation and the gradual evolution of a musical public—at first rather loosely defined, but eventually of increasing significance. It may seem injudicious at this stage to introduce the concept of a 'musical public', yet this term does denote a community of taste and inclination which is manifested in different ways; and without that, fruitful patronage of any art is hardly possible. Patronage, as we shall see, was an essential condition of English music-making in the Renaissance period. The manner in which composers and performers sought it will appear in due course. But as a background to this we need to discuss certain aspects of sixteenth-century life and thought which have a distinct bearing on musical custom at that time.

I

The Tudor succession and all its ramifications have been the subject of many detailed studies. The aspect of it which most concerns us is the gradual change-over in Henry VII's reign (but especially under Thomas Cromwell in the 1530s) from a 'household' administration to a form of government based roughly on departmental lines. For this called into being a Civil Service made up of laymen who had received a fair amount of formal

48

education. The custom of bringing up potential statesmen and ambassadors in noble households did not, of course, cease for a long time to come, but in the earlier part of the sixteenth century the prestige of the better grammar schools and the universities increased as the prejudice declined that only chivalric prowess and high birth could qualify a man for responsible political activity. And it was from such institutions that government servants were increasingly recruited. At any rate, the age-old contempt for 'learning' was diminishing among the more influential sections of the laity.

The curricula of sixteenth-century schools, though all having much in common, varied from place to place. In the Middle Ages most religious foundations maintained grammar schools and song schools, the work of which was closely related to the day-to-day needs of the institutions themselves. After the Reformation this situation changed, and in many cases the teaching of music was left to chance. In some schools (like that at Coventry, for example) music was freely taught; elsewhere it was neglected entirely. 'Grammar schools', writes D. G. T. Harris, 'had to make fresh provisions for teaching music [after 1547]: and as time-tables were becoming crowded with new subjects, music was either relegated to a secondary place, or omitted altogether.'[1] Yet many of the English humanists—Sir Thomas More, for instance—were great lovers of music, and some account of the importance of music in education is given in most of the treatises written on this subject in the early sixteenth century. It was usually considered under two heads—the utilitarian and the recreational. It was believed that the exercise of singing (quite apart from any devotional significance it might have) was beneficial to health: 'a knowledge of singing is found to be of the greatest use for clear and distinct elocution' is a proposition laid down in the Westminster School statutes—though the boys at this school were allowed only two hours' instruction in music each week. On the question of recreation one of the most interesting statements occurs in Sir Thomas Eylot's *Boke Named the Governour* (Book I, Chapter 7). Elyot recommends the pursuit of music; but he insists that this must not become an obsession: 'that is to say, that it onely serveth for

[1] David G. T. Harris, 'Musical Education in Tudor Times (1485–1603)' in *Proceedings of the Musical Association*, LXV (1939), p. 120.

recreation after tedious or laborious affaires, and to shewe him [the potential governor] that a gentilman, plainge or singing in a commune audience, appaireth his estimation'.[1] This attitude, however, was not universal. The anonymous author of *The Institution of a Gentleman* (1555) allows 'the use of musicall Instruments' as suitable for the training of his 'gentle Gentle' nobleman; and Richard Mulcaster, in his *Positions* (1581) is more explicit. To him singing is highly desirable because it serves to 'sprede the voice instrumentes within the bodie': and playing on instruments enables us 'in forme of exercise to get the use of our small joyntes, before they be knitte, to have them the nimbler, and to put Musicianes in minde, that they be no brawlers, least by some swash of a sword, they chaunce to lease a jointe, an irrecoverable jewell unadvisedly cast away'.[2]

Humanistic thought on music and its effects was invariably coloured by the theories of Plato and Aristotle, who maintained that there was a connection between the music a man heard and the quality of his moral behaviour. There is a reflection of this in Ascham's *Toxophilus* (1545) when Philologus tells Toxophilus that he has overstated his case for shooting as a pastime. But Toxophilus will not accept the argument that performing on musical instruments is just as good an exercise as handling the long-bow. He points out that in the *Politics* Aristotle condemned 'lutes, harpes, all maner of pypes, barbitons, sambukes, with other instrumentes every one, whyche standeth by fine and quicke fingeringe' as irrelevant to the pursuit of learning and virtue. Such 'nice, fine, minikin fingering', he declares, 'is farre more fitte for the womannishness of it to dwell in the courte among ladies, than for any great thing in it, whiche shoulde helpe good and sad studie, to abide in the universitie amonges scholers'.[3] After taking note of his friend's sarcasms, Philologus laments that 'the laudable custome of Englande to teache chyldren their plainesong and priksong' is so sadly neglected, and this gives him an opportunity to observe that for every student then entering the university who had learned to sing there were six who had received no musical education whatever. There may

---

[1] Elyot, *The Boke Named the Governour* (Everyman ed.), p. 27.
[2] R. H. Quick, ed., *Mulcaster's Positions* (1888), p. 39.
[3] English Works of Roger Ascham (Cambridge, 1904), pp. 13, 14.

not, indeed, have been much formal music teaching in schools at this time, but there was a great deal of informal instruction and private tuition. Despite Elyot's warning that it ill becomes a man of standing to behave as though he were a common minstrel, executive musicianship was coming to be regarded as an important social acquirement.

The career of Henry VIII, indeed—to whom the *Boke Named the Governour* is dedicated—is almost a refutation of Elyot's words. Elyot takes as a pertinent example the Emperor Nero, whose unquenchable thirst for music rendered him a vicious tyrant. Yet Henry VIII was likewise an implacable autocrat who was also an enthusiastic devotee of music—more so, perhaps, than any English king since Henry VI. Henry was not only a composer and a performer of vocal and instrumental music: he was a patron, over a long period, of a very large number of musicians. His motets and part-songs are not regarded by scholars as of any great distinction, but his interest and personal example acted as a powerful stimulus to other composers and performers. John Stevens has studied in detail the kind of music enjoyed at Henry VIII's court and has come to the conclusion that, although court life and entertainment were still very much as they had been in the reigns of previous monarchs, a decisive change in mode came about somewhere between 1530 and 1540. 'The mid-sixteenth century gets its character', he writes, 'from the appearance of such "newfangilnes" as the consort of viols, the pavane and galliard, the metrical psalm, the art-song for voice and lute, the new polyphonic style, semi-professional musicians as servants, popular instrumental tutors, and increased musical literacy.'[1] Dr. Stevens has discussed the part played by music in the pageants, interludes and dramatic 'shows' which were common at this time. By the 1540s the work of those responsible for organizing the royal revels was very full and exacting, and the musicians employed at court in a secular capacity stood on a different footing from the members of the Chapel Royal. Some of the most favoured musicians appearing at the English court were visitors from foreign countries.

In the *Calendar of State Papers (Milan)* there is a note to the effect that in October 1471 the Duke of Milan sent his Maestro di Capella to England to recruit singers for the Ducal Chapel.

[1] John Stevens, *Music and Poetry in the Early Tudor Court* (1961), p. 109.

This was no doubt an expedition authorized to use the press-gang methods such as had been common in England since the time of Richard III to obtain choristers for the Royal Chapel. But it is also evidence of a musical interchange between England and Italy which more frequently brought musicians to England than vice versa, though companies of English musicians and actors did tour the Continent in the sixteenth century. The Italian influence on our musical culture thus antedates by more than two centuries the vogue for Italian opera which was so strong after about 1710. By the fifteenth century English contact with Italy was very intimate in the intellectual as well as the economic sphere: the Papacy engaged important emissaries to conduct negotiations between the two countries; of these may be mentioned Polydore Virgil, the historian. It is a commonplace of literary criticism that poets like Wyatt and others visited Italy and then tried to 'Italianize' English poetry by means of translations and imitations of Italian verse forms. Humanist thinkers had for some time past been appropriating the ideas of Italian theorists and philosophers. At the court of Henry VII and Henry VIII Italian, Flemish and French musicians were in constant employment. Among the 'vialls' engaged at 12d. a day in 1540, for instance, were Alberto da Venitia, Vincenzo da Venezia, Alexander, Ambrosio and Romano di Milano and Joan Maria da Cremona.[1] From this period the status of English minstrels declined. They were still very much in request for occasional music to plays and other amusements, but they did not command the respect accorded to foreign instrumentalists and to the practitioners of 'art' music in general. We know from the papers of ambassadors and others that Italian keyboard players were particularly admired in England. What music such *virtuosi* performed is not exactly known, but it is assumed that a great many of them were highly skilled at improvisation.

An inventory of musical instruments belonging to Henry VIII was compiled during the time that Philip Welder (or van Velder) was in charge of them (1547). This shows that the king possessed an unusually large number of regals, virginals, clavichords, organs, etc., for the most part richly decorated. There were also many bowed string instruments and wind instruments,

---

[1] See Lady Mary Trefusis, *Songs, Ballads and Instrumental Pieces composed by Henry VIII . . .* (Roxburghe Club, 1912), p. xiv.

many of them bespeaking a high standard of craftsmanship. A typical entry reads:

> Item a little venice Lute w^t a case to the same
> Item sondrie Bookes and skrolles of songes and ballattes
> Item an olde cheste covered w^t blacke fustian of Naples
> Item a cheste collered redd w^t vi Vialles havinge the Kinges Armes.

There is no reason to believe that all the instruments mentioned —'cornetts, gitterons, phiphes', recorders and flutes—were of transalpine origin, but their variety and richness of decoration suggests that most of them had not been produced by English makers. We can only guess at the contents of the 'bookes and skrolles', though it is well known that three-part songs (of which Henry VIII himself wrote several examples) were popular among the musically 'literate' in this period. The occasionally profane nature of these is hinted at in an exclamation which occurs in the dedication to William Baldwin's *The Canticles or Balades of Salomon* (1549): 'Would god that suche songes myght once drive out of office the baudy balades of lecherous love that commonly are indited and song of idle courtyers in princes and noble mens houses.'[1] A collection of songs and serious ballads published by John Hall in 1565 under the title of *The Court of Virtue* included items such as Baldwin approved; it provided music as well as words and was obviously intended to displace an earlier volume, *The Court of Venus* (*c.* 1550), on which it is apparently modelled.

On the question of musical literacy in the sixteenth century, it is as well to exercise caution. At one time it was considered reasonable to take a certain passage in Thomas Morley's *Plaine and Easie Introduction to Practicall Musick* (1597) as evidence that in the later part of the period nearly all educated men were accomplished sight-singers. But, as several writers have pointed out, the situation imagined in Morley's dialogue is much more likely to be in the nature of a 'puff' for his book than a strictly accurate record of the prevailing state of affairs. Nevertheless, the musical efflorescence which took place in Queen Elizabeth's time could never have come about if there had not been available a fair amount of private tuition, and if there had not been an

---

[1] Quoted in Lily B. Campbell, *Divine Poetry and Drama in Sixteenth-Century England* (1959), p. 42.

active interest in music among those classes who could afford to encourage it.[1] In schools, as we have noted, musical instruction was often perfunctory, but 'singing men' and others were in demand—so much so that in 1577 William Byrd complained to the queen that his constant attention at the Chapel Royal (of which he was a Gentleman) prevented him from 'reaping such commodity by teaching as formerly he did'. Music-teaching as a sole source of emolument is comparatively rare before the seventeenth century. But before dealing with the specifically Elizabethan period, in which this profession is already taken seriously, we must return to the earlier part of the sixteenth century and examine some of the effects of the Reformation. In passing, however, it is worth noting that advances in the technique of printing, which were so important in other directions during this period, had very little effect on the music written before 1550; and whereas the development of English poetry and prose was unquestionably affected by the skill and enterprise of typographers, the rapid duplication of songs and instrumental pieces was comparatively slow in coming to perfection.

II

The Reformation in England did not take place with dramatic suddenness. Looked at in retrospect the period from, say, 1520 to 1560 appears to be one of continuous persecution and violence, yet in the country at large the old faith was powerful enough to withstand the force of statutory enactment. In any case, it should be recalled that attempts were made within the Catholic Church itself to revise the Liturgy in the early sixteenth century, and Luther's 'Kirchen-Ordnungen' belong to the period just before the English Reformation—though even when formal proclamations had been issued it was some time before their intentions were fully carried out. The anti-prelatical arguments of such a pamphlet as Simon Fish's *Supplicacyon for the Beggars* (*c.* 1529) are difficult to refute. Yet, as Sir Maurice Powicke says, 'The horror of monastic depravity which is expressed in the Act of 1535 was not a true reflection of popular opinion.'[2]

---

[1] A brief, but valuable, account of private teaching occurs in the *Autobiography of Thomas Whythorne* (ed. James Osborn, 1961): see also Harris, *loc. cit.*, p. 131.

[2] F. M. Powicke, *The Reformation in England* (1941), p. 28.

The exact state of 'popular opinion' at any time in the sixteenth century is not easily arrived at, but it is fair to say that the immediate result of the Reformation—as understood by its severest advocates—was a degree of general deprivation which was not confined to those it was intended to penalize. To take one consequence of the general upheaval which indirectly concerns us—the demise of the mystery plays and pageants: according to one authority, 'it was not the expense or the changes in the formation of the trade gilds' which led to their abandonment but 'a gradual revulsion of feeling on the part of the people, due to the work of religious reformers and the changing spirit of the age'.[1] It is difficult to be convinced that this revulsion was universal, for the mystery plays, after surviving mutilation in the reigns of Henry VIII and Edward VI were continued right until the 1560s and '70s because, among other things, Elizabeth and the Privy Council could not count on co-operation from subordinate officials when it came to suppressing the popular religious dramas.[2]

The Reformation threw into prominence the question of lay participation in religious services, and this was in turn related to the problem of admitting the use of the vernacular. Both Catholics and Protestants agreed that music had an important part to play in the acts of worship, but they differed in their notion of its proper use. In the Dialogue between Pole and Lupset, for instance, the writer (Thomas Starkey) makes Pole say 'touching the singing (in churches), they use a fashion more convenient to minstrels than to devout ministers of the divine service; for plainly, as it is used, this is truth, especially considering the words be so strange and so diversely descanted, it is more to the outward pleasure of the ear and vain recreation, than to the inward comfort of the heart and mind with good devotion'.[3] This is a familiar argument, but it does not necessarily follow that those who objected to descanting and the 'effeminate and over-refined strains' of Catholic service music would approve of the singing in public which Bishop Jewel described in a letter to Peter Martyr. 'Religion', wrote Jewel on 5 March

---

[1] M. Lyle Spencer, *Corpus Christi Pageants in England* (1911), pp. 249–50.

[2] See Harold C. Gardiner, *Mysteries' End . . .* (Yale, 1946), p. 70.

[3] Printed in *England in the Reign of Henry VIII* (E.E.T.S., 1878: E.S., xxxii), pp. 134 *et seq.* (spelling modernized).

1560, 'is now somewhat more established than it was. . . . The practice of joining in church music has very much conduced to this. For as soon as they once commenced singing in public, in only one little church in London, immediately not only the churches in the neighbourhood, but even the towns far distant, began to vie with each other in the same practice. You may now sometimes see at Paul's Cross, after the service, six thousand persons, old and young, of both sexes, all singing together and praising God. This sadly annoys the mass-priests, and the devil. For they perceive that by these means the sacred discourses sink more deeply into the minds of men, and that their kingdom is weakened and shaken at almost every note.'[1] The idiom of Latin church music had evolved under circumstances which did not favour voluntary expression on the part of the congregation. The Injunctions of Edward VI calling for the simplification of the music to be sung during religious services were in some ways the most radically Protestant of all the measures intended to ensure what Archbishop Parker referred to as a 'reverent mediocrity' in common ministry.

The demand that the Scriptures should be rendered in English was made repeatedly by the Reformers. *The Book of Common Prayer* is, of course, a form of vernacular liturgy in which the Roman rite is reduced in size and made available for all who can read English. The Preface to the First Prayer Book, indeed, harps on the extent to which things are now made 'plain and easy' for worshippers; whereas in the proper performance of the Catholic liturgy four books were necessary (namely the Missal, the Breviary, the Manual and the Pontifical), now the whole of the service material was contained under one cover. The section 'Of Ceremonies' speaks out boldly against the 'excessive multitude' of such superadditions, but in other parts of the volume much of the Catholic procedure and terminology is retained. As for the music, here again the break with Roman practice was not as extreme as might have been expected. John Merbeck's *Book of Common Prayer Noted* (1550) did indeed employ the one-syllable-one-note style as recommended in Cranmer's famous letter to Henry VIII, but Merbeck's melodic lines are very near to plainsong, this being adapted to suit the accentuation of the English language. By this means, as H. C. Colles pointed out, Merbeck

[1] Hastings Robinson, ed., *The Zurich Letters* (Parker Society, 1842), I. 71.

'called attention to the existence of certain natural verbal rhythms inherent in the English language'.[1] His work was therefore instrumental in helping to supplant plainsong in the consciousness of the ordinary churchgoer.

The mid-sixteenth century Injunctions, by means of which the intentions of the Reformers were put into effect, are all of great interest to the musical historian. Perhaps the set issued by Queen Elizabeth in 1559 is the most far-reaching of all. Article XLIX of this gives prominence to the necessity of rendering the service distinctly in English; it adds: 'and yet, nevertheless, for the comforting of such that delight in music, it may be permitted, that in the beginning, or in the end of the Common Prayers, either at morning or evening, there may be sung an hymn, or such like song, to the praise of Almighty God, in the best sort of melody and music that may be conveniently devised, having respect that the sentence of the hymn may be understanded and perceived'. The consequences of this enactment were more widespread than its promoters probably imagined: it was a concession to those who looked forward to hearing music in church; and it raised the question of musical literacy in an acute form. For while it might be highly desirable to have the congregation taking its full share in the music of the service, an unhappy situation could arise if members of the general public asserted their right to join in without really knowing what they were trying to sing. To the *Book of Common Prayer Noted* was added a preface together with a simple table setting out the four note values ('strene', 'semibreve', 'minim', 'crotchet') used in the book itself. This may be regarded as a prototype of the brief manuals of instruction placed at the beginning of several sixteenth- and seventeenth-century psalters, of which the most comprehensive is the 1561 edition of 'Sternhold and Hopkins'. This famous rendering of the Psalms—it did not bear the title of *The Whole Book of the Psalms* until 1562—included a 'Short Introduction into the Science of Musicke' in which it is taken for granted that men will want to sing psalms 'aswel in common places of prayer where al together with one voyce render thankes and praises to God, as privately by themselves or at home in their houses'. Such references to private performances are not uncommon in other collections of the period.

---

[1] Foreword to J. Eric Hunt, ed., *Cranmer's First Litany, 1544*, and *Merbeck's Book of Common Prayer Noted, 1550* (1939), p. viii.

Sternhold and Hopkins, by recasting the language of the Psalms in ballad metre, made a determined effort to appeal to the populace. But they were not the first to produce metrical psalms in English: Miles Coverdale's *Goostly Psalmes and Spirituall Songes* dates from about 1538, and this also uses the stanza form of the *Whole Book of the Psalms*. Coverdale's work, which drew heavily on Luther's earlier collection, has something in common with Sternhold and Hopkins; it proclaims an earnest desire to lead men's minds away from degrading secular songs. In his preface Coverdale announces that 'to give our youth of England some occasion to change their foul and corrupt ballads into sweet songs and spiritual hymns of God's honour, and for their consolation in him, I have here, good reader, set out certain comfortable songs grounded on God's word, and taken some out of the holy scripture, specially out of the Psalms of David, all whom would God that our musicians would learn to make their songs'.[1] Such sentiments as these are repeated in other volumes; they are important because they reveal the extent to which (as it seems) popular music was able to divert attention from the serious concerns which the Reformers had at heart. And what is more, they hint at a rather pharisaical attitude towards popular amusements. There is no need to labour this point, but whereas the zeal for total reformation in the religious sphere unquestionably contributed to the musical enlightenment of ordinary people, it also helped to discredit music which did not bear an exalted 'ditty'.

In another passage from the Injunctions of 1559, Queen Elizabeth declared her intention to refrain from making any alteration in the arrangement which already prevailed at parish and collegiate churches in respect of 'the laudable science of music'. The dissolution of the monastic houses had, obviously, thrown a great many musicians on the general labour market, and it is difficult to be sure how far the establishments of the 'new foundation' were able to make use of their services. The conflict of loyalties brought about by religious changes could not help but affect composers as well as poets and playwrights. Marbeck, for instance, was at one time under sentence of death for subscribing to Calvinistic heresies. John Taverner, on the

[1] George Pearson, ed., *Remains of Miles Coverdale* (Parker Society, 1846), p. 538.

other hand, supported Henry VIII's policies and towards the end of his life returned to Lincolnshire to 'arrange matters for the suppression of the four friaries at Boston in August 1538'.[1] The 'father of English cathedral music', Thomas Tallis (c. 1505–85), was organist at Waltham Abbey, Essex, at the time of the Dissolution; as compensation for the loss of his post he was allowed a monetary award. But not all 'singing men' were as fortunate as this. Numbers of them were compelled to accept menial employment or to desert music altogether. We must note that the Injunctions of Edward VI required that 'all antiphoners, missals, grayles, processionalles, manuelles, legendes, pies, portasies, journalles and ordinalles' should be defaced and abolished in case their use might prove prejudicial to the general reception of the Prayer Book. In this way a great deal of music came to be wantonly destroyed, thus depriving us of much written evidence that would throw light on pre-Reformation musical custom. In addition, some of the more puritanical among the prelates in their diocesan visitations put down the use of organs in places of worship. Thus at York in 1552 Archbishop Holgate decided to 'will and command that there be no more playings of the organs, either at Morning Prayer, the Communion, or the Evening Prayer . . . but that the said playing do utterly cease and be left the time of Divine Service within the said Church'.[2] Such prohibitions were not, however, universal, and in some places new instruments were installed in churches during the Edwardian and Elizabethan periods. To some of the overscrupulous, indeed, the organ stood as a symbol for popish luxury and superstition. A more enlightened attitude was that shown by Archbishop Parker when in 1564 he assured the French ambassador and his colleague the Bishop of Constance that 'our musick drowned not the principle regard of our prayer'.[3]

During the reign of Queen Mary the Catholic liturgy was restored. But this did not materially affect the trend of musical history. In actual fact, many of our composers seem to have been able to work just as well under a Catholic as under a Protestant régime, and vice versa. But the Reformation, though it swept

[1] W. H. Grattan Flood, *Early Tudor Composers* (1925), p. 51.
[2] W. H. Frere, ed., *Visitation Articles and Injunctions* . . . (Alcuin Club Collections, XV, 1910), p. 320.
[3] T. T. Perowne, ed., *Correspondence of Matthew Parker* (Parker Soc., 1853), p. 215.

away a great deal, had a number of positive effects on our musical culture. One of these—again an attempt to get rid of a superstitious practice—was the establishment of the Anthem in English as an important part of the full church service. Among the Royal Injunctions issued to Lincoln Cathedral in 1548, for instance, occurs the following passage: 'Item, they shall from henceforth sing or say no anthems of our Lady or other Saints, but only of our Lord, and them not in Latin; but choosing out the best and most sounding to Christian religion they shall turn the same into English, setting thereunto a plain and distinct note for every syllable one; they shall sing them and none other.'[1] The Royal Injunctions to Winchester College (1547) called for the omission of the 'Regina Caeli', the 'Salve Regina' and 'any suchlike untrue or superstitious anthem'.[2] The importance of proclamations like these rests in the fact that composers were given a fair amount of licence provided that certain conditions were honoured. The anthems of mid-sixteenth-century composers were virtually motets to English words; later, in the hands of Byrd, Morley, Tomkins and Orlando Gibbons, the English anthem achieved a power of devotional expression calculated, in Hooker's words, 'both to move and to moderate all affections'.[3]

III

The 'golden age' of English music stretches roughly from 1570 to 1645. There have been many attempts to account for its occurrence at this particular period. Thus, after reviewing some of the political events of the '70s and '80s, E. H. Fellowes writes: 'Small wonder that the whole country felt relief with the turn of events in 1588. It was possible to settle down to the Arts of Peace with a quiet mind in conditions that endured for a considerable period.'[4] This view of the age comes near to that which represents the contemporaries of Shakespeare, Donne, Dowland, Wilbye and Weelkes as living in a world of romantic pastoral fancy untroubled by the rigours of economic necessity. The 'Arts of Peace', however, include activities other than literature,

---

[1] Frere, *op. cit.*, p. 168.
[2] *Ibid.*, p. 151.
[3] Hooker, *Laws of Ecclesiastical Polity*, Book V, chapter xxxviii, paragraph 1.
[4] E. H. Fellowes, *English Cathedral Music* (1941), p. 70.

music and painting, and the careers of men like Shakespeare and Morley plainly indicate that they were neither of them entirely untouched by the commercial spirit. Elizabethan and Jacobean literature, not to mention parliamentary enactments as well, leave us in no doubt that men were preoccupied with problems arising from the inequitable distribution of wealth. There are constant references to the rising prices of commodities, the fall in the purchasing power of money, and the existence of much unnecessary poverty. The poorer classes felt keenly the periodic dearth so frequently alluded to in tracts and pamphlets, though on the other hand the great price rise of that era made possible a degree of prosperity among other sections of the population, which in turn was reflected in the state of the fine arts.

As a consequence of monastic dissolution, hundreds of estates changed hands between the Reformation and the Civil War. The only aspect of this phenomenon that need concern us is the one touched on by the writer of B.M. MS. Cole xii. This anonymous author states that the disruption of property brought about earlier in the century 'made of yeomen and artificers, gentlemen, and of gentlemen knights'. He also goes on to complain that, conversely, the Reformation made the poor of this country poorer than they had been before. These statements suggest a reason for the growing disrespect shown towards the concept of 'degree' which is said to have been predominant in Tudor society. The recent prolonged discussion on the Elizabethan gentry has, among other things, brought out the fact that despite oft-quoted proclamations and deference to revered notions there was a great deal of social mobility in the Elizabethan and Jacobean periods. Some evidence of this is contained in William Harrison's *Description of England* (1577–87) in which the customs of various social classes are discussed. At one stage Harrison considers four 'degrees' of people—gentlemen, citizens, yeomen and artificers. Citizens and burgesses come next in order to gentlemen as being 'of some (likelie) substance to beare office in (the cities)'; along with them Harrison places the merchants '(although they often change estate with gentlemen, as gentlemen doo with them, by a mutuall conversion of the one into the other) whose number is so increased in these our daies, that their onelie maintenance is the cause of the exceeding prices of forreine wares'.[1] This last contention is, of course, wide of the mark, but Harrison's observations suggest the nature of the forces which were helping to strengthen the *bourgeois* elements in Elizabethan and Jacobean society. And it is the cultural tastes of the well-to-do which now call for investigation.

The establishment of a workable money economy gave citizens, burgesses and merchants an important position in Renaissance life. 'In England in the sixteenth century', writes G. N. Clark, 'the markets for so many kinds of goods expanded that the money-market, which fed them all with capital, expanded too. More people made it their business to deal in money, so that borrowing was less a mere touting round among those who might have money to spare. The money-market was in some ways very well organized.'[2] The acquisition of large fortunes by men who had speculated in industries and finance or acquired landed property had its inevitable outcome—conspicuous expenditure. But in this case 'conspicuous' is not a term of reproach: and Pope's sarcasms in the Fourth Moral Epistle (line 100) about Timon's villa would not have applied to the majority of the houses, great and small, which were built in town and country during the later half of the sixteenth century. That this was a truly great age of domestic architecture few will deny. Moreover, these newly built houses were furnished with well-designed chairs, tables, beds and other items hitherto regarded as luxuries. Glazed windows were now becoming more common: the old-fashioned wooden platters and spoons were gradually being replaced by silverware and pewter, and as Harrison pertinently observed, 'whilest I behold how that in a time wherein all things are growen to most excessive prices . . . we doo yet find the means to obtein & atchive such furniture as heretofore hath been unpossible'.[3] The wills of prominent Elizabethan and Jacobean citizens reveal a considerable partiality for exquisite jewellery and miscellaneous *objets d'art*. Harrison mentions the vogue for Venetian glass, and fine embroidery was often worn as part of everyday dress. The secular music admired in the milieux created by these conditions must now be considered.

[1] F. J. Furnivall, *Harrison's Description of England* (New Shakespeare Society, 1877), p. 131. (The complicated question of the relationship which Harrison's work bears to that of Sir Thomas Smith does not have relevance here.)

[2] Clark, *The Wealth of England* (1946), p. 78.

[3] *Harrison's Description* . . . ., p. 239.

For the most part it consisted of vocal and instrumental chamber music suitable for performance among small parties of friends gathered together in private apartments. Concerted music for more than a few instruments does not make an independent appearance in England until well into the seventeenth century. There were, of course, small ensembles in the theatres: but as yet no instrumental groups engaged to play for the general public. Between 1587 and 1630 over eighty collections of vocal music, most of it in several parts, were published; but before discussing this, something must be said about instrumental music during the period.

The three main instruments in general use were the virginals, the viol and the lute. They are often mentioned together in household accounts, of which a particularly good example is that made available in F. G. Emmison's study of Sir William Petre.[1] The lute—of which Sir William's son John seems to have been particularly fond—has been called the most serious solo instrument of the sixteenth century; its complicated tuning made it difficult to handle, though it was impressive when played by a virtuoso. The lute and other fretted instruments such as the cittern and orpharion were in demand for accompanying the voice, and instruction books for them began to appear in the middle of the century. A striking testimony to the esteem in which this 'king of instruments' was held by serious-minded people is provided in the manuscript instruction book compiled for Mary Burwell in the 1660s (or thereabouts) and reprinted in the *Galpin Society Journal* (May 1958). 'It maketh alone a consort of music,' says the writer; 'it speaks without any origin; and out of dead and dumb things it draws a soul that seems reasonable. . . .' A similarly reverential tone was adopted by Thomas Mace in his great apologia for the lute and the viol, *Musick's Monument* (1676).

As for the viols, it has sometimes been maintained that these bowed instruments are more suited to amateur ensemble performance than their successors, the violin family. It may be that a player can attain a tolerable standard more easily on a viol than, say, on a viola, and consequently that he may confidently bear his part in a sixteenth-century fantasy after a few years' tuition (whereas a longer period would be necessary for the performance

[1] F. G. Emmison, *Tudor Secretary* . . . (1961), pp. 210–16.

of modern music). But this does not mean that capable viol-playing is accomplished without serious study. One reason why the viol was so suitable for group performance in the kind of milieu we are discussing, however, lies in the fact that it has an even and subdued tone, which enables the players to hear the other parts of a consort without much difficulty. A great deal of music written for viols in this period was not published, because it was produced for private use. But those collections which did get into print reveal a considerable interest in consort-playing during the hundred years before the Restoration. Such publications as Anthony Holborne's *Pavans, Galliards, Almains . . .for Viols, Violins, or other Musicall Wind Instruments* (1599) and Morley's *First Book of Consort Lessons* (1599) show that composers were willing to make allowance for the fact that ensembles had to be made up from whatever instruments were available. As Professor Westrup observes, following up a point made in Roger North's *Musicall Grammarian*, 'A chest of viols was not a universal possession',[1] a fact which explains the existence of the 'broken' consort. The violin, though well known in Henry VIII's time, did not make its début as the main treble stringed instrument until late in the seventeenth century; at first it was employed alongside viols, but in due course its stronger and more alluring tone gave it a prominence which the viol could not rival. Mace's *Musick's Monument* bemoans the fate of the 'sprightly, generous, and heroic viol', but Mace did not record that there were social as well as purely musical reasons for its gradual disappearance. The frisky and nimble violins, in short, led to the composition of music which was more congenial to Restoration musical taste than the intricate polyphonic textures to which the viol had been so well suited, and 'Restoration taste' is in turn associated with that desire for novelty and bravura which characterized all aspects of cultural life after 1660.

Curiously enough, comparatively little instrumental music of any kind was published in England before the seventeenth century. But this does not mean that it was not written down and collected. The Fitzwilliam Virginal Book is only one of a number of such compilations made up from the work of many composers. But the virginal was a well-established domestic instrument by

[1] J. A. Westrup, 'Domestic Music under the Stuarts', *Proc. Mus. Ass.*, LXVIII (1942), p. 27.

the beginning of the sixteenth century, and indeed traditions of performance at the keyboard date from a much earlier period than this. As we see from Philip Welder's inventory, there were several kinds of portable keyboard instruments in Henry VIII's royal establishments, but the virginal itself is the simplest of them all. In appearance it resembles a small piano: its strings, lying at right-angles to the keys, are plucked by a set of 'jacks' which are brought into contact with the string when the keys are pressed down. This comparatively simple action, and the fact that the virginal has a compass of barely four octaves made it an easy instrument to carry from room to room. It could, of course, be mounted on a trestle, but in any case the virginal's small body of tone made it inaudible in large halls. The clavichord, which is sometimes confused with the virginal, has a different kind of action, the strings being struck rather than plucked. Generally speaking, it was less popular in England than in other European countries. The virginal, however, continued in vogue until the eighteenth century; in the shop kept by John Playford, virginals and harpsichords were offered for sale together. In the sixteenth century English makers of keyboard instruments were not numerous, though there were more of them during the Stuart period. Their number was constantly being increased by refugees who had fled from the Low Countries as a result of religious persecution.

The various virginal books—the Lady Nevell's Book, Benjamin Cosyn's Book, etc.—consist of short pieces, fantasies, dances, 'toys' and movements in variation form. Some of these items were simply harmonizations of melodies already existing in some other version, but most of the better-known sixteenth-century composers left many examples of original music written for the keyboard. None of this, however, was published before 1611, when an engraved volume entitled *Parthenia or the Maydenhead of the first musicke that ever was printed for the Virginalls* was issued. For the modern musician this book is extremely difficult to read, partly because the six-line stave is used and partly because no attempt is made to ensure that the notes in the bass part fall into their appropriate places underneath their counterparts in the treble. Incidentally, the virginal was not played exclusively by females: in Sir William Petre's accounts it is twice referred to as 'my master's' and not 'my lady's', and

John Petre had his own virginal as well as a viol.[1] The difficulty of reading the music of the sixteenth century is not so acute (assuming the note values are understood) when it comes to vocal compositions, which were issued in sets of small books, one to each part. It would be interesting to know something at first hand of the manner in which ballets and madrigals were performed in this period. No full scores appear to have survived, though it is too much—especially in the absence of bar lines—to expect that such ensembles could keep together for long without some such aid. Denis Stevens assures us that so far as sacred music was concerned, the music 'certainly existed in score before it was copied out according to its component voice-parts, since it is obviously difficult to compose complex polyphony other than in score'.[2] Admittedly; and since so much virginal music has been handed down to us in manuscript form, we are prompted to ask what happened to, say, the score of *The Triumphs of Oriana* and the numerous other madrigal collections.

Anyone who has studied Professor Westrup's paper on 'Domestic Music under the Stuarts'[3] will hesitate before accepting too facile a view of music at the turn of the sixteenth century. All the same, Morley's *Introduction* does give us some notion of contemporary customs. It needs, however, to be read in conjunction with other pieces, in particular the dedications and prefaces to the various sets of madrigals and airs published in the late Elizabethan and Jacobean periods. Perhaps the most informative of all these is that given in *Musica Transalpina* (1588), a second volume of which appeared in 1597. This was compiled by Nicholas Yonge, whose address to Gilbert, Lord Talbot has often been quoted. It is memorable, however, for its reference to the 'Gentlemen and Merchants of good accompt (as well of this realme as of forreine nations)' who met at Yonge's house in the City of London, and also for its confirmation of the fact that Italian madrigals and English imitations of them found favour with such amateur performers. The vogue for Italian part-songs was followed up by other composers and translators, Morley publishing two sets (untranslated) and Thomas Watson the *First Sett of Italian Madrigalls Englished* (1590). In this way

---

[1] Emmison, *op. cit.*, p. 214.
[2] Denis Stevens, *Tudor Church Music* (1961), p. 13.
[3] Westrup, *op. cit.*, p. 28.

the works of composers like Marenzio, Croce and Lassus gained a restricted circulation in this country.

The Elizabethan attitude towards Italian affairs in general was an ambiguous one. From a work like William Thomas's *Historie of Italie* (1549) it appears that the courage, spontaneity and 'civility' of the Italians was admired. On the other hand their quick resort to violence and their haughty conception of honour gave rise to a kind of fascinated distrust. But to amateur musicians such as those Nicholas Yonge speaks of, the Italian style in secular vocal composition represented a very desirable standard of attainment. All the same, it is legitimate to speak of a distinctly English idiom of madrigal-writing represented in different ways by the works of Byrd, Morley, Wilbye and Weelkes. The volumes published by these and lesser composers are too numerous to mention in detail, but it is worth observing that their titles—especially in the case of solo-songs—indicate a readiness on the composer's part to accommodate the abilities of the moderately capable performer. The elaborate title-page of Thomas Whythorne's *Duos* (1590), for example, tells us that this volume (issued in parts) contains songs of which 'some be playne and easie to be sung, or played on Musicall Instruments, & be made for yong beginners of both these sorts. And the rest of these Duos be made and set foorth for those that be more perfect in singing or playing'—the whole being arranged so that various combinations of instruments and voices are possible. John Dowland's *First Book of Airs* are, as the composer observes, 'So made that all the partes together, or either of them severally, may be sung to the Lute, Orphereon, or Viol de Gambo.' In this, as in similar volumes, the inclinations of the average performer are studied. The desire to obtain *rapport* without condescension, however, was not necessarily a subterfuge intended to increase sales: composers were well aware that such provisos were called for by the conditions of the time.

An analysis of the dedications prefixed to the madrigal collections shows that composers expected to find patronage for their work among the nobility, the lesser gentry, the 'ungentle gentle' and the minor government officials of the day. After quoting the dedication (to Sir George Carey) from Morley's *Canzonets* (1597), Professor Westrup writes: 'How pompous the whole thing is, and how clear a picture it presents of the environment in which these pieces were sung—the stately house, the elegant furniture, the rich hangings, and the patron either performing in dignified solitude or engaging others to do it for him.'[1] Yet it should be recalled that Morley's four-part *Canzonets* (published the same year) were dedicated to 'Master Henrie Tapsfield Citizen and Grocer of the Cittie of London'; Weelkes's *Balletts and Madrigals* (1598) were addressed to Edward Darcye, Groom of Her Majesty's Privy Council; while Richard Alison's *Howres Recreation in Musick* (1606) (inscribed to Sir John Scudamore) was 'Framed for the delight of Gentlemen and others which are well affected to that qualitie' (of music). Other examples would bear out that these compositions were not intended for an exclusively aristocratic audience. And the presence of a famous name on a title-page does not necessarily guarantee that the person concerned was able to live up to all that is said of him in the dedication. At the most it indicates a modest hope that notice will be taken of the composer's work and some kind of reward given either in the form of ready money or relevant 'influence'.

Not all the recipients of these fulsome addresses were able to advance the fortunes of composers and performers. Yet unquestionably there were men in responsible positions who could afford to give musicians more or less permanent employment. The Earl of Leicester, for instance, maintained a company of musicians on much the same basis as the dramatic company which performed in his name; Lord Berkeley likewise had a 'band of musicians' under his patronage; and Sir Arthur Hevingham kept liveried servants to perform musical duties.[2] These, obviously, were in a different category from those whose names have been mentioned above, yet many of the major composers of the time enjoyed the intimate acquaintance of the great. William Byrd was familiar with and greatly respected by the Petre family; Robert Dowland, the son of John Dowland, was educated at the expense of Sir Thomas Monson; and Philip Rosseter, in his *Lessons for Consort* (1609), speaks warmly of the favours he received from Sir William Gascoyne of Sedbury. But perhaps the most famous of all noble patrons of music in this period was Sir

[1] *Ibid.*, p. 22.
[2] See J. T. Murray, *English Dramatic Companies* (1910), II. 337; see also Walter L. Woodfill, *Musicians in English Society from Elizabeth to Charles I* (Princeton, 1953), Appendix B, pp. 252–79 (Household Records).

Thomas Kytson, of Hengrave Hall, Suffolk. Inventories from the Elizabethan and Jacobean periods quoted in John Gage's *History and Antiquities of Hengrave* (1822) show that the Kytson family had a great partiality for instrumental music and were lavish in their emoluments to players, teachers and instrument-makers. John Wilbye (1574–1638) was at one time the Kytsons' 'resident' composer, and the furnishings of 'Wilbee's Chamber' at Hengrave were anything but niggardly. The Hengrave accounts have been quoted many times, but it is worth noting that they were not confined to expenditure on just one or two musicians: a great many disbursements were made to actors, minstrels and players of unspecified kinds. This is enough to remind us that in the large and medium-sized country seats, of which Hengrave is only one, dramatic entertainments which made a considerable use of music were a fairly common occurrence.

The most important of such devisings was, of course, the masque, which was wholly aristocratic in tone. It was a form of entertainment in which the monarch and members of the aristocracy delighted, and it constituted another channel by which Italian styles and artistic devices were introduced into England. 'From the time of Henry VIII to the outbreak of the Civil War', writes Enid Welsford, 'the history of our English masque is the history of the absorption (and modification) of influences coming from Italy, either directly or by way of France.'[1] The tradition of masquing in one form or another goes back a long way, and records of it exist throughout the Tudor and Stuart periods; the office of the Master of the Revels, which involved the arrangement of such productions, grew in importance during the late sixteenth century. But the presentation of masques was not confined to the court circle: other social groups such as the Inns of Court were active in devising and performing them. Without going too deeply into the history and structure of the masque, we may notice that at its most sophisticated it is essentially a formalized festival—a 'triumph' to which many kinds of creative activity were made to contribute. As it developed it became an ordered celebration of some particularly notable event—a wedding, a state visit, a meeting between eminent people—in which aspects of the occasion were given symbolic recognition. It is impossible to do justice to the immense variety of the Elizabethan

[1] Enid Welsford, *The Court Masque* (1927), p. 81.

and Jacobean masques, so rich are they in their appeal to the five senses. In the spoken parts the main themes are announced: these are embellished with songs and accompanying instrumental music, and there is always an elaborate *mise en scène*. But the one feature of the masque which surpassed all others was the profusion of dances. These were of many kinds, and included conventional measures such as galliards and courantes as well as more fantastic gesticulations.[1]

The presentation of masques involved an enormous expenditure of money and labour. But their very existence in the period is evidence of a sensitive relationship between the monarch and the more illustrious nobility. In her various 'progresses', for example, Queen Elizabeth was greeted with a 'show' at the country houses she visited, and her hosts vied with each other in the magnificence and ingenuity displayed on such occasions. A distinction is usually made between an 'entertainment' and a full-scale masque, but from a musical point of view both types of diversion are of roughly equal significance. This can be illustrated from the work of Ben Jonson, whose genius was very fertile in this direction. Jonson's entertainments vary in length and impressiveness. For example, the first part of that given at Althorpe Park in June 1603 on the occasion of Queen Anne's visit to Lord Spencer's household, contained some 'excellent soft Musique' by way of introduction to the main business, several dances, and the song 'This is She', together with the concluding 'noyse of cornets, hornes, and other hunting musique'. In the *Entertainment at Highgate* (1604) there is a three-part song, and for the *Entertainment . . . at Theobalds* (1607) a choral group was engaged to bear the burden of the song 'O blessed change'.

In the masques proper the musical requirements were much more ambitious than this. *The Gipsies Metamorphosed* (1621), for example, contains nine songs and eleven dances, not to mention other incidental music; and *Neptune's Triumph* (1624), after the performance of several songs divided between soloists and chorus, concludes with a 'Song to the whole Musique, five lutes, three Cornets, and ten voyces'. An ensemble of about the same size is required for William Browne's *Inner Temple Masque* of

[1] See Otto Gombosi, 'Some Musical Aspects of the English Court Masque' in *Journal of the American Musicological Society* (Fall, 1948), p. 4.

1641, in which 'the music was composed of treble violins with all the inward parts, a bass viol, bass lute, sagbut, cornamute, and a tabor and pipe'.[1] By comparison with this, Campian's *Masque in Honour of Lord Hayes* (1607), in which two instrumental consorts and a double chorus took part must have seemed a veritable musical banquet. Jonson's *Love Freed from Ignorance and Folly* (1611) also employed upwards of fifty musicians. In several of Ben Jonson's masques the *stylo recitativo* was introduced for purposes of musical declamation, and there were other anticipations of operatic devices. Perhaps the grandest of the Caroline masques was *The Triumph of Peace* (1633), for which the words were provided by James Shirley, and the music by William Lawes and Simon Ives.[2] Generally speaking, the masque gave composers scope for the invention of songs in a variety of styles, as well as dance music and entr'acte pieces. Many of these incidental items needed careful timing, and in both vocal and instrumental music the masque invited the cultivation of a 'dramatic' approach to the art of composition. This in turn favoured the adoption of homophonic musical textures. 'Acting in song, especially in dialogues,' wrote Francis Bacon in his essay 'Of Masques and Triumphs', 'hath an extreme good grace', especially if the words were 'high and tragical, not nice or dainty'.

The masque retained its popularity throughout the Caroline period, but as a histrionic form in its own right it did not long survive the Civil War. In a sense it never died out completely, for masque-like scenes are fairly common in eighteenth-century operas. But the upheavals of the 1640s destroyed the social cohesion which made such productions possible. After all, the presentation of masques depended on the goodwill of numerous amateur performers (many of them menial servants) whose talents were at the disposal of those in charge of affairs. And though a number of masques were given in the late seventeenth century, the rise of professionalism in the theatre completely altered the spirit in which they were presented. Yet the association between music and the drama was throughout this period a very full and intimate one. In this connection the year 1576 is important.

It was in the earlier part of 1576 that James Burbage and his

---

[1] Gordon Goodwin, ed., *The Poems of William Browne* (1894), II. 181.

[2] See Leslie Hotson, *The Commonwealth and Restoration Stage* (1928), p. 152.

associates opened the Theatre in Shoreditch. This was followed by the construction of the Curtain close by and subsequently by the Bankside playhouses which became the *venue* of the leading acting companies of the time. In December 1576 Richard Farrant, who was then in charge of the Children of the Chapel Royal, leased a part of the old monastic site at Blackfriars for the purpose of setting up what has come to be known as the 'first' Blackfriars Theatre. Originally this structure was intended to serve as a place in which the Children could rehearse plays; later it came to be something more than this. For the Children did not perform merely to amuse themselves: they were a source of diversion for the monarch and members of the court. In the late sixteenth century there was a considerable tradition of dramatic production by the choristers attached to several religious establishments, and the officials in charge of the various chapels were employed as much for their literary ability as for their musical talents. Such men as William Cornyshe, John Heywood and William Crane were expected to write plays as well as to compose service music. Their interludes and other dramatic pieces do not strike us now as living literature, but they wrote to meet a specific need, and from the musical point of view their dramatic ventures have one or two points of special interest.

At this time of day it seems incredible that the performances of child actors could exert a fascination for adult audiences, but it is quite clear that during the sixteenth century the presence of juveniles on the stage was a perfectly acceptable convention. The stiff and formal dialogue of a piece like *Damon and Pythias* which was played 'before the Queenes *Maiestie*, by the Children of her *Graces* Chappell' about 1565 makes one wonder how its lumbering slowness was ever endured. But the author, Richard Edwards (? 1523–66), was a composer of some note who had grasped the principle that the musical expression of emotion is called for in moments of tension and despair. Thus when Pythias knows that Damon is condemned to die he sings a lament, 'Awake ye wofull Wightes', which foreshadows the kind of thing found in many later dramas. Elsewhere in the play there is some convivial ensemble singing while Grimme the collier is being given a shave. In his lecture on 'Elizabethan Choirboy Plays and their Music', G. E. P. Arkwright cited other examples of music from chorister plays by composers like Nicholas Strogers, Robert

Parsons and Nathaniel Patricke.[1] The latter was sometime organist at Worcester Cathedral; and in 1593 John Hilton, another ecclesiastical musician, received payment for helping to prepare plays to be acted by the choristers at Lincoln.

A famous passage in *Hamlet* (Act II, Scene 2) (omitted in the Quarto of 1604) shows that as late as 1600–1 the popularity of the children performing in 'private' theatres could still be an embarrassment to the common players. But in the public playhouses such as the Fortune and the Swan the main actors were men, with a small number of boys to take the women's parts. The apprenticeship system obtained in acting just as in other trades, and the younger members of the more important professional troupes were occasionally drawn from the ranks of the choristers. In any case, from a professional point of view musicians and actors were not then as distinct as they have since become. In the various companies with which Shakespeare and Ben Jonson were associated there were several actors—such as William Kempe and Augustine Phillips—who were fine musicians. The place of music in the drama of the period can be looked at from two angles—the functional and the textural: or, in other words, we must ask what use music and musicians were put to in the various types of plays presented, and we must also examine the kind of musical knowledge the dramatists expected their audiences to have.

'Primitive English comedy', wrote W. J. Lawrence in 1912, 'was nothing if not musical.'[2] But inter-act music such as is found in Udall's *Ralph Roister Doister* (*c.* 1560) and the anonymous *Gammer Gurton's Needle* (*c.* 1575) is also used in tragedy of the same period. Sackville and Norton's *Gorboduc* (1560–1), for instance, has an elaborate musical accompaniment for the dumb show which precedes each act. At a later stage the public companies made careful provision for incidental music, which was required by nearly all plays. In the *Diary* of Philip Henslowe, who for many years acted as a financier for theatrical affairs in London and opened the Rose Theatre in 1587, there are many references to payments made for musical instruments; and E. K. Chambers quotes an inventory of 1598 which included among the properties acquired by the Admiral's Men 'iij trumpettes

---

[1] In *Proc. Mus. Ass.*, XL (1913–14), p. 131.
[2] Lawrence, *The Elizabethan Playhouse and Other Studies* (1912), p. 75.

and a drum, and a trebel viall, a basse viall, a bandore, a sytteren
. . . j chyme of bells . . . iij tymbrells . . . j sack-bute'.[1] Practically all of these items are put to use—not merely spoken of—
in the plays of Marlowe and Shakespeare. The trumpet figures
in countless stage directions, two or more being required on
military and processional occasions. The drum beats Macbeth's
approach; a bell 'invites' him to enter Duncan's chamber. The
viol, either as a solo instrument or in consort, is found in several
episodes such as that in *Pericles* (Act III, Scene 2) where Thaisa
is restored to life by the strains of music, and in *Troilus and
Cressida* (Act III, Scene 1) where Pandarus promises 'good
broken music' to Helen. An instrument of the lute family is
required in the fourth act of *Julius Caesar* when Brutus, just
before encountering the ghost of Caesar, calls on his boy Lucius
for some music. Towards the end of *Coriolanus* (Act V, Scene 4)
we are told by the Second Messenger that

> The trumpets, sackbuts, psalteries, and fifes
> Tabors and cymbals, and the shouting Romans,
> Make the sun dance . . .

though only trumpets, hautboys and drums are mentioned in the
First Folio stage directions. Hautboys were commonly used to
provide 'loud music'. Songs are, of course, very numerous in the
comedies of Shakespeare. In the major tragedies they underline
the pathos of Ophelia's suicide and Desdemona's undeserved
murder; the last plays utilize musical accompaniments in association with miraculous happenings, as in the statue scene of *The
Winter's Tale* and throughout *The Tempest*. An interesting indication of divergence of custom between the private theatres and
the public stage during the Jacobean period occurs in the epi-
logue to John Marston's *Sophonisba* (1606), where the author
plainly states that 'the Entrances and Musique' as given in the
printed text reflect only the manner of its performance 'by
youths, and after the fashion of the private stage'.

The size of the instrumental ensemble found in the playhouses
of Shakespeare's time obviously varied from one production to
another. An historical drama needed a more ambitious accompaniment than a trivial comedy, and a play in which the elements
figured spasmodically called for percussive effects that would be

[1] Chambers, *The Elizabethan Stage*, II. 542.

out of place in a domestic farce. But the general importance of music was recognized by the inclusion of a 'music room' in the layout of the Elizabethan and Jacobean theatres. This compartment for the musicians was situated—as the stage directions again and again indicate—above the heads of the players and out of sight of the audience, or, alternatively, curtained off so as to make possible the illusion of music coming from an unspecified source.

As for the occasions on which music was introduced into drama, these were too numerous to mention in detail. Music creates 'atmosphere' in *Twelfth Night* and *The Tempest*; it serves as an accompaniment to courtship in *Volpone* and *The Taming of the Shrew*; it ushers in a miniature masque at the conclusion of *A Tale of a Tub*; it heralds supernatural occurrences in *Julius Caesar*; it acts as light relief in *As You Like It*; and it emphasizes the magniloquence of *Tamburlaine*. These are well-known examples, but music is equally important in the work of dramatists less celebrated than Shakespeare and Jonson, such as Lyly, Middleton and Fletcher. Most of these dramatists introduce dance measures into their plays, and musicians contributed to the numerous 'jiggs' which formed the concluding item at most public theatrical performances. By Shakespeare himself music is frequently made the subject of verbal play—some of it quite unsubtle and on the level of the simple pun, some much more ingenious and assuming an exact knowledge of musical phraseology. There is the famous episode in *Hamlet*, for instance, when Hamlet challenges Rosencrantz to play the recorder: after Rosencrantz has protested his ignorance, Hamlet goes on to reveal not only a very profound understanding of Claudius's motives for sending Rosencrantz and Guildenstern to him, but also an intimate acquaintance with the terms actually in use among wind players. To what extent we should be justified in taking Shakespeare's detailed references to such things as 'proportion', 'divisions' and so on as evidence that his audience was in possession of recondite information it is difficult to decide. But the casual nature of such allusions in the work of Webster, Nashe and others supports the view that the average Elizabethan playgoer understood musical terminology as readily as he did the language in which, say, fencing, falconry and indoor games were spoken of. We do not know for certain how far Shakespeare was personally acquainted with major composers. But he was familiar with a very large range of popular songs and dance music, and in his plays the popular and sophisticated varieties of musical art coalesce in an extraordinary manner. On the one hand we have the exquisite lutenist songs in *Twelfth Night* and the *Two Gentlemen of Verona*, on the other the 'dildos and fadings' so relished by the clown in *The Winter's Tale*.

IV

To the social historian of music *The Winter's Tale* is perhaps the most interesting of Shakespeare's plays, because it not only presents a pedlar of ballads in the person of Autolycus but also gives one very good reason for the popularity of the simple broadsheets then on sale. 'I love a ballad in print, a' life,' says Mopsa, 'for then we are sure they are true.' The unsophisticated person's assumption that whatever comes to be printed must be authentic could hardly be better put. Yet Shakespeare's caricature of contemporary ballad literature is not unduly extravagant. In 1562, for instance, there was printed in London a 'True reporte of the forme and shape of a monstrous childe borne at Much Horkesleye, a village about three miles from Colchester . . .' and in 1604 a ballad of a 'strange and monstruous fishe seene in the sea on friday the 17 of february 1603' was entered in the Stationers' Register. The invention and refurbishing of ballads in this period engaged a number of writers such as Richard Tarlton, Martin Parker and William Elderton who had acquired the knack of paraphrasing earlier accounts and then regurgitating them in a jog-trot metre. Shakespeare and Ben Jonson held such individuals in contempt: they regarded it as a serious punishment to be 'traduced by odious ballads', yet they did not scruple to introduce ballad strains into their plays when occasion demanded such things. Upwards of twenty different ballad tunes are either named or alluded to in the plays of Shakespeare.

'Of the passion for the ballad among the people there can be no doubt,' writes C. R. Baskervill.[1] In his *Principles of Musik* (1636) Charles Butler speaks of 'the infinite multitude of Ballads (set to sundry pleasant and delightful tunes, by cunning and witty composers), with country dances fitted unto them'. This process

---

[1] C. R. Baskervill, *The Elizabethan Jig* (Chicago, 1929), pp. 31–32.

of adapting simple ballads to existing music was a very common practice, and one tune occasionally became associated with several different sets of words. Ballad tunes were frequently used as dance melodies, as is apparent from several passages in contemporary literature.[1] On the subject-matter of the ballads we need not dwell. They covered a wide range of topics—historical, political and religious—and exploited the 'human interest' side of current affairs. A great number of them were straightforward moralizations. At all times music is effective in helping unlettered people to memorize words: thus throughout the sixteenth and seventeenth centuries it had a certain importance in the formation of public opinion. In the *Strange Histories* (1602) of Thomas Deloney, for instance, the dangers of sedition and the duplicity of the papists form the subject of several ballads; and Catholic ballad-writers were also active during this period, some of them singing (like the author of '*Hierusalem*, my happie home') the joys of heaven on earth.[2] In the 1640s a good deal of Royalist and anti-Royalist propaganda was set out in ballad form. It must be recalled, of course, that there were any number of purely *literary* ballads that were not sung, but where, as in so many cases, the tunes were printed along with the words, the possibility of performance was at least envisaged.

There exist (or existed) several ballads from the Tudor and Stuart periods dealing with the subject of music. Of particular interest in this connection are Nicholas Whight's *Commendation of Musicke, And a Confutation of them which disprayse it* (*c.* 1562) and the anonymous 'Sweet music mourns and hath done long'.[3] The former justifies the art of music on historical and scriptural grounds; the latter addresses itself, early in the reign of James I, to a contemporary situation. Evidently not meant to be sung, this 'songe in praise of musique' attributes the present decline of music in large measure to the 'puritanes',

> Whose hautie, proude, disdainfull myndes
> Much fault agaynst poore musique findes,

---

[1] *Ibid.*, p. 10, where William Webbe's *Discourse of English Poetrie* is quoted in support of this.

[2] Hyder E. Rollins, ed., *Old English Ballads, 1553–1625* (1920), p. 164.

[3] For Whight see Herbert L. Collman, ed., *Ballads and Broadsides Chiefly of the Elizabethan Period* (1912), No. 92; also Hyder Rollins, 'Concerning Bodleian MS Ashmole 48' in *Modern Language Notes*, XXXIV (1919), p. 341.

and goes on to lament the fact that despite Queen Elizabeth's provisions for the maintenance of singing men and boys, things have so turned out that the funds intended for their support have been misappropriated.[1] In his *Popular Music of the Olden Time*, William Chappell quoted from a British Museum manuscript (Roy. 18 B. xix) which sets out this position in some detail and recommends that the statutes of every cathedral and collegiate church should be looked into so that 'poor singing men' might have their rights fully restored. 'As to the Puritans,' writes William Chappell, 'many of the clergy who were raised to preferments in Queen Elizabeth's reign, spent the time of their exile in such churches as followed the Genevan form of worship, and returned much disaffected to the rites and ceremonies that were re-established, and especially to cathedral service.'[2] The Puritan attitude towards music and entertainment generally is reflected in a number of tracts, of which Phillip Stubbes's *Anatomie of Abuses* (1583) may be quoted, because it draws on classical writers who provide arguments quite contrary to those set out in Nicholas Whight's *Commendation*. In Stubbes's view music is seductive and thus likely to allure men to effeminacy, pusillanimity and depraved living. It *has* a rationale; but this is very different from the one in estimation at present. Music is degraded by its association with dancing; minstrels and other such 'bawdy parasits as range the Cuntreyes, ryming and singing of uncleane, corrupte and filthie songs' are simply agents for the dissemination of scurrility. 'But if musick openly were used . . . to the praise and glory of God, as our Fathers used it, and as was intended by it at the first, or privatly in a mans secret Chamber or house . . . If Musick were thus used it would comfort man wunderfully, and moove his hart to serve God the better; but being used as it is, it corrupteth good minds, maketh them womannish, and inclined to all kinde of whordome and mischeef.'[3] Strictures of this sort were, of course, repeatedly uttered in the early seventeenth century. It will be noticed that Stubbes does not reject music altogether—indeed, its 'sollacious' aspects attract him: he merely insists that it must be made to minister to

---

[1] See Rollins, *Old English Ballads*, p. 142.

[2] Chappell, *Popular Music of the Olden Time* (1855–9), II. 403.

[3] F. J. Furnivall, ed., *Phillip Stubbes's Anatomy of the Abuses in England in Shakespeare's Youth* (New Shakespeare Society, 1877–9), pp. 170–1.

the life of the spirit rather than to the gratification of the senses. Other writers could be quoted in this connection. But we shall not understand the Puritan standpoint properly if we fail to bear in mind the lengths to which hatred of Rome—the subject of dozens of ballads—was carried during this period. The fierce determination to take the process of reformation to its ultimate end had repercussions in all branches of life. To such fanaticism can be attributed the ransacking of churches which followed enactments like the 'Ordinance for further demolishing of Monuments of Idolatry and Superstition', dated 9 May 1644. This decreed that 'all Organs, and the Frames or Cases wherein they stand in all Churches and or Chappels aforesaid, shall be taken away, and utterly defaced, and none hereafter set up in their places'. It would be absurd to whitewash the men who ordered and engaged in the destruction of church property such as went on at places like Norwich, Worcester, Exeter and elsewhere, but as Percy Scholes has argued, this did not after all amount 'to anything beyond the carrying into effect of one of the Injunctions of Edward VI, of nearly a century earlier, which was repeated by Elizabeth (1559) in almost the same words'.[1] The characteristic severity of the Puritan iconoclasts was the result of literal interpretation taken to its absurdest limits. At the same time it must be observed that the kind of ransacking described by Bishop Hall was the work of extremists who acted too zealously on the instructions given them to 'demolish' and 'deface'. As W. H. Hutton put it, 'Designed for the purification of the sanctuary, it (Puritanism) became merely an occasion of sacrilegious outrage.'[2] It is small consolation to know that the mid-seventeenth century destruction of organs gave rise, at a later stage, to the church bands which will be discussed in the next chapter.

Percy Scholes's work on the Puritan attitude to music has done much to discountenance the view that the Civil War and its aftermath put a stop to serious music-making in England. Scholes was not the first to suggest that the Puritans had been 'much maligned' in this connection, but the evidence he drew on was disarmingly conclusive. What had been overlooked by some authors was the fact that such things as the ban on full-scale

---

[1] Scholes, *The Puritans and Music* (1934), p. 235.

[2] W. H. Hutton, *A History of the English Church from the Accession of Charles I to the Death of Queen Anne* (1903), p. 127.

service music in churches could not be *totally* effective, any more than the closing of the public theatres in 1642 could entirely obliterate the drama. Roger North's often-quoted passage to the effect that 'during ye troubles & when most other good arts languished musick held up her head, not at Court nor (In ye cant of those times) profane theatres, but In private society, for many chose rather to fidle at home, then to goe out & be knockt on ye head abroad; and the enterteinem^t was very much courted & made use of not only In country but citty familys'[1] gives a plausible summing-up of affairs. The disposition of the times towards plainness of life and away from frivolous ostentation helped to promote a respect for what contemporary writers called 'grave' music; later in the seventeenth century, as North explains, 'the old English music . . . passed for dull entertainment, *and I must agree it is so to impatient hearers*'.[2] This last phrase is revealing. In the private music-making of the Commonwealth period which Scholes has discussed with reference to Bulstrode Whitelock and his family, the sober and often profound contrapuntal works by writers like Jenkins, Lawes, Simon Ives and the Ferraboscos found favourable reception. 'Oliver's mutable reign' did not prevent men like Colonel Hutchinson from enjoying all sorts of music, or from giving their children the kind of education which included 'music, dancing, and all other qualities befitting their father's house'.[3] And the Hutchinson family was not an isolated case. According to Anthony à Wood, the Presbyterians and Independents during the Commonwealth period loved and encouraged instrumental music, but 'did not care for vocall, because that was used in church by the prelaticall partie'.

During the Civil War period, if we are to believe Charles Burney, 'Oxford . . . seems to have been the only place in the kingdom where musical sounds were allowed to be heard'—a view which is based on the fact that a number of musicians from London found refuge in Oxford at the time of the 'troubles'. Burney goes on: 'Ten years of gloomy silence seem to have elapsed before a string was suffered to vibrate, or a pipe to

[1] Hilda Andrews, ed., *The Musicall Grammarian By Roger North* (1925), pp. 18–19.

[2] Augustus Jessopp, ed., *The Lives of the Norths* (1890), III. 84 (my italics).

[3] Lucy Hutchinson, *Memoirs of the Life of Colonel Hutchinson* (Everyman ed.), p. 292.

breathe aloud, in the kingdom; as we hear of no music-meetings, clubs, or concerts, till the year 1656.'[1] The reference here is to the periodic gatherings of musicians at Oxford which are alluded to in *The Life and Times of Anthony à Wood*. But in any case concerts of the kind Burney was accustomed to were not a feature of English musical life until after the Restoration, and it is misleading to regard Oxford as the only place in which consort music was heard. Within the ten gloomy years, as Burney himself makes clear, a large number of musical publications were brought out, and in a typical example from 1651, *A Musicall Banquet*, a list is appended containing the names of twenty-seven music teachers in London alone (*cum multis aliis*, as we are informed). The *Musicall Banquet* is one item out of a very large number issued by John Playford (1623–86), a Norwich-born stationer who established a business in London about 1648. Although many of Playford's best-known publications date from after 1660, he did bring out important collections in the 1650s. Scholes has devoted a chapter to 'The Playford Publications', and the fact that *The English Dancing Master* was issued by Playford in 1651 is a very strong support for Scholes's case that the Puritans were not joyless repressors of all light recreation. The nature of the volumes issued by Playford up to 1660, however, reveals one or two other significant features.

In the first place, they are not exclusively devoted to 'serious' music: included among them are books of rounds, catches and other mirthful items. Then it is noticeable that the instructional element is predominant. *Musicks Recreation* (1652), for instance, is stated to be 'a choice Collection of New and Excellent Lessons for the *Lyra Viol*, both easie and delightful for all young Practitioners'. In the Preface to the second (1682) edition of this work, Playford expressed an anxiety to encourage 'such as desire to Learn who live in remote Parts, far from any profest Teacher'; he retained the adjective 'new' on the title-page, even though the work was thirty years old. His *Introduction to the Skill of Music* (1654) ran into many editions, though in his less formal instruction books (such as the *Booke of new lessons for the gitterne* (1652)) he continued to keep in mind the needs of the less-experienced performer. Playford was also a voluminous publisher of dance music. *The English Dancing Master* is his

[1] Charles Burney, *General History of Music* (ed. Frank Mercer, 1935), II. 334.

most famous compilation. It was made up of over a hundred tunes, the majority of which had not appeared in print before. 'With only one or two exceptions,' writes Margaret Dean-Smith, 'the previous appearance of these tunes in Britain is in manuscript—the *Fitzwilliam* and *Lady Nevell's Virginal Books*, very occasionally in Cosyn's *Virginal Book*, Ballett's, Dallis', Elizabeth Rogers' and Jane Pickering's *Lute Books*, and a few in the lute collections at Cambridge. A very few have been discovered in madrigals, rounds and catches.'[1] Primarily a tune book for fiddlers accompanying the dance, the *English Dancing Master* also gives details of the steps to be learned by prospective dancers. It went through eighteen editions in all, these being altered and augmented as in the case of other volumes issued by Playford. In this field as elsewhere John Playford and his son Henry were—at any rate after the Restoration—capturing an expanding market.

The Playfords were not, of course, the only London publishers of any consequence during this period. But their work does serve to indicate the existence of what at the outset was called a 'musical public'—a public, that is to say, eager to acquire a practical knowledge of music and prepared to spend money liberally in order to enjoy it. After the Restoration, music again held an important place in the theatre. Songs and instrumental items were included in most serious plays, the action being held up now and then to permit the introduction of brief recitals. The music written by Purcell and others for the dramas of Congreve, Dryden, Otway and Crowne was often collected in such volumes as *The Theatre of Music* (1685) and *The Banquet of Music* (1688–92), both published by John Playford. After Purcell's death, his widow arranged for selections from his theatrical music to be issued in *Orpheus Britannicus*, of which the first edition appeared in 1698.

So far we have said nothing of English opera, which from its beginnings in the Commonwealth period became a popular diversion in London after various French operas—of which *Albion and Albanius* by Dryden and Louis Grabu (1685) was a notorious imitation—had failed to capture the theatrical public.

---

[1] See Dean-Smith, 'English Tunes Common to Playford's "Dancing Master", the Keyboard Books and Traditional Songs and Dances' in *Proc. Mus. Ass.*, LXXIX (1952–3), p. 10.

Just why an authentic English opera did not materialize when the conditions for it seemed so favourable has baffled many historians; yet the hybrid form of 'semi-opera' was not without its attractions for an audience accustomed to masques rather than to opera on the Italian model. It is significant that masque-like spectacles form an integral part of Purcell's *Dioclesian* and *The Fairy Queen*, though from a dramaturgical point of view a résumé of the origin and nature of these works would lead us into complicated discussion. One characteristic of the English opera at this stage must be noted, however—its usefulness as a vehicle for the expression of nationalistic sentiments. The feeling of national pride which we associate with Arne's 'Rule, Britannia' (1740) was already much in evidence on the Restoration musical stage.

Although the Restoration theatre made extensive use of musicians, it was in the sphere of formal chamber music that the musical public asserted itself most noticeably. Conditions were now suitable for the establishment of the public concert. The first genuinely *public* musical recitals ever given—apart, that is, from the theatres—were those arranged by John Banister in 1673. Banister was a musician of some note who had composed music for a number of plays. According to Pepys he was displeased by the favourable reception given in this country to the Frenchman Louis Grabu. In the *London Gazette* for 30 December 1672 he advertised 'musick performed by excellent masters' at his house in Whitefriars, to commence at four in the afternoon each day. Banister's concerts were followed by those given by the musical small-coal man Thomas Britton. And from the State Papers we learn of a rather later venture in 1689 by Robert King, one of the royal musicians, who obtained a licence to commence musical concerts with sole control of them, on the understanding that 'none shall force their way in, without paying such prices as shall be set down, and no person shall attempt rudely or by force to enter in or abide there during the time of performing the said music'.[1] This rather stringent wording ('All officers, civil and military, are required to be abiding and assisting herein') suggests that considerable competition for seats was anticipated at the Charles Street premises where Robert King's concerts were held. It was in this period, too, that music began

[1] W. J. Hardy, ed., *State Papers Domestic, 1689/1690* (1895), p. 367.

to be provided more liberally at taverns. Roger North even recalls that Banister's Whitefriars room 'was rounded with seats and small curtains, alehouse fashion'. But though the public concert developed along the lines of the music meetings such as Anthony à Wood describes, this was also a great age of private concert-giving, as the *Diary* of John Evelyn makes clear. 'I dind at the Master of the Mints with my Wife,' wrote Evelyn on 20 November 1679, 'invited to heare Musique which was most exquisitely performed by 4 the most renouned Masters, *Du Prue* a *French-man* on the *Lute*: Signor *Batholomeo* Ital: on the *Harpsichord*: & *Nicolao* on the Violin; but above all for its swetenesse & novelty the *Viol d'Amore* of 5 wyre-strings, plaied on with a bow, being but an ordinary *Violin*, play'd on *Lyra* way by a *German*, than which I never heard a sweeter Instrument or more surprizing: There was also a *Flute douce* now in much request for accompanying the Voice: *Mr Slingsby* Master of the house (whose Sonn & Daughter played skillfully) being exceedingly delighted with this diversion, had these meetings frequently in his house.'[1] At such gatherings as this, chamber music in the French and Italian styles was given frequent performance.

It is a commonplace of English musical history that after his exile in France Charles II returned to this country with a decided preference for the light and airy music he had heard on the other side of the Channel. But there were many people who deprecated the facile compositions which the French masters were then producing so readily. In the Preface to *Musick's Delight on the Cithern* (1666) John Playford wrote: 'It is observed that of late years all solemn and grave music is laid aside, being esteemed too heavy and dull for the light heels of this nimble and wanton age; nor is any musick rendered acceptable, or esteemed by many, but what is presented by foreigners.' And Thomas Mace in *Musick's Monument* issued what was probably the last serious plea for the reinstatement of the lute and the viol which, as he saw, were gradually being superseded by more superficially attractive instruments. The standpoint Mace adopts is openly reactionary, but it is comprehensible if we bear in mind the background against which it was formulated. In the 1660s, 1670s and 1680s it was only natural that mature men and women should

[1] Evelyn, *Diary* (ed. E. S. de Beer, 1959), p. 675.

reflect ruefully on the social changes brought about by the late 'rebellion'. Clarendon, for instance, who can hardly be accused of partiality towards the Puritans, speaks of the 'dilapidations and ruins of the ancient candour and discipline' noticeable in his time, and laments the way in which the country has been 'corrupted from that integrity, good nature, and generosity, that had been peculiar to it, and for which it had been signal and celebrated throughout the world; in the room whereof the vilest craft and dissembling had succeeded'.[1] It would be unwise to apply these remarks to our subject but for the fact that, as has been observed, musical customs mirror the shift in human relationships. In the madrigals and viol fantasies, which were almost outmoded by 1660, there was of necessity a voluntary subjugation of the individual performer: the music might not be altogether easy to sing or to play, yet it was designed for corporate enjoyment and not in order to show off personal prowess. The art of playing 'divisions' on the viol may seem to contradict this notion, but the skill entailed in this was essentially one of musical invention (i.e. variation) rather than purely mechanical dexterity. But with the rise of competitive professionalism—particularly when prominence came to be given to the solo voice or violin—this state of affairs underwent a significant change.

But the ascendency of the 'scoulding violins', as Mace called them, is only one aspect of the situation. Generally speaking, the tacit contempt for the 'rare chest of viols', which is discernible in many quarters after the Restoration, implied a certain antipathy towards the values and standards by which men of an earlier period lived. A grave and 'solid' demeanour now commanded less respect than it did in Clarendon's youth. In music, the older consort style gave place to easily assimilated melodies ('passionate and well turned', as Dorimant puts it in Etherege's *Man of Mode*) supported by harmonies which did not leave the ear in much doubt as to how they should be resolved. The musical public at the end of the seventeenth century was unquestionably larger than it had been in Elizabethan times, but the political and religious events of the intervening period had, in a subtle way, helped to make it more superficial. Writers like Playford, Mace and Roger North are inclined, obviously, to overstate their case, yet they had at least witnessed the social changes

[1] G. Huehns, ed., *Selections from Clarendon* (World's Classics, 1955), p. 381.

to which their comments on musical taste must be related. For this reason their observations have a greater relevance than, say, the theorizing which emerged from the controversy over the relative merits of the French and Italian styles of composition.

III

<hr>

The Eighteenth Century

<hr>

I

During the late seventeenth and early eighteenth centuries unprecedented developments took place in the spheres of commerce and finance. From 1688 onwards the standard of living in this country gradually rose, and in spite of occasional setbacks all classes benefited from the improved trading conditions which had slowly developed since the Restoration. Admittedly, England was at war with France after 1689, and later became involved in other conflicts, yet in 1718 William Wood, a Secretary to the Customs, was able to report that 'upon the whole, from the Year 1688 to this Time, we have gone on, *Encreasing* our Stock, notwithstanding the many Convulsions this Nation has had in respect of its *Trade* abroad and Credit at home'.[1] A consequence of this state of affairs was that the mercantile classes rose in general esteem. 'All other Subjects of our Island, from the highest to the lowest,' wrote the Whig journalist Richard Steele in *The Englishman* for 13 October 1713, 'are as much below the Merchant in political Merit, as that ravenous Worm in the Entrails of the State the Stock-jobber.'[2] But an Act of 1697, introduced into Parliament to curb the dealings of unscrupulous speculators, had virtually established stockbroking as a profession. Henceforth the pursuit of wealth as an end in itself became a respectable calling. The careers of many prominent figures

[1] William Wood, *A Survey of Trade . . . Together with Considerations on our Money and Bullion* (1718), p. 48.
[2] Rae Blanchard, ed., *The Englishman* (1955), pp. 20–21.

from various walks of life could be cited in this connection. But if any one individual may be said to have stood in symbolic relationship to both the economic situation *and* the art of his time, that man was James Brydges, first Duke of Chandos (1673–1744). Patron of architects, friend to men of letters, and a generous sponsor of musical performances, Brydges improved upon his position in the government service by judicious investment at a time when innumerable projectors were busily forming new companies in an attempt to profit from the expanding market. Few of his contemporaries were able to survive the South Sea *débâcle* of 1720 as triumphantly as did the Duke of Chandos; yet Brydges's aspirations—so typical of that age— were shared by dozens of lesser men who could not possibly lay claim to his abundant riches.

In various ways, music as well as literature and the drama was affected by a situation in which opulence stimulated a desire for novelty and encouraged unfamiliar forms of artistic expression. It is a commonplace of musical history, for instance, that throughout this period England showed an extraordinary hospitality to foreign musicians. According to the German traveller von Uffenbach, the orchestra for a performance of Francesco Mancini's *Hydaspes* which he saw at the Haymarket Theatre in 1710 was made up entirely of foreigners, 'mostly Germans and then French, for the English are not much better musicians than the Dutch, and they are fairly bad'.[1] Whatever the grounds may have been for this rather extreme view, foreign vocalists and instrumentalists would never have settled here, as many of them did, if there had not been a considerable demand for their services. We seldom hear of those foreign musicians who *failed* to establish themselves in our midst, but late-seventeenth-century drama has many references to French and Italian teachers or performers of music. Since before the Restoration, indeed, Italian musicians had been coming to England in increasing numbers.[2] By 1680 Siface, the well-known *castrato*, was appearing in England, and many more of his countrymen took part in private concerts during the last decades of the century. One of the most distinguished visitors from Italy whose career is characteristic of

---

[1] *London in 1710, From the Travels of Zacharias Conrad von Uffenbach* (trans. and ed. by W. H. Quarrell and Margaret Mare, 1934), p. 17.
[2] See J. A. Westrup, *Purcell* (1937), chapter viii.

the time was Per Francesco Tosi. Celebrated in musical literature for his treatise on the art of florid song (1742), Tosi—who
lived from 1646 to 1732—ran a series of concerts in the York
Buildings during the season of 1693. This was not, of course, an
isolated enterprise. Other singers and instrumentalists organized
similar recitals for their own personal benefit and in the hope of
attracting pupils.

The early years of the eighteenth century witnessed a modest
development of the public concert very much in the form we are
familiar with today. Semi-public gatherings for musical purposes
had been taking place for the last fifty years at least; not only
were musical parties common at country and town houses belonging to the nobility, but we also find less ambitious musical
meetings taking place in taverns and coffee houses. In 1713,
however, a dancing master by the name of Thomas Hickford
opened a music room in premises just off the Haymarket, and
this seems from the first to have been devoted to the presentation
of formal concerts. So successful was Hickford in meeting the
needs of famous performers that he later (1738) took over
another room in Brewer Street which served as a venue for subscription concerts until the 1770s. It may be wondered why some
arrangement of this kind had not been thought necessary before
this. But the period was one in which technical prowess was
beginning to command a high market value. Musicians who had
come to England with the intention of securing engagements
and of reaping rich rewards needed to make contact with a public
larger than the small circles of friends who gathered in private
houses. Musical recitals, it is true, frequently formed part of
theatrical entertainments; but Hickford's Rooms and the York
Buildings offered greater scope to solo performers. Hickford's
premises were the home of some notable musical ventures.
Among those who performed there over the years were Geminiani, Matthew Dubourg, Signora Cuzzoni, Mrs. Arne, Guadagni
and John Beard. The limited accommodation forced up the prices
of admission, and at one time the subscription for twenty concerts from December to the following April was as much as four
guineas. But Hickford's Rooms were not suitable for orchestral
concerts, and when the symphonies of J. C. Bach, Haydn and
Mozart became known in England these were performed in the
more commodious Hanover Square Rooms.

II

By far the most fashionable type of musical entertainment in early eighteenth-century London was the Italian opera. Excerpts from Italian operas had been heard in England for some years past, but it was the appearance in this country of expert performers from foreign opera houses which encouraged certain theatrical managers to stage full-scale Italian works as well as the English operas of Locke, Leveridge and Purcell. For a long period opera was in serious competition with other theatrical exhibitions, and the difficulties of those attempting to promote opera arose mainly from the fact that the day-to-day costs for this kind of production far exceeded those of the non-musical drama. This is clear from the correspondence which passed between Sir John Vanbrugh and the Earl of Manchester in 1708. Writing on 11 May 1708, Vanbrugh informs Manchester that his colleague Owen Swiney is now 'entire Possessor' of the Haymarket Theatre business and proposes to subsidize opera from the profits he has made out of 'the Acting Company'. While relying on Manchester (who was then in Venice) to obtain the services of some of the 'Top Voices' of the time, Vanbrugh goes on to reveal that Swiney is prepared to allow Nicolini a thousand pounds for two London seasons and the same amount for two equally eminent women performers.[1] Few actors in this period earned more than two hundred pounds a year. But the fees demanded by visiting singers rose as time went on, and in a letter to Jacob Tonson (18 February 1719–20) Vanbrugh wrote : 'The Opera will begin about the 10th of March under the Academy of Musick. It will be a very good one this year, and a better the next. They having engag'd the best Singers in Italy, at a great Price. Such as I believe will bring the Expences to about twice as much as the Receipts.'[2] The exorbitant costs of the Italian opera were met by appeals for handsome subscriptions, but there was a limit to which such demands could be made. The state of affairs revealed in Vanbrugh's letters, however, made the opera the preserve of the rich and was prejudicial to the interests of what Vanbrugh called 'the Gallery People'.

[1] Bonamy Dobree and Geoffrey Webb, eds., *The Complete Works of Sir John Vanbrugh* (1928), IV. 20–21.
[2] *Ibid* , p. 125.

The phrase 'theatrical exhibitions' is used advisedly. For in this period dramatic productions were, by modern standards, strangely varied and disparate. The *Daily Courant* for 26 April 1703 advertised a production of Southerne's *Oronooko* at the Royal Theatre, Drury Lane, 'in which will be performed several Italian Sonatas by Signor Gasperini and others . . . Likewise the famous Mr. Evans, lately arrived from Vienna . . . will vault on the manag'd Horse, where he lies with his Body extended on one Hand in which posture he drinks several Glasses of Wine with the other, and from that throws himself a Sommerset over the Horses head, to Admiration.' A performance of Wycherley's *The Country Wife* at Lincoln's Inn Fields on 29 December 1702 included a dance performed by sixteen people in grotesque habits, and 'Sir Roger de Coverley' done 'Originally after the Yorkshire manner'. In conditions such as these the dividing lines between legitimate drama, pantomime, 'opera' and 'show' were not clearly defined. On the Restoration stage, act tunes and songs were an important part of the performance; they remained so well into the eighteenth century, along with dances and various other stage turns.

The Restoration audience was made up chiefly from the higher reaches of 'the gentry' and 'the nobility'. But after the turn of the century representatives of a greater variety of social classes were to be found in the playhouses. The literature of the time reveals that though the courtly tone persisted within the theatres themselves, there was a distinct shift in the nature of patronage towards the *nouveaux riches* in general, the upper middle classes, the professional ranks and their servants. So much, at least, can be inferred from the writings of John Dennis (1657–1734), a well-known antagonist of the Italian opera. As the outspoken opponent of Swift and Pope, Dennis has for a long time been regarded as one of the black sheep of English criticism. But his remarks on music and the drama present the views of a perceptive writer whose own career was greatly affected by changes in taste in the post-Revolution era. What Dennis says about theatrical audiences can be taken as applying just as much to operas as to spoken drama itself.

In 1702 Dennis's play *The Comical Gallant; or, The Amours of Sir John Falstaffe* was produced at Drury Lane. It was later published with a dedication to George Granville, himself a dramatist and distinguished Cabinet Minister. The play itself (an adaptation of *The Merry Wives of Windsor*) was a failure, but the *Large Account of the Taste in Poetry, and the Causes of the Degeneracy of it* which makes up its dedicatory epistle is a shrewd discussion of the comic mode and the public's response to it. Dennis takes the view that although there was in the time of Charles II a 'public' capable of appreciating drama at its true value, the playwright of 1702 has to deal with audiences which have less opportunity to cultivate the three main qualities necessary for the serious judgement of a play, namely, '1. Great Parts. 2. A generous Education. 3. A due Application.' Dennis attributes this to the drift of national events, and claims that since 1688 men's minds have been engaged by matters which inhibit true appreciation. 'Besides,' he goes on, 'there are three sorts of People now in our Audiences, who have had no education at all; and who were unheard of in the Reign of King *Charles* the Second. A great many younger Brothers, Gentlemen born, who have been kept at home, by reason of the pressure of the Taxes, Several People, who made their Fortunes in the late War; and who from a state of obscurity, and perhaps of misery, have risen to a condition of distinction and plenty.'[1] Is it to be wondered at, Dennis argues, that an audience of this kind cannot be relied upon to give sustained attention to the legitimate drama? Besides, there are now a great number of foreigners in London who, being unable to follow what is going on in the play, are only too ready to give countenance to the introduction of 'Sound and Show, where the business of the Theatre does not require it, and particularly a sort of a soft and wanton Musick, which has used the People to a delight which is independant of Reason, a delight that has gone a very great way towards the enervating and dissolving their minds.'[2] Apart from these considerations, Dennis maintains that in these days of speculation and commercial turmoil, these people who *are* capable of forming rational judgements have neither the leisure nor the serenity requisite for a fair assessment of the dramatist's intention. In the present reign there are, on Dennis's calculations, ten times more gentlemen in business than in Charles II's time, and 'By reason that they are attentive to the events of affairs, and too full of great and real events, to

---

[1] Edward Niles Hooker, ed., *The Critical Works of John Dennis* (1939), I. 293.
[2] *Ibid.*, pp. 293–4.

receive due impressions from the imaginary one of the Theatre'[1] they come to the playhouse merely to *unbend*, and are therefore 'utterly incapable of duly attending to the just and harmonious Symetry of a beautiful design'.[2]

In another polemical work, *The Person of Quality's Answer to Mr. Collier's Letter* . . . (1704), Dennis lists the reigning diversions of 'the Town' as four—gaming, music meetings, balls and meetings for dancing, and going to plays; and in *The Grounds of Criticism in Poetry* (1704) he states that 'even they who pretend to like nothing, will at the Play-houses be pleas'd with ev'ry thing; and they who would be thought to approve of every thing, like nothing long'.[3] And when men come to the theatre, as he puts it, 'full of some business which they have been solliciting, or of some Harrangue which they are to make the next day',[4] their impatience with serious drama is understandable. Hence their readiness to sample a new form of entertainment—one which promised to be in good taste, was highly gratifying to the senses, and left some kind of impression even though imperfectly understood. Such was the Italian opera.

III

The Italian operas of the early eighteenth century are so seldom performed on the modern stage that it is difficult for us to appreciate the kind of satisfaction which they originally gave. Writing at the end of the century, Samuel Johnson characterized the Italian opera as 'an exotic and irrational entertainment which has always been combated, and has always prevailed'. This description is a shrewd one, and worthy of further comment. In the sense that it adopted conventions which at first sight seem rather more absurd than those of spoken drama, the Italian opera was certainly 'irrational', but it was no more exotic than many of the heroic plays of a slightly earlier period. It was opposed by critics like Dennis on the ground that it was below the dignity of Britons to sit and listen to seductive airs sung by eunuchs; 'precisians' such as William Law objected to the artfulness with which the opera seemed to recommend Pagan degeneracy. But the Italian opera prevailed—after many struggles—because it

[1] *Ibid.*, p. 294. [2] *Ibid.*, p. 294. [3] *Ibid.*, p. 328.
[4] *Ibid.*, p. 294.

flattered the vanity of an audience which liked to think that *virtù* was its most conspicuous quality. At a time when most young men of well-to-do families undertook the Grand Tour as a matter of course, a taste for Italian art and culture was well established; and as Dr. Burney pointed out, the love of opera was 'most powerfully excited in such of our nobility and gentry as (had) visited Italy in their youth' and desired a replica in their own country of the productions they had seen abroad.[1] But quite apart from this, the Italian opera was congenial to the frame of mind John Dennis was at pains to notice.

As is well known, opera in seventeenth-century Italy had developed in a remarkable manner. 'Radiating from Venice with its public opera houses,' writes Professor Grout, 'it established itself on a firm basis of public interest and support which made it by the end of the century the most widespread and most popular of all musical forms.'[2] Composers in other countries produced imitations or adaptations of the music dramas that were given in the theatres of Naples, Rome and Parma. Purcell's 'operas' are not, in the case of *King Arthur* (1691), *The Indian Queen* (1695) and the rest, sung throughout; his *Dido and Aeneas* (1689) is the only one of his works which properly resembles an authentic Italian opera—though its smallness of scale puts it in a rather different category from the innumerable musico-dramatic pieces which were imported into England after Purcell's time. Historians have never ceased to deplore the fact that *Dido and Aeneas* had no successors, and that Purcell's death seems to have defeated all hopes of an indigenous English operatic tradition. Formally speaking, however, as Professor Dent pointed out, Thomas Clayton's *Arsinöe, Queen of Cyprus* (Drury Lane, 16 January 1705) was for all its inadequacies a fully developed Italian opera 'and in that respect a complete novelty to the English theatre'.[3] It was advertised as 'After the Italian manner, All sung, being set to Musick by Master Clayton'.

Arsinöe was based on a *drama per musica* of the same name by Tomaso Stanzani, and was something of a *mélange* to which others besides Clayton contributed. Hard things have been said

[1] Charles Burney, *Account of the Musical Performances in Westminster Abbey . . .* (1785), 'Sketch of the Life of Handel', p. 15.

[2] D. J. Grout, *A Short History of Opera* (1947), I. 179.

[3] E. J. Dent, 'Italian Opera in London', in *Proc. Royal Mus. Ass.*, LXXI (1945), p. 20.

about it, but in its own time it was a reasonably popular piece. Although deriving from Italian sources, it was sung entirely in English, as was the same composer's ill-fated *Rosamond* (1707), for which Joseph Addison supplied the words. During the first decades of the century English and Italian were used indifferently in operatic performances. But from the time of Handel's *Rinaldo* (1711) the principle that operas should be given entirely in Italian was generally accepted.

It was by his operas that Handel, who counts for so much in the social history of English music, first became really well known in this country. The cabals and intrigues associated with the early history of the Italian opera concerned Handel intimately. They were largely the outcome of competitive endeavours on the part of composers and performers to secure adequate patronage. No one knew better than Handel how to humour his audience. In this connection there is a distinction to be drawn between opera *pur sang* and the type of composition known as a *pasticcio*. The latter is an agreeable miscellany put together without much thought of essential thematic unity. In one sense *Rinaldo* itself is a *pasticcio*, since it was made up from music that Handel had already composed, but a better example is *Muzio Scevola* (1721), to which Handel contributed one act. Other composers like Hasse, Galuppi and Scarlatti wrote *pasticcios* when required. But at their best Handel's operas have a symmetry and logical development that is lacking in the average medley of this kind.

Not, of course, that Handel wished to free himself from the stylistic conventions of his age. The titles of his operas—*Alessandro, Atalanta, Orlando, Scipione*—indicate the kind of legendary material upon which his librettists drew; it was either classical antiquity or the dark mediaeval past which seemed to offer the most promising subjects. And on the purely musical side Handel adhered fairly closely to the arrangement by which a small number of singers of both sexes were given a few significant appearances: in these they sang arias, duets and ensemble pieces describing their feelings and aspirations. The pattern of Handel's operas differed from one season to another, and they were occasionally altered when revivals took place. But for the most part they tell the story of exalted personages who are distinctly larger than life; their virtues and vices are laid boldly before us and the virulence of their passions is fully revealed. The fables used are generally fairly simple in construction and the devices of disguise, failure in recognition and blatant coincidence are applied unsparingly. A great deal of the music is, unquestionably, designed to display the capacities of particular vocalists. But too much must not be made of this. Handel more than adequately served the needs of musical characterization as demanded by his libretti; and bearing in mind their limitations, we are justified in saying that Handel's operas have as much claim upon our attention as all but the very finest of his oratorios.

Some idea of the kind of appeal exerted by an Italian opera of this period can be gained from a brief examination of one of Handel's more ambitious scores. What is said of Handel does not necessarily apply to other composers. We can now appreciate his superiority over men like Pepusch, Matteis or Buononcini, but his reputation in 1711 did not then place him very far ahead of them. Things were very different ten or fifteen years later, when he had satisfied 'the Town' of his outstanding ability. Works like *Serse* (1738), *Rodelinda* (1725) and *Faramondo* (1738) are full of individual beauties, but from Handel's thirty or forty operas, *Giulio Cesare in Egitto* is perhaps one of the most striking examples of his work.

Giulio Cesare was produced in February 1724 at the King's Theatre, Haymarket. It was published later in the same year by John Cluer and his partner in a 'neat large Octavo Pocket Size', Handel having disposed of the copyright to those publishers. The libretto, by Nicola Haym, deals with Caesar's campaign in Egypt during A.D. 48, and represents Caesar as having arrived in that country shortly after the murder of Pompey by Achillas. Since Caesar is displeased at this outrage, the triumphal exuberance of the Overture and the opening chorus is soon tempered by the lamentations of Pompey's widow, Cornelia: these are followed by frantic recitatives from Pompey's son Sextus and some more restrained rebukes by Caesar himself. Achillas is banished from Caesar's sight, but not before he (Achillas) has revealed a partiality for Cornelia. Together with Ptolomaeus, Achillas contrives a conspiracy against Caesar—unaware that Sextus is in league with Cleopatra, whose charms have captivated Caesar. Meanwhile Cornelia, after the arrest of Sextus by Achillas and Ptolomaeus, is herself captured by these would-be suitors, but while Ptolomaeus is attempting to subdue her stubbornness, Sextus, by means of bribery, manages to free himself from bondage. Achillas and Ptolomaeus quarrel over Cornelia. Achillas weakens, and in returning a sword to Sextus rekindles Sextus's courage. Ptolomaeus has all along been at odds with his sister Cleopatra, who refuses to rule Egypt jointly with him. But Caesar manages to evade the conspirators sent to slay him and reappears to find that Achillas has betrayed Ptolomaeus, whose jealousy in respect of Cornelia has turned him against his former associate. Now, however, Sextus inflicts a mortal wound on Achillas. It remains for Caesar to reassert his power in Egypt and make Cleopatra his consort, the worthy Sextus having proved himself a dutiful son by avenging Pompey's death. The opera ends with a four-part 'apotheosis' in which Cleopatra, Cornelia, Sextus and Caesar welcome a propitious future.

So much for the plot of *Giulio Cesare*. Musically the action is carried on by means of recitatives sung by several of the characters; the arias denote the states of mind experienced by the contending parties. In this connection we may compare the plaintive arioso of Act I, Scene viii ('Nel tuo seno'), in which Cleopatra pays homage to Pompey's memory, with the defiant 'Si spietata, il tuo rigore' sung by Ptolomaeus to the reluctant Cornelia in Act II; or contrast the simple lament 'Piangero la sorte mia', through which Cleopatra voices her woes, with the more confident 'Da tempeste il legno in franto', sung by Cleopatra when she is aware that Caesar is safe.[1] The latter is a powerful and florid aria making full use of trills and rapid semi-quaver passages. The duets and choruses display a typically Handelian majesty, and the purely instrumental music includes several sinfonias which for the festive scenes of Act II are scored in a most unusual manner, with harp, theorbo and viola da gamba added to the main orchestral ensemble.

In *Giulio Cesare* the balance between instrumental and vocal music is very much the same as that in other operas by Handel. The augmented orchestra is called for by the pomp and regality of certain scenes, and the style of writing, despite a certain conventionality in the male parts, is pleasantly variegated. The whole makes up a grand concert in which the variety provided by

[1] References are to pp. 34, 67 and 100 of *Giulio Cesare* as printed in Volume 68 of the German Handel Society's complete Handel Edition (1875).

eight solo voices, a chorus and a sizeable orchestra could be enjoyed. As music drama it is less striking than such works as *Alcina* (1735) and *Deidamia* (1741), but it shares with *Rodelinda* and *Scipione* one or two other commendable qualities. Writing in 1728, Roger North complained of a lack of unity in the music meetings of a few years back. The kind of thing offered at the York Buildings was marred by a spirit of emulation among the performers, 'all which together scandalized the company, and poysoned the enterteinement. Besides the whole was without designe or order . . . whereas all enterteinements of this kind ought to be projected as a drama, so as all the members shall uninterruptedly follow in order, and having a true connexion, set off each other.'[1] The Italian opera fulfilled this stipulation exactly, and to some extent set the pattern for the large-scale concert in years to come. Addison spoke of the opera as encouraging an 'indolent attention' on the part of the audience; and indeed some of the lesser works of the period do not call for any great efforts of concentration. But the three-act structure found in so many operas had much to recommend itself to concert-promoters; most later-eighteenth-century concerts were, in fact, nothing more than operatic selections interspersed with instrumental items—though in time symphonies and concertos came to occupy a predominant part of the programme.

IV

The stages by which Handel turned from the composition of operas and became the creator *par excellence* of oratorio have often been detailed. For all his 'temperamental' disposition and eccentricity of manner, Handel did not conform to the popular notion of an unworldly musical genius. Quite apart from his skill as a great executive musician, he was an eminently practical individual. He had several friends in financial circles and was able to recoup his heavy losses by prudent investment. As Percy Young explains, Handel 'was capable of dealing with the business fraternity on equal terms and (despite popular tradition) he was never bankrupt or anywhere near it'.[2] Handel was very

[1] John Wilson, ed., *Roger North on Music* (1959), p. 353.
[2] Percy M. Young, 'Handel the Man', in Gerald Abraham, ed., *Handel: a Symposium* (1954), p. 5.

much alive to trends in contemporary taste, and when in the late 1720s a recession in the demand for opera set in, he had no option but to try out alternative modes of entertainment. This change did not, of course, take place suddenly: for a number of years Handel worked concurrently on both operas and oratorios, and in some cases there is not much to choose between the style of composition used for each. In producing a long series of sacred musical pieces to exclusively English texts, Handel was in a sense submitting to the trend away from the genre in which he was an acknowledged master.

It was only to be expected that sooner or later an effective burlesque of the Italian opera would make its appearance. An early instance of this was Richard Estcourt's *Prunella*, which was put on at Drury Lane in February 1708 along with Bayes's *The Rehearsal*. Handel's *Rinaldo* was the subject of a 'skit' published in Walsh and Hare's *Monthly Mask of Vocal Music* for May 1711[1] and there are earlier instances of opera being travestied. But the outstanding example was *The Beggar's Opera* of 1728. Opinions vary on whether Gay's political satire or musical parody is the more prominent. Suffice it to say that Gay did intend to ridicule some of the characteristics of the Italian opera. At the end of the work the Beggar retorts to the Player's objection that the catastrophe is 'manifestly wrong' by saying 'You must allow that in this kind of Drama, 'tis no matter how absurdly things are brought about.' As it happens, *The Beggar's Opera* is only one of a number of literary productions which focused attention on certain anomalies in Walpole's administration, and its artistic merits are not in question. For us its interest centres around its great popularity on the one hand and its allegedly dubious moral influence on the other. Its success in 1728 was unparalleled in English theatrical history, and the reasons for its finding favour are not hard to seek. The chief character, Captain Macheath, whose contempt for the rigours of the law is calculated to endear him to any audience, exhibits in his conversation all the nonchalance of a born gentleman; his readiness to engage in intrigues ('I must have women . . .') gives rise to dramatic entanglements which merely serve to emphasize the comparative naïvety of Polly Peachum and Lucy

[1] See W. C. Smith, *Bibliography of the Musical Works Published by John Walsh . . . 1795–1720* (1948), pp. 115–16.

Lockit. Part of Gay's aim was to dramatize the contention (advanced by other writers of the time) that despite class differences a 'similitude of manners' could be discerned between high and low life. The dialogue of *The Beggar's Opera* is extremely witty, and the arias are adaptations of familiar ballads and dance tunes, together with music taken from Purcell, Eccles, Handel and other composers. Yet the work is not simply a re-hash of attractive bits and pieces. As W. E. Schultz puts it, 'No one can accuse Gay's opera of slipping by inattentive playgoers through some trick of legerdemain.'[1] Indeed, the design of the whole is controlled by a sharp satiric sense; and it was this which enabled Gay to please not only the accepted patrons of opera, but also a much wider audience. To these was demonstrated very pertinently that a musical entertainment on the stage need not have as its main point of interest the lives of heroes and heroines as remote from eighteenth-century life as those of Italian opera.

These considerations, however, do not go very far to explain the vogue for ballad opera, which continued until about 1740. The many imitations of *The Beggar's Opera* were popular because they contained satirical references to affairs of the day, relied on sentimental characterization and introduced attractive songs. But in all of them the music served to break up the dramatic action, which was reduced in complexity so as to make the main issues stand out boldly. This could be demonstrated from pieces like *The Quaker's Opera*, the *Village Opera* and *Polly*. But by reason of its smallness of scope, Henry Fielding's *The Lottery* (1732) is a very suitable example to discuss. The heroine, Chloe, entertains the idea that a lottery ticket in her possession is about to bring her a large fortune; she accordingly prepares for a grand life in London. Unfortunately for her, these illusions are spoiled when she encounters Jack Stocks who, taking Chloe for a wealthy woman, courts her under an assumed name. Posing as 'Lord Lace', Jack Stocks makes Chloe his wife only to find after the wedding that the lottery ticket is worthless. The disappointed and impecunious Jack denounces all lotteries. But in the finish Chloe is rescued from shame by her real suitor, Lovemore, who offers Jack Stocks a thousand pounds if he will

---

[1] William Eben Schultz, *Gay's Beggar's Opera: Its Content, History and Influence* (1923), p. 15.

renounce Chloe. This Jack is only too willing to do, and for her part Chloe is glad to be rid of this self-styled nobleman. 'A lord!' she says, 'faugh! I begin to despise the name now as heartily as I liked it before.'

This is a typical ballad-opera situation: pretentiousness and mean advantage are foresworn and an honourable conclusion is reached in which all parties are satisfied. Some of the procedures used in the ballad operas may, indeed, seem relatively unsubtle. But they help to explain the popularity of this genre. In London itself *The Beggar's Opera* and *The Beggar's Wedding* (by Charles Coffey, 1729) were presented before the populace in booths at Bartholomew Fair and Southwark Fair. Soon they were being taken round the countryside by troupes of strolling players like those described in the memoirs of Charlotte Charke.[1]

The moral issue associated with the presentation of *The Beggar's Opera* is neatly summed up in a passage from Daniel Defoe's *Augusta Triumphans* (1728). Speaking of the contemporary underworld Defoe writes: 'We take pains to puff 'em [rogues] up in their villainy, and thieves are set out in so amiable a light in "The Beggar's Opera" that it has taught them to value themselves on their profession, rather than be asham'd of it by making a highwayman the hero and dismissing him at last unpunished.'[2] Samuel Johnson thought that this kind of criticism was exaggerated. But Defoe's assertion reminds us that the age of Handel, Pope and Gay was also the age of Jeremy Collier (1650–1726), Arthur Bedford (1668–1745) and other puritanical opponents of stage entertainment. Throughout the period Italian opera, along with all other theatrical amusements, was under constant surveillance from the guardians of religion and public morality. In March 1728, Thomas Herring (afterwards Archbishop of Canterbury) actually preached against *The Beggar's Opera* at Lincoln's Inn Chapel, and almost simultaneously Herring's friend William Duncombe wrote to the *Whitehall Evening Post* a letter which began: 'It has, I think, been generally agreed among moralists, that all public sports and entertainments should be so regulated, as to have a tendency to the

---

[1] Charlotte Charke was the daughter of Colley Cibber. Her *Narrative of the Life of Mrs Charlotte Charke* (1755) gives a very vivid description of conditions among low-ranking theatrical people in the middle of the eighteenth century.

[2] Quoted in Schultz, *op. cit.*, p. 237.

encouragement of virtue, and the discountenancing of vice and immorality.'[1] In the knowledge that four years earlier Bishop Gibson had censured Handel's partner, Heidegger, for presenting masquerades, we can appreciate the extent to which Handel needed, in the interests of his own reputation, to play for safety by exploiting the taste for oratorio. He did not turn from opera simply to oblige those who, like Aaron Hill, had asked him to clothe English words in suitable musical language. His earlier oratorios were performed by Italian singers, and except for the absence of acting were almost indistinguishable from operas. They did not catch on immediately, and many opera-lovers were disconcerted by their solemnity. But in time Handel came to appreciate that he could appeal to a species of piety which finds expression in many items of contemporary literature. By setting sacred texts to music which occasionally exhibited a true sublimity, Handel produced something that was virtually a supplement to formal worship. As Mrs. Dewes wrote to Bernard Granville on 3 December 1750, 'It is only those people who have not felt the pleasure of devotion that can make any objection to that performance [i.e. *The Messiah*], which is calculated to raise our devotion, and make us truly sensible of the power of the divine words he has chose beyond any human work that ever yet appeared, and I am sure I may venture to say ever will.'[2] Rigid purists might object to the treatment of Scriptural subjects even in mature Handelian oratorio, but by the late 1740s these poems accompanied by music and yet emancipated from the atmosphere of the dramatic exhibition were generally accepted as morally sound. So much so that Mrs. Eliza Haywood, in her *Epistles for the Ladies* (1749), expressed the desire that 'Oratorios (might be) established in every City and great Town throughout the Kingdom . . . to be given gratis'.[3] In a note on Handel's librettist Charles Jennens, the Rev. R. B. Nickolls observed that 'Perhaps that Sacred Musick may have contributed more than any modern Sermons to spread diffusely the knowledge of the finest and most interesting parts of Scripture, to which many besides the Great World might otherwise have paid little or no

[1] Thomas Herring, *Letters . . . to William Duncombe* (1777), p. 179.

[2] Lady Llanover, ed., *The Autobiography and Correspondence of Mary Granville, Mrs Delany* (1861), II. 623.

[3] Quoted in Winton Dean, *Handel's Dramatic Oratorios and Masques* (1959), p. 137.

attention.'[1] How far eighteenth-century oratorio did actually promote this kind of awareness no one can say. But such a remark testifies to the thoroughness with which Handel's idiom associated itself in the public mind with the notion of spiritual well-being.

V

So far we have been considering music as an activity which engaged the attention and esteem of the wealthier and more privileged classes. We must now turn to some of the agencies by which a taste for serious instrumental and vocal music was diffused among those orders of society which were below the highest ranks. In this connection we shall first examine the part played by music and musicians in some of the more familiar places of public resort.

The London pleasure gardens are of considerable importance in the social history of English music. Nearly all of them paid homage to the value of music and dancing as a means of pleasing their patrons, and even the more modest establishments saw the advantage of engaging the services of reputable singers and instrumentalists. At Lambeth Wells we hear of a 'consort' performing every Wednesday during the summer of 1697, an ensemble of about thirty performers making music 'after the manner of the musick-meeting in York buildings, the price only excepted'.[2] In 1698 the Sadler's Wells Music House was providing music twice a week, and other gardens followed much the same arrangement.[3] Later on it became a common practice to install an organ and to make this instrument a major feature of the musical activities, and many organ concertos, especially those of James Hook,[4] were written for performance at Vauxhall Gardens.

The larger pleasure gardens favoured the construction of an 'orchestra' around which vocal and instrumental groups could be assembled. When, for instance, Daniel Gough became the proprietor of the Marylebone Gardens in 1738, he 'selected a band

---

[1] John Nicholls, *Literary Anecdotes of the Eighteenth Century* (1812), III. 126.
[2] Warwick Wroth, *The London Pleasure Gardens of the Eighteenth Century* (1896), p. 279.
[3] *Ibid.*, p. 45.
[4] C. L. Cudworth, 'The English Organ Concerto', in *The Score*, No. 8 (Sept. 1953), pp. 56–57.

from the Opera and the Theatres to play, from six to ten (at night), eighteen of the best concertos, overtures and airs'.[1] In their days of prosperity the gardens provided a great variety of musical programmes; apart from orchestral items, there were vocal performances of all kinds. Well-known violinists and organists became associated with particular gardens, and most of the larger ones, such as Ranelagh and Vauxhall, had their favourite singers. Prodigies, performers on novel musical instruments, and other curiosities of the musical world made their appearance at the pleasure gardens, and George Colman the younger speaks with particular enthusiasm of the *burlettas* given at Marylebone Gardens when Samuel Arnold (1740–1802) was musical director there.[2] Music was, of course, only a part of the entertainment as a whole. Nevertheless, an enormous repertory of contemporary music was performed at the gardens over the years. In some cases 'resident' composers and conductors were engaged, and there was a considerable demand for *commemorative* music such as J. F. Lampe's grand martial composition in honour of Admiral Vernon (1741), and Samuel Arnold's Ode 'in the manner of a Oratorio' composed to celebrate the Prince of Wales's coming of age in September 1772. In compositions like these, the patriotic strain, cultivated by such composers as Arne and (later) Charles Dibdin, makes a frequent appearance. Selections from operas and oratorios were very popular. Thus in 1774 a comparatively unimportant rendezvous, the Lord Cobham's Head, was offering excerpts from *Samson* and *Saul* to its patrons. But it was at Vauxhall that Handel was in most demand. In 1738 Jonathan Tyers, the manager, ordered from the sculptor Roubillac a white marble bust of the 'bold Briarius' to be set up in the great Grove of Vauxhall Gardens, 'where his Harmony has so often charm'd even the greatest Crouds into the profoundest Calm and most decent Behaviour'.[3]

At this time Jonathan Tyers was doing well out of Vauxhall, so the three hundred pounds spent on the Handel statue was a tribute to his own success as well as that of the composer. Some of the other gardens were less profitable, and moreover they attracted disreputable members of society. An interesting feature

---

[1] Wroth, *op. cit.*, p. 95.

[2] George Colman, *Random Records* (1830), I. 49.

[3] Otto Erich Deutsch, *Handel A Documentary Biography* (1955), p. 456.

of the gardens generally, though, was that within them social distinctions tended to be disregarded. Henry Fielding remarked that these places of pleasure 'set apart for the use of the great world' were 'seldom frequented by any below the middle rank', though he had to admit that they were, 'by reason of their price . . . not entirely appropriated to the people of fashion'.[1] Looking back to the 1780s, Sir Samuel Egerton Brydges observed that of the various London amusements 'Ranelagh was the chief evening resort; and it was very entertaining, as all ranks were there mingled'.[2] It is not to be supposed, of course, that the musical performances at Ranelagh, Cuper's Gardens and Sadler's Wells were of a uniformly high standard. All the same, the repertory drawn upon was a large one. The programmes given at the more ambitious gardens (quite apart, that is, from the music for dancing) suggest that they made available to a wide cross-section of the London public a great deal of music which it would otherwise have had no reasonable chance of hearing.[3] And even if, as Rowlandson's drawings would persuade us to believe, the audiences were not as solemn and attentive as they are expected to be in a modern concert hall, full provision was made to meet a variety of tastes. Writing to *Common Sense: or The Englishman's Journal* from Dick's Coffee House, Temple Bar, on 10 April 1738, one 'A.D.' complained of Handel's oratorio performances that 'every Body knows his Entertainments are calculated for the Quality only, and that People of moderate Fortunes cannot pretend to them'.[4] This was only too true: Handel's decision to charge a guinea for admission to *Deborah* (March 1733) made him appear an 'insolent and rapacious Projector' (to quote *The Craftsman* for 7 April 1733), the usual price for a box at the opera being only half that.[5] But in the pleasure gardens people like 'A.D.' could go to hear representative items from Purcell, Boyce, Arne, Festing and many others (in some cases performed by the composers themselves) under conditions specially intended to accommodate individuals 'of moderate

[1] Fielding, *An Enquiry into the Causes of the Late Encrease of Robbers* (Complete Works of Henry Fielding, 1903), XIII. 28.

[2] Sir Samuel Egerton Brydges, *Autobiography* (1834), I. 193.

[3] See T. L. Southgate, 'Music at the Public Pleasure Gardens of the Eighteenth Century', in *Proc. Mus. Ass.*, XXXVIII (1912), pp. 141 *et seq.*

[4] Deutsch, *op. cit.*, p. 460.

[5] *Ibid.*, p. 312.

Fortune'. And the pattern of entertainment which prevailed in London itself was imitated at provincial centres of population. In 1761 William Herschel was appointed to direct a 'weekly garden concert' at Newcastle; Birmingham had its Vauxhall, at which, thirty years later, the oboist W. T. Parke became a leading performer;[1] Norwich boasted at least three pleasure gardens; and the spas such as Bath, Tunbridge Wells and Scarborough all provided musical attractions. These *al fresco* performances were the forerunners of the modern promenade concerts.

VI

The abundant musical life of the pleasure gardens provided a considerable amount of business for music publishers during the eighteenth century. Not only were hundreds of Vauxhall, Marylebone and Ranelagh songs published separately; they were made up into innumerable collections. Typical of these is *Universal Harmony* (1743), which contains a song called 'Spring Gardens', set by William Boyce, describing the joys of a *rus in urbe* complete with colonnades, pavilions and attractive walks. A writer in Abraham Rees's *Cyclopedia* (1809) claimed that after being heard at Vauxhall the ballads, dialogues and duets of Thomas Arne were 'circulated all over the kingdom'. Another Vauxhall composer whose work afforded many collections was John Worgan (1724–90); but from a later generation the name of James Hook (1746–1827) is perhaps the most outstanding. Hook was connected with Vauxhall for over fifty years and had an incredible facility in the composition of operas, concertos, sonatas, catches and ballads.

The amount of music published in England during the eighteenth century was, of course, prodigious. And the great name in English music publishing up to 1766 is that of Walsh, famous for (among other things) its association with Handel. John Walsh the elder had started publishing in 1695, and is said to have made fabulous profits out of the sale of *Rinaldo* in 1711. With his son, John Walsh, jnr., he extended the scope of his business and also imported music from abroad. The important feature of the Walshes' publishing policy was their considerable use of advertisement, either by means of catalogues or by the

[1] W. T. Parke, *Musical Memoirs* (1830), I. 191.

insertion of announcements in vacant spaces on title-pages. The catalogues show that the Walsh concern kept in stock large quantities of Italian music by composers such as Corelli, Albinoni, Vivaldi and Buononcini; they also published the songs and instrumental music in plays as well as full operatic scores. Among their many rivals was John Cluer, who dabbled in patent medicines in addition to music. Cluer was one of the first to try to popularize the pocket-size musical volume, the virtues of which were advertised in the Preface to *A Pocket Companion* (1724–5). Cluer also sold musical playing cards, and claimed in a publication called 'The Pedigree of a Fidler' that he had hit upon a method of producing music 'at a much cheaper rate'.

But cheap music—for works of any size, that is—did not come in until later in the century. Most of Handel's works (in score) were published by subscription at a cost of two guineas; to James Harrison belongs the credit of having produced a vocal score of *The Messiah* at no more than seven shillings. This was made possible by the application of a principle which had obvious parallels outside the sphere of music, namely periodical publication. Harrison's *New Musical Magazine* (1783) included oratorios, ballad operas and other items. But this had been anticipated by many other periodical collections of (in particular) vocal music. In the first years of the century there had been several numbers of a *Mercurius Musicus* (published by Playford), but Walsh and Hare made a greater success of *The Monthly Mask of Vocal Music* between 1702 and 1724. This was largely a selection of current theatrical music. Yet despite the craze for opera and a large trade in such things as 'The Airs in the Opera of Almahide for a single Flute', the demand for dance music was even greater than for vocal pieces. Indeed, dances and psalm tunes may be regarded as the staple items of eighteenth-century music publishing. Playford's *Dancing Master*, as we know, had an enormous popularity, but by the middle of the century, dances were being published not in dozens but in hundreds. Every publisher of note issued yearly sets of country dances, and in practically every case emphasis was laid on the novelty of the tunes being presented. An instance of this—and also an example of the publisher's flair for discreet advertisement—is an item from the firm of Walsh: 'Twenty Four New Country Dances for the year 1716 With New Tunes and New Figures or Directions to each

Dance Humbly dedicated to Walkin Williams Esqr., by his most Obedient and most humble Servant Natl. Kynaston. Note the New Country Dancing Master is Publish'd Containing the Country Dances of the last Ten Years.'[1]

Country dance tunes, like songs, were published fairly frequently in the *Gentleman's Magazine*. And we must give several of the monthly journals credit for popularizing music so far as it was possible for them to do so. Handel, for instance, is represented in such periodicals as the *London Magazine*, the *European Magazine*, the *Aberdeen Magazine* and others. The *Christian Magazine* for October 1760 printed 'Sin not, O King' (*Saul*) under the title of 'How long wilt thou forget me, Lord'. Admittedly such journals as these were only able to offer separate songs (sometimes no more than thirty or forty bars), but taken over a period they provided their readers with a fairly substantial repertory of contemporary music. They also gave obscure composers a chance to appear in print. The *Gentleman's Magazine* for 1750 (to single out one particular year) included upwards of a dozen songs—among them an air from Handel's *Triumph of Time*; 'Contented all day I will sit at your side' from Boyce's *The Chaplet*; and 'The Highland Laddie Written long since by Alan Ramsay, and now sung at Ranelagh and all the other gardens; often fondly encor'd, and sometimes ridiculously hiss'd'. This last observation is an interesting one. For despite the attempts by Arne and other composers to arouse a decisive response to specifically English sentiments, the taste for Caledonian music and dances increased towards the end of the eighteenth century.

James Harrison's more ambitious ventures should be described as serial rather than periodical publications. Under this heading comes his *Piano-Forte Magazine* (1797–1802), which sold for half a crown a number. By 1800 the pianoforte had almost superseded the harpsichord as the principal keyboard instrument. According to John ('Estimate') Brown there was a time about 1750 when the guitar was taking the place of the harpsichord, but the arrival in this country of a number of German instrument-makers (mostly political refugees) at more or less the same time did a great deal to popularize the piano. At first such instruments were of rather large dimensions, but

[1] Noted in W. C. Smith, *Bibliography of John Walsh*, item 488.

Johann Zumpe, who had worked under the Swiss harpsichord-maker Tschudi, constructed small pianofortes about the same size as a virginal. Of these a writer in Rees's *Cyclopedia* says: 'from their low price, and the convenience of their form, as well as power of expression, [they] suddenly grew into such favour, that there was scarcely a house in the kingdom where a keyed-instrument had ever had admission, but was supplied with one of Zumpe's piano-fortes, for which there was nearly as great a call in France as in England'.[1] The advantages of the 'Piano-forte' over the spinet and harpsichord are too numerous to mention here. But as Rosamond Harding observes, whereas a large amount of music had been written for 'Harpsichord or Piano Forte', as we approach the end of the eighteenth century 'the heading is frequently reversed and we read "for Piano Forte" often printed in large letters whilst "or Harpsichord" if not omitted is often printed in smaller type.'[2] Both the harpsichord and the pianoforte inspired a host of inventors who worked to achieve perfection of design; and the possibility of using a variety of stops on both instruments was followed up by craftsmen such as Broadwood, Kirkman and Isaac Hawkins. When inaugurating the *Piano-Forte Magazine* James Harrison introduced a modern touch: each number of the journal was to include a note signed by Harrison himself, and any reader who purchased the entire 250 numbers and produced 250 signed certificates was entitled to receive from the publisher a 'Brilliant toned and elegant Piano Forte, far superior to many instruments sold for twenty-five guineas each'.

VII

'The Love of Musick is now descended from the Opera-house in the *Hay-market* to the little Publick Houses about this Metropolis, and common Servants may be now met with, who pretend as much Judgement of an Opera Tune as my Lady Duchess.'[3] So wrote the author of *An Enquiry into the Melancholy Circumstances of Great Britain*[4] about 1775. Certainly in the pleasure gardens

[1] Rees's *Cyclopedia*, article on 'Harpsichord'.
[2] Rosamond E. M. Harding, *The Pianoforte* (1933), p. 68.
[3] Quoted in J. J. Hecht, *The Domestic Servant Class in Eighteenth Century England* (1956), p. 217.
[4] N.d., but *c.* 1775?

the commonalty may well have enjoyed much the same entertainments as the nobility and even royalty itself, but in general men and women of the eighteenth century were extremely conscious of rank and station. The lives of authors like Savage, Johnson and Crabbe shows how sensitively well-bred individuals reacted to any suggestion that they might at some time be unable to live up to the position they had assumed in society. And a common argument against Methodism was that it fostered 'impertinence and disrespect towards . . . superiors, in perpetually endeavouring to level all ranks and do away with all distinctions'.[1] It cannot be denied that in Handel's day the national wealth was very unequally distributed. This was in part responsible for the prolonged outcry against Luxury which, as David Hume said in an essay on *Refinement in the Arts* was named by men of 'severe morals' as 'the source of all the corruptions, disorders, and factions, incident to civil government'.[2] In this connection should be mentioned an ingenious proposal put forward in 1729 by Daniel Defoe to 'prevent the expensive importation of foreign musicians, &c., by forming an academy of our own'. Under this scheme the governors of Christ's Hospital would arrange for musical instruction to be given to a selected number of children who in course of time would be qualified to stage operas at reasonable cost; 'so that instead of 1,500 l. per annum, the price of one Italian singer, we shall for 300 l. once in ten years, have sixty English musicians regularly educated, and enabled to live by their science'.[3] This proposition evidently did not recommend itself to Defoe's contemporaries.[4]

We have only to study the works of Hogarth and Fielding to get some idea of the extremes of wealth and poverty in this period. Throughout the century charitable institutions were constantly being established to ameliorate the condition of the poor.[5] In this connection music played an honourable and important part. 'Where the riches are engrossed by a few,' wrote

[1] The Duchess of Buckingham in a letter to the Countess of Huntingdon, quoted in Alfred Plummer, *The Church of England in the Eighteenth Century* (1910), p. 124.

[2] David Hume, *Writings on Economics* (ed. Eugene Rotwein, 1955), p. 20.

[3] 'Augusta Triumphans', in *The Novels and Miscellaneous Works of Daniel de Foe* (1841), XVIII. 16.

[4] A scheme not unlike it, however, was adopted when Kneller Hall was set up in 1857.

[5] See M. Dorothy George, *London Life in the XVIIIth Century* (1925), pp. 319–22.

David Hume in his tract *Of Commerce*, 'these must contribute very largely to the supplying of the public necessities.'[1] From the early years of the eighteenth century musical endeavours aided this process. Right at the end of the period the Rev. William Coxe praised Handel for so often lending his talents to promote 'religion's best fruit, charity',[2] and many other leading composers engaged in philanthropic efforts to which music gave valuable assistance.

The era of the joint-stock company and the state lottery provided new opportunities to people actuated by a serious 'concern' for charity. A 'feeling for the power of association' was, according to B. Kirkman Gray, 'the conscious and subconscious idea of the age'.[3] Certainly, a great deal of eighteenth-century music-making had its origin in the awakening spirit of voluntary association, which was characteristic of other than strictly charitable enterprises. There were then no such things as agencies in the modern sense of the term; concerts had to be arranged either by individual efforts or through the combined activities of groups of people—such as the 'Academy of Ancient Music'—who had interests in common. One incentive to concert-giving was found in the exercise of charity.

For example, in 1678 Charles II granted a Royal Charter of incorporation to the Charity for the Sons of the Clergy. Each year this event was celebrated by a service in St. Paul's Cathedral at which Purcell's *Te Deum* and *Jubilate* were performed. A ticket for the Feast of the Sons of the Clergy (which took place in Merchant Taylors' Hall) carried with it two Rehearsal tickets and two Choir tickets for the Festival itself.[4] Another charitable fund was established for the Support of Decayed Musicians (afterwards called the Royal Society for Musicians), to which Handel was a generous contributor. The custom of arranging musical gatherings in aid of private individuals who had suffered particularly grievous misfortunes was a fairly common one in Handel's time. In 1748, for instance, the *London Evening Post* carried an advertisement for a 'grand Entertainment of Musick, Vocal and Instrumental' organized to relieve the wants of those

[1] Hume, *ed. cit.*, p. 15.
[2] W. Coxe, *Anecdotes of George Frederick Handel* (1799), p. 29.
[3] B. K. Gray, *History of Philanthropy* (1905), p. 80.
[4] E. H. Pearce, *The Sons of the Clergy* (1904), p. 198.

who had been victims of 'the late dreadful Fire in Exchange-Alley', and the *London Courant* in April 1757 spoke of a benefit concert at the Great Room in Dean Street, Soho, for a widow whose husband had been lost at sea in particularly distressing circumstances.[1] Handel's own exertions on behalf of the Foundling Hospital and Mercer's Hospital, Dublin, are well known. Less famous than *The Messiah*, though equally typical of its period, is William Boyce's *Ode to Charity*, which was produced at a music festival in Leicester held during September 1774 at St. Martin's Church in aid of the Leicester Infirmary. On that occasion a Snetzler organ was used for the first time, and the nobility and gentry supported the festival in strength. Lord Sandwich, a musical patron of distinction, was particularly interested in this Ode and arranged for it to be repeated at Hinchingbrooke Hall, his Huntingdonshire seat; it was afterwards given at Covent Garden.

Several provincial festivals—of which the Three Choirs Festival is the oldest—originated in the close association of music with charity. Like the Sons of the Clergy Festival, the Three Choirs meeting was in the first place an extended church service; but, as Dr. Thomas Bisse, Chancellor of Hereford, put it in his charity sermon of 1729, 'It was in like manner a fortuitous and friendly proposal, between a few lovers of harmony and brethren of the correspondent choirs, to commence an anniversary visit, to be kept in turn; which voluntary instance of friendship and fraternity was quickly strengthened by social compact; and afterwards, being blessed and sanctioned by a charity collection, with a word of exhortation added to confirm the whole, it is arrived to the figure and estimation as ye see this day.'[2] Dr. Bisse went on to extol the virtues of mutual improvement as brought about by 'a choral and collegiate fraternity' based on the solid foundation of authentic piety.

From its inception the Three Choirs Festival brought a great deal of pecuniary help to the widows and orphans of clergymen in the West of England. But like other festivals it achieved very much more than this. It introduced to wider public notice many

[1] W. S. Lewis and R. M. Williams, *Private Charity in England, 1747–1757* (1938), pp. 47 and 91.

[2] Quoted in Daniel Lysons and others, *The Origin and Progress of the Meetings of the Three Choirs* (ed. of 1895), p. 4.

fine singers who seldom performed outside the cathedrals and larger churches. Thus we hear of Walter Powell, a counter-tenor from Christ Church, Oxford, who sang at the Gloucester Festival of 1733,[1] and the Rev. Benjamin Mence, Vicar of St. Pancras, who appeared in *The Messiah* at Hereford in 1759 and whose 'vocal powers as an English singer' were highly praised by the *Gentleman's Magazine*.[2] The Festivals also drew on talent from farther afield than the West Country. Daniel Lysons mentions 'the celebrated female chorus singers, as they were called, from the North of England', among whom was the soprano Sarah Harrop, afterwards Mrs. Joah Bates.[3] This and other references to these 'nameless singers' is enough to show that in the larger towns during the second half of the century choral unions were coming into being and were achieving a tolerable standard of performance. Joah Bates, who directed the great Handel Festival in 1784, was a native of Halifax, a thriving industrial centre with strong evangelical connections. Here, in 1788, Charles Dibdin found a great veneration for the works of Handel. 'I have been assured, for a fact,' he writes, 'that more than one man in HALIFAX can take any part in chorusses from the *Messiah*, and go regularly through the whole oratorio by heart; and, indeed, the facility with which the common people join together throughout the greatest part of YORKSHIRE and LANCA-SHIRE, in every species of choral music, is truly astonishing.'[4] Admittedly, the music heard at the provincial festivals which from about 1760 were beginning to flourish in towns like Salisbury, Derby, Leicester, and Sheffield was almost entirely Handelian in character. But they gave an opportunity for 'provincial musicians of character', as Charles Burney called them, to prove their abilities alongside professionals from London.[5] Until the 1770s women chorus singers were frowned upon. But in the later decades of the century provincial music-making (especially in the vocal departments) became so ubiquitous that it was impossible to do without them.

One of the most extraordinary charity schemes which made direct use of music was that at Church Langton in Leicestershire.

[1] *Ibid.*, p. 17.   [2] *Ibid.*, p. 36.   [3] *Ibid.*, p. 49.
[4] Charles Dibdin, *The Musical Tour of Mr. Dibdin* (Sheffield, 1788), Letter XLVII, p. 196.
[5] In *An account of the Musical Performances in Westminster Abbey* (1785), 'Introduction', p. 13.

This was proposed by the Rev. William Hanbury, the famous botanist and cultivator of rare trees. Hanbury conceived the idea of a music meeting in the parish church at which well-connected people in the locality would be given a chance to contribute towards an ambitious charity administered, as usual, by a board of trustees. In arranging a two-day festival in September 1759 (parts of which were repeated for the benefit of 'the common people') Hanbury thought he was breaking new ground, for he wrote later: 'An oratorio in the country was never heard of before.'[1] In fact, music from the oratorios of Handel had been given in places as far removed from London as Chester, Norwich, Lichfield, Bridgnorth and Walsall long before the composer's death in 1759. Birmingham, for instance, developed as an important musical centre from about 1750. There, as in other large towns, musical societies sprang up under the auspices of enthusiasts like James Kempson, who organized the Musical and Amicable Society in that city. On 26 December 1766, this Society, with Kempson as director, performed music by Purcell and Handel in St. Bartholomew's Chapel in aid of distressed housekeepers, Kempson also officiating at festivals in Staffordshire, Warwickshire and Worcestershire.

In other parts of England musical clubs—sometimes merely convivial assemblies, but frequently of an entirely serious nature —could be found in such towns as Hull, Liverpool, Leeds and Bristol well before the opening of the nineteenth century. Glee clubs and catch clubs flourished exceedingly between 1760 and 1860 and sociable music for (largely) unaccompanied voices was produced in considerable quantities by composers with a special gift for appropriate harmonization. The London 'Noblemen's and Gentlemen's Catch Club', which was founded in 1761, was very fashionable in its day and had as its first secretary Thomas Warren, editor of a collection entitled *Vocal Harmony* (one of a number of such works). The Madrigal Society, which is still in existence, dates from 1741. An offshoot of the Academy of Ancient Music (which was started in the 1720s), this association was run in its earlier days on the lines of a friendly society, with a code of rules and fines for disregarding them. 'The whole structure of the society', says Reginald Nettel, 'was based on the

---

[1] William Hanbury, *The History of the Rise and Progress of the Charitable Foundations at Church-Langton* (1767), p. 87.

old trade guilds system, adapted to a recreational scheme of musical and intellectual improvement.'[1] Although the Madrigal Society later became a more specialized fraternity, it originally admitted to membership amateur musicians of comparatively humble capacities.

Corporate musical activity—as we may gather from the lists of subscribers to musical works—was not confined to the growing industrial towns and the cathedral cities. Indeed, the practice of yearly subscription was frequently invoked in quite small places to establish what were generally called 'Gentlemen's Concerts'. Music flourished at the universities, where its indulgence was justified on the ground that the enjoyment of it was preferable to less worthy pursuits. As a writer of a letter to *The Student* on 5 April 1750 observed, 'As to the concerts we frequently have in our halls, do they not in some measure contribute, by bringing us into company, to the wearing off that rust and moroseness which are too often contracted by a long continuance in college?'[2] Much the same kind of associational impulse was responsible for the promotion of subscription concerts which, as Stanley Sadie has shown, prevailed in comparatively remote localities.[3] At the Gentlemen's Concerts the practice was for a select band of (mostly) string players to come together at regular intervals to perform music by composers like Corelli, Geminiani, Handel and Vivaldi. In some cases these meetings were wholly private, but on certain occasions the public was admitted. Some of the Gentlemen's Concerts acquired sizeable libraries of orchestral music, and their needs were met by publishers such as John Preston and Robert Bremner, who issued symphonies and concertos on a periodical basis. As may be imagined, these bands of amateur instrumentalists differed in quality from place to place; but even when 'professional stiffening' was brought in to avoid frequent breakdowns, the participants did not lose sight of the fact that their 'concerts' were held

[1] R. Nettel, 'The Oldest Surviving English Musical Club', in *Musical Quarterly*, XXXIV (1948), p. 102.

[2] Quoted in R. Brimley Johnson, *The Undergraduate* (1928), p. 220. This book is an abridgement of Christopher Wordsworth's *Social Life at the English Universities in the Eighteenth Century*. The correspondent signs himself 'Granticola' from 'C.C.C. Cambridge'.

[3] Stanley Sadie, 'Concert Life in Eighteenth Century England', in *Proc. Royal Mus. Ass.*, LXXXV (1958–9), pp. 17–30.

for purposes of mutual enjoyment rather than exact rendering. The subscription (a guinea or two guineas a year) tended to make the Gentlemen's Concerts rather exclusive, and in most places they were kept in being by enthusiasts drawn from the upper social ranks. It was among such informed dilettanti that a taste for 'modern' music took root.

VIII

Whatever else it may have been, the eighteenth century was —so far as English musical life was concerned—a period of bickering and controversy. The squabbles which took place among the patrons of the Italian opera early on in the century were commented upon in the letters of Lady Mary Wortley Montague and Lord Hervey; references to the supposed *irrationality* of opera occur in the writings of Dennis; and Henry Carey was speaking for a great number of his contemporaries when he pronounced a 'Curse on this damn'd Italian pathic mode'.[1] Later there were long discussions on the legitimacy of oratorio, most of which turn on the notion that sacred words are somehow immolated when given a musical setting. The Rev. John Newton, for instance, was scandalized to think that his generation chose 'to make the solemnities of their impending trial, the character of their judge, and the awful sentence to which they are exposed, the ground-work of a musical entertainment', as he put it in the fourth sermon of his fifty discourses on *The Messiah* (1786). The famous Ancients-versus-Moderns dispute extended to music, especially instrumental music. This has some slight connection with the growth of musical antiquarianism, but broadly speaking it takes its rise from the conviction that the so-called 'Baroque' style of composition had had its day by the middle of the century, and that only triteness and repetition would in future be possible for composers in that idiom. This position is stated (and answered) in John Potter's *Observations on the Present State of Music and Musicians* (1762). It led to a somewhat paradoxical situation, for a good many older musical enthusiasts were not anxious to welcome new schools of composition. 'The present fashion', wrote Richard Gregory in 1767,

---

[1] Carey, 'A Satire on the Luxury and Effeminacy of the Age' (line 22), in F. T. Wood, ed., *The Poems of Henry Carey* (1930), p. 98.

'is to admire a new style of composition lately cultivated in Germany, and to despise Corelli as wanting spirit and variety. The truth is, Corelli's style and this will not bear a comparison.'[1] Musical conservatism was not easily broken down in the eighteenth century; and at this time of day it seems incredible that Charles Dibdin could have seriously described Haydn's music as 'strong effusions of genius turned into frenzy, and labouring as ineffectually to be heard as a flute in a belfry, or equity in a court of justice'.[2] But although Dibdin mistrusted the 'floods of German nonsense' then being brought into our concert halls, he did not side with the faction which maintained that Handel's music represented the ultimate perfection of this art. In his *Musical Tour* he placed a higher value on the works of Arne and Purcell than upon those of Handel, but though there is some point in what he says about all three composers, it is clear that jealousy on behalf of 'British' musicians as against insolent foreigners forms the mainspring of his comments. This was not the case, however, with those who objected to what Gregory called the 'spirit of wild luxuriancy' in early romantic music: these critics took their stand on what they believed to be the unnecessary difficulty in the works of composers such as Richter, Stamitz and Haydn himself.

Haydn did not visit this country in person until 1791; but his music was well known here long before then. Since the 1760s, in fact, more and more works by German composers were being introduced as an alternative to what Mrs Delany in 1775 called 'modern flimsy Italian music'.[3] The Italian opera still attracted its habitual patrons, but after the arrival of J. C. Bach and K. F. Abel, who gave concerts in partnership for upwards of twenty years from 1764 onwards, performances of large-scale instrumental sinfonias were increasingly called for. The Concerts of Ancient Music, established in 1776, sought to repress the 'intemperate rage for novelty' by excluding from their programmes music written within the last twenty years, but these efforts were unavailing. The 'modern' style of writing prevailed, for reasons admirably summed up by John Marsh in a 'Comparison between the Ancient and Modern Styles of Music', which was published

---

[1] Richard Gregory, *A Comparative View of the State and Faculties of Man* (4th ed., 1767), p. 145.

[2] Dibdin, *Musical Tour*, Letter XLIV, p. 182.

[3] *Autobiography and Correspondence, ed. cit.*, Second Series, II. 91.

anonymously in the *Monthly Magazine* for 1796.[1] The 'Ancients', according to Marsh, were anxious to achieve correctness rather than 'what is understood by modern amateurs, under the general denomination of *effect*';[2] they were casual about dynamic contrasts, and seemingly indifferent to tone colour (though in fairness it should be remarked that the mechanical improvements which made accurate performance on wind instruments possible were of comparatively recent origin). Moreover, their modulations were unadventurous. As Marsh put it, 'The fashionable composers, HAYDN and PLEYEL, by avoiding occasionally the regular and studied uniformity of modulation and style which has been generally adopted by most of their predecessors, have certainly attained far more originality and greater variety.'[3] With specific reference to Haydn, a writer in Rees's *Cyclopedia* takes Marsh's appreciation a stage further when he says that 'There is a general cheerfulness and good humour in Haydn's allegros, which exhilarate every hearer. But his adagios are often so sublime in idea and the harmony in which they are clad, that though played by inarticulate instruments, they have a more pathetic effect on our feelings than the finest opera air united with the most exquisite poetry.'[4] There could hardly be a more outspoken championship of classical instrumental music than this, and other writers extol the grandeur and intricacy of Haydn's scoring. John Marsh even went so far as to wonder whether the instrumental symphony could give *general* pleasure (as, presumably, the oratorio did) simply because its appreciation depended on repeated hearings. With this, of course, we recognize the emergence of a new attitude towards music and an assertion of status on the part of an educated *élite*. In the *Musical Times* for 1 January 1875 Henry C. Lunn wrote that the Hanover Square Rooms in which so much of Haydn's music was first heard in England 'were especially adapted for the nobility and those moneyed aristocrats who, either from taste or fashion, were content to devote a portion of their time and capital to the support of struggling music'.[5] The Professional Concerts and

[1] Reprinted in *Music and Letters*, XXXVI (April 1955).
[2] *Ibid.*, p. 158.
[3] *Ibid.*, p. 159.
[4] Rees's *Cyclopedia*, article on 'Haydn'.
[5] H. C. Lunn, 'The Hanover-Square Rooms', in the *Musical Times*, 1 January 1875, p. 741.

the Salomon-Haydn concerts did indeed receive support from a 'brilliant patronage'. But it was an enlightened patronage, not merely an indulgent one. This much is deducible from newspaper comments of the 1790s.[1] Impresarios like Salomon constantly solicited the support of the gentry and the nobility, but the existence of a fair percentage of discriminating listeners among the eight hundred people who were able to crowd into the Hanover Square premises is recognized in many respectful references to 'the connoisseurs' and 'the amateurs' who, according to the *Morning Chronicle* for 30 December 1780, were in the habit of looking up to Joseph Haydn as 'the *god* of Science'.

The Ancients-and-Moderns issue did not involve the less sophisticated lovers of music. But the lower and middle classes of society were affected directly or indirectly by another musical controversy which was prolonged right through the eighteenth century and continued into the nineteenth. This concerned the performance of church music, and had quite as many ramifications as the dispute mentioned above. In this period sacred music played an important part in the informal education of the masses. The majority of people attended some place of worship, and few denominations proscribed music altogether; so that even in localities where oratorios were seldom heard some form of service-music was usually attempted. During the eighteenth century the music in our cathedrals lost a great deal of the vigour it had enjoyed for some years after the Restoration. It is perhaps an exaggeration to say that the services (in the cathedrals) were 'droned out day by day with diminishing thoughtfulness',[2] yet there is a fair amount of evidence to show that organists in this period were negligent and worldly.[3] In parish churches the musical parts of the service received perfunctory and occasionally eccentric treatment. The argument that music had no legitimate place in worship was still heard quite late in the century, though it had been refuted many times in sermons on the excellence of divine music and the rationale of sacred song. But more interesting for the student of social history is the discussion of parochial music which occupies a place in the lesser ecclesiastical literature

[1] The subject is fully documented in H. C. Robbins Landon, *The Symphonies of Joseph Haydn* (1955), chapter xii, pp. 435–551.

[2] C. Henry Phillips, *The Singing Church* (1945), p. 147.

[3] See John E. West, *Cathedral Organists Past and Present* (1899), pp. 33, 49 and 68.

of the Augustan period. This is taken up in countless tracts and episcopal charges, and hardly a decade passes without some serious pronouncement being made upon it.

The dispute concerned the status of congregational psalmody and the proper use of instrumental music in places of worship. The latter is to some extent a secondary matter, as comparatively few country churches possessed organs until late in the century (if then); so Addison's complaint about frisky voluntaries could not have had a wide application. The question of psalmody was more weighty, however: for as Bishop Secker pointed out in his second Charge to the Clergy of the Oxford diocese in 1741, the performance of psalms is 'a part of Divine Worship . . . clearly appointed in Scripture, both expressive and productive of devout Affections, extremely well fitted to diversify long Services, and peculiarly to distinguish the several Parts' of the Anglican rite.[1] In most churches the custom was for the parish clerk to intone each line of the various psalms and then for the congregation to follow on after him. But this practice could lead to misunderstanding, as at St. George's Church, Doncaster, where the parish clerk had the choice of both the psalm itself and the tune it was to be sung to. 'His custom', writes Edward Miller, 'was to send the organist not the *words*, but only the *name* of the tune, and how often it was to be repeated. Strange absurdity! How could the organist, placed in this degrading situation, properly perform his part of the church service? Not knowing the words, it was impossible for him to accommodate his music to the various sentiments contained in different stanzas; consequently, *his* must be a mere random performance, and frequently producing improper effects.'[2] Where few of the congregation knew the appropriate tunes, a lead was given either by the charity-school children or by groups of voluntary singers who took it upon themselves to supply the place of a choir, thereby assuming 'an exclusive right, which belongs not to them but (to) the congregation at large'.[3]

In many later-eighteenth-century accounts of church music the 'Village Practitioners' come in for a good deal of notice. At some places they were not encouraged, but in many parts of the

[1] Thomas Secker, *Eight Charges* (1769), p. 64.
[2] Miller, *History and Antiquities of Doncaster* (n.d.), p. 88.
[3] William Jones, *The Nature and Excellence of Music* (1797), p. 17.

country they flourished much as the glee clubs did in the towns.[1] Nor were they confined to Anglican churches: a remarkable musical ensemble in the Dean area of Rossendale (Lancs.), known locally as the 'Deighn Layrocks', was made up mostly of Baptists who produced psalm tunes and chants in considerable numbers.[2] William Mason went so far as to say of such music-making that 'since the rage of Oratorios has spread from the Capital to every Market Town in the Kingdom, [country musicians] can by no means be satisfied unless they introduce chaunts, Services, and Anthems, into their Parish Churches, and accompany them with . . . *scolding Fiddles*, squalling Hautboys, false-stopped Violoncellos, buzzing Bassoons; all ill-tuned and worse played upon, in place of an Organ, which, if they had one, they would probably wish to improve by such instrumental assistance'.[3] Not all clerics were as contemptuous as this. Some bishops did, indeed, take the view that these unofficial singers should not be permitted, as their presence in church tended to make the rest of the congregation diffident about joining in the psalm-singing; but others approved of the parish singers, and there are instances of the lesser clergy being directed to remunerate them. James Woodforde, Rector of Weston Longeville, Norfolk, made payments to the 'Weston Singers' in 1792;[4] in the following year there was friction between the Rector and his musicians, for on 21 April 1793 he writes, 'No singing this Aft. at Church. The Weston Singers talk of giving it up, which I think is behaving towards me very shabby';[5] but in due course 'the Singers took it into their heads to sing again'—and all was well. At Newmarket in 1757 Thomas Holcroft, then a stable-boy, chanced to hear pleasant sounds coming from a church; he went inside and found Mr. Langham, a local breeches-maker, instructing a group of 'acknowledged learners' in four-part singing. Holcroft asked if he might join them as he wished to learn music 'and was answered, yes; they should be very glad to have me, for they much wanted a treble voice, and all they required was that I should conform to the rules of the society. I inquired what those rules were, and was told, they each paid five shillings

[1] See W. E. Tate, *The Parish Chest* (1960), pp. 167, 168.
[2] William Jessopp, *Methodism in Rossendale* (1880), pp. 252 *et seq.*
[3] William Mason, *Essays on English Church Music* (York, 1795), pp. 217–18.
[4] John Beresford, ed., *The Diary of a Country Parson*, III (1927), p. 400.
[5] *The Diary of a Country Parson*, IV (1929), p. 22.

entrance, five shillings a quarter to Mr. Langham, another five shillings for Arnold's Psalmody; and they paid forfeits of pennies and twopences, if they were absent on certain days, at certain hours, or infringed other necessary bye-laws'.[1] This organization is reminiscent of the Madrigal Society; and Mr. Langham was evidently authorized to give tuition, though in many places itinerant psalm teachers were frowned upon by church dignitaries. A pointed reference to those 'men who travel, and style themselves professors of, and instructors in psalmody' occurs in the Address prefixed to William Tattersall's *Improved Psalmody* (1794).

The church bands which William Mason found so uncongenial were very numerous at one time. Canon Macdermott has accounted for a fair number of them, but there were a great many of which no record survives.[2] Thomas Webster's famous painting of the musicians in the gallery of the church at Bow Brickhill, Beds. (1847) is, like Hardy's descriptions in *Under the Greenwood Tree* and elsewhere, a sentimental idealization. But, as is evident from *The Early Life of Thomas Hardy* (1928), the Hardy family played an important part in maintaining a long tradition of musical accompaniment to worship in the church at Stinsford, Dorset. Speaking of the county of Sussex, Canon Macdermott writes: 'These bands seem to have flourished very well till the fatal advent of the harmonium or American organ brought about their doom.'[3] But it should be recalled that from the middle of the eighteenth century, hand-operated barrel organs were occasionally used in the smaller churches for the accompaniment of hymns and chants.

IX

Among the innumerable books and pamphlets which deplored the contemporary state of psalmody and expressed the hope that church music might again be restored to a position of dignity and influence, one of the most interesting is William Vincent's *Considerations on Parochial Music* (1790). Taking the view that 'a scientific knowledge of the art of music' is now more generally diffused among 'all the higher and middling ranks throughout

[1] Elbridge Colby, ed., *The Life of Thomas Holcroft* (1925), I. 94.
[2] K. H. Macdermott, *The Old Church Gallery Minstrels* (1948), pp. 67–71.
[3] K. H. Macdermott, *Sussex Church Music in the Past* (Chichester, 1922), p. 35.

the kingdom', Vincent goes on to praise the Methodists for their treatment of music, which in some respects is more estimable than that of the Established Church. 'That the harmony arising from the voices of a well regulated Methodist Congregation is delightful,' he writes, 'no one who has heard it, can deny. Let us not envy them the enjoyment of it, but draw our own instruction from it.'[1] Other writers declared that it was the musical part of the Methodist service which enticed large numbers of people away from the Anglican fold. The brothers Wesley certainly attached great importance to the congregation's participation in the service, and left strict instructions as to how this might be secured. Much has been written on Methodist hymnody, for hymn-singing as we know it was largely an outcome of the eighteenth-century Evangelical revival. Charles Wesley's great literary gifts have long been recognized; but the general enthusiasm for Methodism is also of great importance in the social history of music during this period.

John Wesley's early acquaintance with the Moravians had brought him into contact with communities among whom the traditions of sociable music-making were especially strong. He realized that many of the old psalm tunes were melodically uninteresting and lacking in distinction. His congregations needed a musical phraseology which was simple without being dull, closely adapted to the words and yet rhythmically alive. The 'people called Methodists' must be able to 'sing with the spirit and the understanding also'. The *Sacred Melody* of 1761, therefore, contained a number of secular melodies as well as more conventional hymn tunes and German chorales. Also included were settings by Lampe, the successful pleasure-gardens composer. Lampe's style resembles that of the lighter theatrical aria, and *Sacred Melody* as a whole is calculated to make the congregation sing 'lustily, and with a good courage'. But John Wesley's attitude to music in general is a cautious one: he sympathized with the 'ancients' rather than the 'moderns'. An entry in his Journal for 25 January 1781 is typical of this: 'I spent an agreeable hour at the concert of my nephews (the musical sons of Charles Wesley). But I was a little out of my element among Lords and Ladies. I love plain music and plain company best.' It is not surprising that he disapproved of counterpoint when it

[1] William Vincent, *Considerations on Parochial Music* (1790), p. 15.

123

destroyed the prose sense of the words sung. This, together with unnecessary repetitions, spoiled his enjoyment of Arne's *Judith* at Bristol on 29 February 1764. But Wesley did not underrate the devotional value of oratorio. In 1758 he went to hear *The Messiah* at Bristol Cathedral and declared afterwards: 'I doubt if that congregation was ever so serious at a sermon, as they were during this performance. In many parts, especially several of the choruses, it exceeded my expectation' (*Journal*, 17 August 1758).

In view of the fact that Wesley's 'Directions for Congregational Singing' commends so wholeheartedly the robust enjoyment of vocal music, it is curious to find one biographer actually apologizing for his (Wesley's) attending the Rev. Martin Madan's oratorio performances at the Lock Chapel. The same writer goes on to explain that Madan was merely imitating his superiors at the cathedral churches. 'Indeed,' he continues, 'some of the early Methodists adopted the same doubtful usage (of sacred edifices). We have before us more than one of Handel's oratorios, specially printed, for performance in Oldham Street chapel, Manchester, only one or two years after Wesley's death. All this was dubious; indeed, we venture to designate it desecration. A Christian sanctuary is a place far too sacred to be used as a place of intellectual entertainment.'[1] This is enough to show that some dissenters as well as orthodox Anglicans were doubtful about the propriety of turning places of worship into concert halls. But from the purely musical standpoint the Methodist Revival had two main consequences: it encouraged numbers of people to take a particular pride in uniting their voices 'so as to make one clear melodious sound', and it helped to promote a taste for the specifically evangelical elements in Handel's oratorios and similar works by lesser composers. Wesley's own tastes in music (as his 'Thoughts on the Power of Music' show) were conventional and unambitious. But the consequences of Methodism (and, for that matter, Nonconformity as a whole) in the musical sphere were manifold. In 1805 an Ipswich clergyman complained that working-class sectaries engaged in 'the almost daily practice of singing their *divine hymns*' at a time when they ought to have been in bed.[2] Twenty years later George Hogarth

[1] L. Tyerman, *The Life and Times of the Rev. John Wesley* (1870), II. 499–500.
[2] *A Letter to a Country Gentleman, on the Subject of Methodism* (Ipswich, 1805), p. 32.

wrote: 'In the densely peopled manufacturing districts of York-shire, Lancashire, and Derbyshire, music is cultivated among the working classes to an extent unparalleled in any other part of the kingdom. Every town has its choral society, supported by the amateurs of the place and its neighbourhood, where the sacred works of Handel and the more modern masters, are performed with precision and effect by a vocal and instrumental orchestra consisting of mechanics and work people; and every village church has its occasional holiday oratorio.'[1] To the strength of Methodism and its appeal to the masses during the closing decades of the eighteenth century may be attributed some of the responsibility for that 'diffusion of taste for music, and the increasing elevation of it' which George Hogarth regarded as so characteristic of the time. It would be a mistake to ascribe too strong an influence to one denomination; but musical associations such as that at Haworth were to a large extent inspired by cultural aspirations which were shared by hundreds of Nonconformists at the turn of the century.[2]

X

The conventional view of English music in the eighteenth century rests on the assumption that musical history is nothing more than an account of well-known composers and their achievements. Looked at from this standpoint, the period between 1700 and 1800 does not—so far as English composers are concerned—seem a very distinguished one. Yet there is no point in dismissing the entire epoch simply because the genius of Arne or Boyce was not equal to that of Handel. Out of a large number of composers contemporary with Handel himself there were a few—including men like Maurice Greene, Charles Avison and Joseph Gibbs—who possessed creative talent of a high order. But this talent was not devoted entirely to composition. Avison and Gibbs were both church organists, the one at Newcastle and the other at Ipswich: and like many others of equal competence they were active proponents of musical culture in their respective

[1] George Hogarth, *Musical History, Biography and Criticism* (2nd. ed., 1838) II. 274.
[2] Referred to in a letter quoted by Mrs. Gaskell in the third edition of her *Life of Charlotte Bronte* (reprinted with an Introduction by Clement Shorter, 1900), p. 32.

localities. The conditions of the time, as we have seen, were favourable to the establishment of a thriving provincial musical life which, though inclined to ape metropolitan fashions, occasionally produced interesting regional variants. This was aided by an increase of wealth in towns distant from London, which in turn led to the erection of churches, theatres and concert halls. There were also tentative developments in a field which was later to occupy the attention of some remarkable people—namely the encouragement of musical potentialities among the masses. It was left to the nineteenth century to solve some of the problems—educational and otherwise—associated with this phenomenon.

IV

Industrial Society and the People's Music

In some ways the most important single event in the history of
English music during the eighteenth century was the Handel
Commemoration held at Westminster Abbey and the Pantheon
in 1784. This confirmed general approbation for the composer
whose best-known oratorios had already attracted large audiences and were to draw even larger crowds during the nineteenth
century. It also demonstrated in London itself that large choral
and orchestral forces could combine successfully in a sustained
act of tribute. For, as Charles Burney explained in his Account of
this festival, it was now evident—perhaps for the first time in
the history of mankind—that as many as five hundred vocal and
instrumental performers could produce such grand masterpieces
as *The Messiah*, the *Dettingen Te Deum* and *Zadok the Priest* with
perfect intonation and unfaltering tempo. The occasion was 'no
less remarkable for the multiplicity of voices and instruments
employed, than for accuracy and precision'. And Burney added:
'When all the wheels of that huge machine, the Orchestra, were
in motion, the effect resembled clock-work in every thing, but
want of feeling and expression.'[1] This figure of speech reminds
us that the English choral tradition has its origins in the period
of the Industrial Revolution. Burney's very phraseology is, indeed, that used by the devotees of applied science: it would

[1] Charles Burney, *An Account of the Musical Performances in Westminster Abbey*
(1785) 'The Commemoration', p. 15. Burney continues: 'And, as the power of
gravity and attraction in bodies is proportioned to their mass and density, so it
seems as if the magnitude of this band has commanded and impelled adhesion and
obedience, beyond that of any other of inferior force.'

hardly have suggested itself fifty years earlier. It is not without significance, too, that the musical director of the 1784 commemorations, Joah Bates, was a substantial investor in the famous Albion Mills; and when these were destroyed by fire in 1791 Bates and his wife, Sarah Harrop (who had formerly been a factory worker in Halifax), lost a large fortune. The patrons of the provincial festivals which came into existence during the later eighteenth century included many well-known manufacturers; and developments in industrial skills—such as the casting of metal and the use of precision tools—brought about great improvements in the art of instrument-making. It is the purpose of the present chapter to examine some of the ways in which English musical life was affected by the changes consequent upon the Industrial Revolution itself.

I

'The Industrial Revolution', said W. C. Smith, 'largely created conditions which compelled the ordinary people . . . to find their own recreations cheaply amongst themselves—and they therefore endeavoured to make their own music. Many tried to play the pianoforte and other musical instruments, and to sing as soloists or in part-songs, choruses, etc. They were able to make the attempts they did, and they were not all bad performers, because the music of the time was mostly very simple, demanding little technical ability of player or singer.'[1] Perhaps the supreme example of self-help in this direction was that of Samuel Crompton, of whom we are told that 'Though his means were but small, his economy in living made him always in easy circumstances. He was fond of music, and built for himself an organ, which he had in his little cottage.'[2] Few had the inventive genius of a Crompton, but most people could make some attempt at vocal music or the rudiments of instrumental technique. By 'the music of the time' Dr. Smith means that of Handel and his imitators. The words most commonly used to describe the works of Handel are 'sublime', 'majestic' or 'magnificent'

---

[1] See Reginald Nettel, 'The Influence of the Industrial Revolution on English Music' in *Proc. Royal Mus. Ass.*, LXXII (1946), p. 39.

[2] John Kennedy, 'A Brief Memoir of Samuel Crompton' in *Memoirs of the Literary and Philosophical Society of Manchester*, Second Series V (1831), p. 322.

rather than 'simple', but the idiom in which late eighteenth-century music in general was written exhibits a freedom from fundamental complexity and a reliable absence of startling or 'unvocal' modulations which makes its performance by untutored amateurs relatively straightforward. This fact told in favour of those whose inclinations towards music were encouraged by their employers, by Sunday-school teachers or by other enthusiasts for self-cultivation.

The early factories employed large forces of child labour; and it occasionally became apparent to factory-owners and overseers that the presence of numerous illiterate and disaffected young people on their premises could easily give rise to serious problems. For this reason some eighteenth-century manufacturers undertook to provide a few educational facilities in order to combat total ignorance. 'In isolated cases, from the earliest years of the eighteenth century,' writes A. E. Dobbs, 'iron-masters and owners of collieries and mines are found building chapels, opening pleasure grounds and supporting schools of the accepted type. . . . To this period may be traced the origin of those organized settlements which have contributed in various ways to raise the standard of social enterprise throughout the country.'[1] Of these communities probably the most remarkable was that described by Robert Owen in his *New View of Society*. Acting on the assumption that a person's character is formed *for* him and not *by* him, Owen set about combating the hostility which was rife in New Lanark in 1797. He did this by ameliorating conditions of life generally, but in particular he discontinued the practice of employing children under ten years of age. Those thus set free were taught reading, writing and arithmetic in the local school, all the 'modern improvements in education' having been adopted and sectarian instruction carefully excluded. 'Another important consideration', wrote Owen, 'is that all their instruction is rendered a pleasure and delight to them; they are more anxious for the hour of school time to arrive than to end; they therefore make rapid progress.'

Part of this pleasure and delight was obtained through music. From the account given by an American visitor who went to New Lanark in 1825, we know that the children in these classes were taught music 'upon the Lancasterian plan, from a large roll

---

[1] A. E. Dobbs, *Education and Social Movements, 1700–1850* (1919), p. 164.

many yards in extent, containing the gamut, with the addition of select tunes. It is placed in a conspicuous part of the room, where the notes can be distinctly seen at the same moment by every pupil. The words are committed to memory from printed cards, embracing a selection of the best songs.'[1] Owen was, of course, an exception to the general run of factory proprietors; and his own descriptions of the New Lanark projects must be taken with some reserve, since they are written in an enthusiastic vein. William Cobbett ridiculed the idea of the children 'bawling' in class and 'singing out something at the word of command'.[2] But there were many manufacturers who were sensitive to the social value of music. In her *Vignettes of Derbyshire* (1824), for instance, Mrs. Sterndale speaks of the cotton-spinners at Cresbrook and notes that 'their highest species of enjoyment, the highest that man can enjoy, is music; this delightfully intellectual source of pleasure is improved, encouraged, and scientifically taught at Cresbrook. Every boy that has a voice, an ear, or a finger capable of participating in the Heavenly science, receives elementary, and practical instruction.'[3] At Belper, John Strutt went to great pains to see that his employees were allowed adequate time from their work to receive musical tuition;[4] the Strutts were a very musical family, and occasionally made it possible for some of their workers to visit places outside Belper— including London—to hear performances. Soon after the commencement of the Strutts' music school, William Gardiner tells us, 'it was found that the proficients were liable to be enticed away, and to commence as teachers of music. To remedy this, the members of the orchestra (were) bound to remain at the works for seven years.'[5] An article in *The Harmonicon* for April 1833 praised John Strutt's 'philosopher-like' exertions on behalf of the Belper workpeople and observed: 'Among these people he truly finds that music *"emollit mores, nec sinit esse feros"*; and it is earnestly to be wished that such an example were generally followed in establishments where great numbers of people are employed.'[6]

[1] Quoted in Frank Podmore, *Robert Owen* (1906), p. 145.
[2] William Reitzel, ed., *The Autobiography of William Cobbett* (1947), p. 217.
[3] Mary Sterndale, *Vignettes of Derbyshire* (1824), pp. 43–44.
[4] William Gardiner, *Music and Friends* (1838), II. 512.
[5] *Ibid.*, p. 513.
[6] *The Harmonicon* (1833), p. 72, col. 2.

Farther north, in the same period, the London Lead Company's Yorkshire and Durham miners were encouraged to form bands, a small 'Band Room' being provided to house the instruments. 'The first bands officially recognized', writes Arthur Raistrick, 'were at Nent Head about 1820; and the Company gave an annual donation of £5 towards it. In 1825, bands were started in Long Marton, Stanhope, Garrigill, and other villages, and in 1835 the Company subscribed £28 9s. 6d. towards new instruments for the Nent Head band.'[1] At Bollington in Cheshire the mill-owner Samuel Greg put into operation some very ambitious plans for the education and recreation of his employees. In his two letters to Leonard Horner he describes the amenities available to those who worked at a mill he opened in 1832. First a Sunday school was started; this was followed by a playground for the younger people, the institution of a drawing class and then of singing classes (music being more popular than drawing). Greg writes: 'Our music and singing engage many of both sexes—young and old, learned and unlearned. We have a small glee class that meets once a week round a cottage fire. There is another more numerous for sacred music that meets every Wednesday and Saturday during the winter, and really perform very well, at least I seldom hear music that pleases me more. A number of men have formed a band with clarionets, horns, and other wind instruments, and meet twice a week to practise, besides blowing and trumpeting nightly at their own homes. A few families are provided with pianos, and here I believe all the children of the household play on them. The guitar also is an instrument not unknown among us, and to these may be added sundry violins, violoncellos, serpents, flutes, and some sort of thing they call a *dulcimer* . . . and when you remember how few families we muster,—not more than 70 or 80,—you will think with me that we are quite a musical society.'[2] Such activities were feasible in relatively small communities: but they were less likely to take place when, for economic reasons, the large-scale employer felt obliged to keep a distance between himself and the workers.

It was, however, under conditions such as those described above that the English brass-band movement had its beginnings.

---

[1] Arthur Raistrick, *Two Centuries of Industrial Welfare* (1938), p. 71.

[2] (Samuel Greg) *Two Letters to Leonard Horner, Esq., on the Capabilities of the Factory System* (1840), 23.

The full evolution of that belongs to a later period; but even in the early years of the nineteenth century towns like Stalybridge, Rochdale and Glossop boasted small wind ensembles which turned out to accompany processions and to provide music for festive occasions: such groups appeared regularly at 'wakes' and contributed the instrumental background to the various May-songs sung annually in the environs of Manchester. Bands of music were usually in attendance whenever newly constructed navigations were opened, and factory musicians were occasionally hired for electioneering purposes. In May 1831, for instance, the band at the Nant Y Glo Iron Works in South Wales was employed by Colonel Wood in connection with the Breconshire election at a cost of £24 for the services of thirteen men and a boy for five days.[1] The paternalism shown by many of the factory-owners in this period may cause us some misgiving: and the benevolence of the Strutts was an openly despotic one. All the same, we have to appreciate that they did their best to meet a situation which had been created largely by their own enterprise. Their exertions proved the truth of George Hogarth's words in 1842 that 'the experience of the present day has shown, and is showing more and more, that even the classes who earn their daily bread by the sweat of their brow, may find in music a recreation within their reach, full of innocent enjoyment, and pregnant with moral and social benefits'.[2]

It is clear, however, that from an educational point of view those workers and their families who came under the supervision of men like the Strutts or Samuel Greg were extremely fortunate. In places other than those mentioned—particularly in the rapidly expanding towns like Manchester and Leeds—it was largely a matter of chance whether young people received any education at all, much less musical instruction. The conditions of life in districts like Hunslet and Salford caused the labouring classes to be thrown on their own resources for recreation and amusement. And from the evidence quoted it would be wrong to imagine that in this period every single artisan was consumed by a desire to bring about his own spiritual and moral betterment.

[1] John Lloyd, *The Early History of the Old South Wales Iron Works* (1760–1840) (1906), p. 175.
[2] Article on 'Music-Art of Singing' in *Chambers's Information for the People*, No. 99 (1842), II. 769.

Similarly, the testimony of Dibdin, George Hogarth and others must not be overstressed. Unquestionably a taste for serious music was developing among a fair section of the factory operatives in the north of England and elsewhere. At the same time, the masses as a whole were satisfied with something less ambitious than the works of Handel, Haydn and Mozart. They had recourse to what, for want of a more precise term, we will call 'urban folk music'.

II

There has long been a tendency to associate English folk music exclusively with rustic life and rural occupations. The reason for this—apart from the obvious one that many folk songs date from a time when few towns were more than a short distance from the open country—lies in the fact that since urban populations frequently contain migratory elements, the memory of songs and ballads handed on by oral tradition has been retained most vividly in country districts and small towns where long family successions have been upheld. This does not always follow, of course; and many writers have shown that few folk songs and ballads are as narrowly localized as was once thought to be the case. Throughout the eighteenth and well into the nineteenth century a large business was done all over England by the printers and vendors of chap-books and pamphlets designed to suit the needs of simple unsophisticated readers. An offshoot of this trade were the broadside ballads, which were enormously popular until comparatively recent times.

Printed on thin—sometimes almost transparent—paper, broadside ballads were retailed by the thousand in towns and villages everywhere. Since they could be easily produced on simple presses, broadsides were often the work of very humble printers using a small stock of type and one or two decorative blocks. Ballads were of two kinds—those meant to be read and those intended for singing. But this somewhat obvious distinction is important, since the whole history of this branch of popular music is bound up with developments in general literacy during the first half of the nineteenth century. The sung ballad with a high proportion of news value (common enough since Elizabethan times) held its own until after the Crimean War; but the mental habits induced by newspaper-reading made such things as 'The Battle of the Nile' and 'The Loss of the Amphi-trite' of less value at a later date than they seemed to earlier generations. But during the period 1780–1850 ballad singers were still comparatively numerous in public places. They did not, in fact, disappear completely until the present century; and many of the buskers who entertained theatre queues up to a very recent time employed devices which were common among the street-ballad singers of an earlier day.

There were several types of ballad singers: some merely relied on a small stock of tunes which they tried out at different 'pitches' before moving on; others had an extensive repertoire to which they added items of their own composition. Sometimes they were vendors as well as performers; in this case they kept in close touch with the printers and took quantities of broadsides to dispose of on their rounds. Broadsides were printed in many centres apart from London—Newcastle, Manchester, Birming-ham and Preston supplying large quantities of ballad sheets to their surrounding districts. And the fact that broadsides were in great demand among the common people indicates at least two significant things: in the first place there was a fair degree of literacy among the masses before about 1840, and secondly there existed a large number of melodies of a wholly secular kind which the majority of people could be expected to know by heart. Musical notation was very seldom given on the broadsides of this period. When a ballad is obviously meant to be sung, its tune is simply indicated by the phrase 'Air—The Pilgrim of Love' or 'To the tune of Gallant Hussar'—a custom which goes back to the sixteenth century at least. Ballads were sold at a halfpenny each; and the fact that relatively few of them (out of the enormous number printed) have survived, indicates that they were regarded as ephemeral productions. Structurally they are of various kinds. The commonest forms are the solo song and the song with unison chorus. At a later stage duologues became more common and also patter songs which introduced spoken passages. Ballads of this type have much in common with nineteenth-century music-hall songs; and a number of techniques later used on the halls were introduced into the comic street songs and sketches of our period. Popular songs and ballads are usually of a heterogeneous nature. They reflect many aspects of national life and popular feeling.

In his *Sketches by Boz* Dickens looked forward to a time when 'penny magazines shall have superseded penny yards of song, and capital punishment be unknown'.[1] The reference here is to the type of ballad which celebrated the crimes and prison reflections of murderers; also numerous were the political and propaganda ballads which were common in times of crisis. Writing in 1840, Douglas Jerrold in *Heads of the People* attributed the decline of the ballad singer to the presence in this country of foreign street entertainers. 'During the war', he writes, 'it was his [the ballad singer's] peculiar province to vend half-penny historical abridgements to his country's glory; recommending the short poetic chronicle by some familiar household air, that fixed it in the memory of the purchaser, who thus easily got hatred of the French by heart, with a new assurance of his own invulnerability. No battle was fought, no vessel taken or sunken, that the triumph was not published, proclaimed in the national gazette of our Ballad-singer . . . It was he who bellowed music into news, which, made to jingle, was thus, even to the weakest understanding, rendered portable. It was his narrow strips of history that adorned the garrets of the poor; it was he who made them yearn towards their country, albeit to them so rough and niggard a mother.'[2] In the revolutionary period, indeed, there were ballad writers who were employed by the Government to compose songs which would arouse the people to the dangers of invasion and awaken a sense of national pride. The outstanding example of this is Charles Dibdin (1745–1814), who was 'instructed [by Pitt] to write, sing, publish, and give away what were termed War Songs'.[3] Dibdin falls into a different class from the ballad composers mentioned above; he was a trained professional musician (albeit of a rather unorthodox kind) who had a sound knowledge of the theatre and could compose with great fluency. But the patriotic motive set out in such songs as 'A Hero's True Glory' and 'The Standing Toast' is also present in the work of less able writers. In the latter part of the eighteenth century, for instance, the Volunteer movement was the subject of a great many ballads issued in Manchester; during the time of the Napoleonic wars the Corsican tyrant was characterized

---

[1] Dickens, *Sketches by Boz* (New Oxford Illustrated Dickens, 1957), p. 69.

[2] Quoted by Charles Hindley, *The History of the Catnach Press* (1887), p. xxxix.

[3] *Songs of Charles Dibdin* (1875), p. xxviii.

in such songs as 'The Bantam Cock' and 'Bony's Last Gasp'; and in 1848 a ballad from the press of John Harkness of Preston was entitled 'France and the Republicans'. These ballads on French affairs are worthy of mention, because they are typical of the bald and unsubtle treatment which political ballad writers employed. The element of wit is more common in songs dealing with controversial local issues. Thus in 1791 the inhabitants of Derby were very much concerned by a proposal to acquire and improve a piece of common land called Nun's Green. Despite protests, this apparent encroachment on ordinary liberties took place: it led to the publication of several ballads, three of which are given in Llewellyn Jewitt's *The Ballads and Songs of Derbyshire* (1867). The topical references would need a great deal of explanation; but a stanza from 'A Birch Rod for the Presbyterians' (to the tune of 'Chevy Chace') will give some idea of the tone which the ballad writer adopted:

> I wish all such Aldermen and folks like them,
>> Was forc'd to change their station;
> And that Greenland hulks for their vile bulks,
>> Might for ever be their station.

The tune for another ballad on the same topic, 'The Nun's Green Rangers', is 'Bow, Wow, Wow', which is said to be identical with 'The Barking Barber' and 'Date obolum Belisario'. For any particular metre there were a great number of different melodies to choose from.

A very good instance of a popular ballad writer who dramatized urban situations in song was Joseph Mather (1737–1804). Mather was a Sheffield tradesman who had some talent in verse composition and scraped a living as an itinerant ballad singer. He had a gift for satire which the mechanics and grinders of the time greatly appreciated, and his sarcasms were directed at local figures in bad odour with the artisan class. Some of Mather's efforts, such as 'The Author's Petition to Fortune' (to the tune of an air in 'Midas') and 'The Royal George' are conventional enough, but others relate specifically to events in Sheffield at the turn of the eighteenth century. In those days the town was a hotbed of radicalism and the scene of frequent disturbance. Mather refers to the uneasy temper of the day in 'Sancho', a song with chorus which is directed against George Wood, a Master Cutler who in 1792 publicly proclaimed his support for the anti-Jacobin party: in 'Norfolk Street Riots' he celebrates an uprising caused in 1795 by the peremptory action of the notorious Colonel Ape-thorpe, who was later responsible for sentencing James Mont-gomery to six months' imprisonment. 'Hallamshire Haman' again satirizes George Wood and refers to the dispute between scissor manufacturers and scissor grinders in 1790, as a result of which five men were committed to Wakefield Gaol. 'God save Great Thomas Paine' was sung by a crowd of radical sym-pathizers who accompanied the editor of the *Sheffield Register*, Joseph Gales, back to his rooms in the Hartshead after a meeting at the Town Hall in 1793 at which a highly illiberal resolution was passed by the 'Church and King' party.

Mather's most famous song, however, was 'Watkinson and his Thirteens'. 'I can never forget', writes John Wilson, the editor of Mather's *Songs*, 'the impression made on my mind when a boy on hearing [this song] sung by an old cutler. This event happened on a "good saint Monday" during a "foot ale" which was drank in the workshop. After the singer had "wet his whistle" he requested his shopmates to assist in chorus, and then struck off in a manly voice, laying strong emphasis on the last two lines in each stanza, at the conclusion of which he struck his stithy with a hammer for a signal, when all present joined in chorus with such a hearty goodwill that would have convinced any person that *they felt* (the true force of the words).'[1] The chorus runs:

> And may the odd knife his great carcase dissect,
> Lay open his vitals for men to inspect,
> A heart full as black as the infernal gulph,
> In that greedy, blood-sucking, bone-scraping wolf.

The vehemence of the language is perhaps excessive, but the point of the song is that Jonathan Watkinson (Master Cutler, 1787) was one of those employers who insisted on his workers' making thirteen knives to the dozen while only paying them for twelve. The question of what really constituted a 'dozen' re-mained in dispute in the cutlery trade for many years.

The case of Joseph Mather could be paralleled in other places. In Birmingham, for example, there was John Freeth (1730–1808),

[1] *The Songs of Joseph Mather* (1862), p. 63–4.

who was for forty-eight years the proprietor of Freeth's Coffee House and a 'facetious bard of Nature', according to the *Gentleman's Magazine* for October 1808. Freeth's audience was a slightly more sophisticated one than Joseph Mather's: and volumes of his songs were published in his lifetime. Typical of Freeth's 'weak, yet willing efforts to please for the moment' is 'Navigation; or, the Canal Fever', to the tune of 'Let us all be unhappy together'. One stanza runs

> Some people cried up *Hampton Gay*,
>   As prospects the greatest possessing,
> The *Grand Junction*, 'tis clear, bears the sway,
>   And the mania still is increasing;
> At *Ell'smere*, don't think I'm in jest,
>   Regardless of lodging or weather,
> Of *Land navigators* at least
>   Full a thousand assembled together.[1]

This appeared in *A Touch on the Times, being a Collection of New Songs to Old Tunes . . . By a Veteran in the class of political Ballad Street Scribblers . . .* (1803). Around Manchester there were a number of popular rhymesters in this period. In his *Ballads and Songs from Lancashire* (1875) John Harland included a song on 'Grimshaw's Factory Fire' (1791) which was attributed to a Gorton hand-loom weaver named Lucas; this, according to Harland, was 'regularly set to music, printed, and sold by the ballad-dealers of Manchester'. The tune is not named; but Lucas's unpolished lines typify the hand-loom weavers' resentment at the introduction of machines. A later song from the same area which decries modern tendencies is 'Gorton Town', composed by John Beswick. In London the famous Seven Dials printer, James Catnach, employed a number of meanly equipped poetasters to turn out songs of many kinds. 'It is said', writes Charles Hindley, 'that he at one time kept a fiddler on the premises, and that he used to sit receiving ballad-writers and singers, and judging of the merits of any production which was brought to him, by having it sung then and there to some popular air played by his own fiddler, and so that the ballad singer should be enabled to start at once, not only with the new song, but also the tune to which it was adapted.'[2] James Catnach died, a moderately

---

[1] Quoted in W. H. Logan, *A Pedlar's Pack of Ballads and Songs* (1869), p. 200.
[2] Hindley, *op. cit.*, pp. 221-2.

wealthy man, in 1841; some idea of the volume of his trade in popular songs can be gathered from the fact that his successor Mrs. Ryle (Catnach's sister) advertised her business in terms which intimated that 'upwards of 4,000 different sorts of ballads are continually on sale with 40 new penny song books'.

When called upon in 1835 to give evidence before the Select Committee on Education in England and Wales, Francis Place reported that the ballads sung about the streets during his youth could not be adequately described in present company. 'I have given you in writing', he told the Committee, 'words of some common ballads which you would not think fit to have uttered [here]. At that time the songs were of the most indecent kind; no one would mention them in any society now; they were publicly sung and sold in the streets and markets.'[1] Although it is not quite clear which kinds of ballad Place had in mind, there is no denying that a fair proportion of the songs disseminated by broadside publishers were coarse and unnecessarily crude: they were often badly printed as well. Their authors were not men of refined sensibility; but they were closely in touch with the conditions of life among the lower orders and well aware of the modes of enjoyment currently experienced by the masses. For this reason the street ballads and broadside songs of this period cover a wide range of topics and are therefore hard to classify. In general, however, four or five headings will suffice to indicate the subject-matter on which the ballad-makers of the period drew.

Love songs, of course, are numerous and many different kinds of situation are exploited. Seduction and betrayal are common themes, and the possibility (or otherwise) of union between partners of different social classes is a frequent theme. An example of this is 'The Knight and Shepherd's Daughter', of which one version, said to be popular in Queen Elizabeth's time, was given in Percy's *Reliques*; this was still being sung in the nineteenth century by the mill girls of Leeds, and is described by Frank Kidson as a 'fly-boat' song, so called because its easy swing and vigour made it a favourite with young people as they went out on fly-boat trips along the canal.[2] This ballad, incidentally, indicates the persistence with which the retailers of ballads

[1] Quoted in G. R. Porter, *The Progress of the Nation* (1847), p. 684.
[2] Frank Kidson, *Traditional Tunes* (Oxford, 1891), p. 19.

hung on to themes and stories which had been current for centuries. Changes of emphasis and corruption of names—Bedford
to Bideford and Newark to Hewart, and so forth—did little to
alter the essential framework on which many of the older ballads
were constructed. There are many songs of faithful love and of
temptations withstood. Jealousy leading to crime is the subject
of such songs as 'Oxford City', in which both the lovers perish.
Sensational murders figure more frequently in the prose broadsides of the period, though there are some sung versions of major
crimes. Disasters and unavoidable calamities, however, provided
the ballad singer with plenty of scope. These topics were especially common in colliery districts such as Newcastle, Nottinghamshire and Derbyshire.

In these areas songs of complaint were also plentiful. 'A New
Song, call'd The Red Wig', printed by Ordoyne of Nottingham[1]
expresses a sentiment which is frequently found in street ballads,
namely, contempt for the upstart:

> His father was a pauper and his uncle likewise.
> And in Greasley workhouse the latter clos'd his eyes,
> But Charley of late such a valiant man is grown,
> He struts about the town like a toad upon his throne.

From Lancashire there are petitions from the hand-loom weavers
who are being displaced by steam power:

> So, come all you cotton-weavers, you must rise up very soon,
> For you must work in factories from morning until noon:
> You mustn't walk in your garden for two or three hours a-day,
> For you must stand at their command, and keep your shuttles in
>   play.[2]

'The Hand-loom Weaver's Lament' (also printed by John Harland) voices the discontent experienced after the Napoleonic
wars and the advent of powered machinery had reduced wages
and forced the workers to look upon their own employers as even
more tyrannical than Bonaparte himself. A little earlier the Lud-
dite risings had brought into being songs—such as 'Come all
you croppers stout and bold'—evidently intended to arouse the
courage of desperate men. 'The Roving Heckler Lad' calls to
mind the practice of heckling, or preparing flax previous to spin-

---

[1] V. de S. Pinto and A. E. Rodway, eds., *The Common Muse* (1957), p. 115.
[2] John Harland, ed., *Ballads and Songs of Lancashire* (1875), p. 189.

ning, which was a highly specialized trade until entirely super-seded by machinery. It must not be imagined, however, that the evolution of mechanized processes was altogether deprecated by the composers of popular song. There are, in fact, a large number of ballads which applaud the advances being made in this direc-tion. The 'New Song in Praise of Willington Colliery' (1838) is an example from the Newcastle area. 'Haswell Cages', which records the 'new invention/Of winding up coal in a cage', was printed by Walker of Durham. The earliest railways were cele-brated in songs, and the application of steam power to operations hitherto performed by hand gave rise to satirical pieces such as 'The Steam Arm', which tells the story of a soldier who, having lost an arm at Waterloo is supplied with an artificial limb worked by steam; this serves him well enough until he finds that he is unable to stop it from working!

Although the power of steam was quickly put to use in con-nection with overland transport, it was some time before it was employed extensively for marine propulsion, and a good many years elapsed between the construction of the first ocean-going steamers and the final abandonment of large sailing vessels. When this did come about, however, it caused one characteristic branch of the people's music—namely sea shanties—to fall into disuse. Shanties are important for two reasons: they relate to vanished and now almost forgotten modes of day-to-day life, and their treatment at the hands of editors and enthusiasts for 'national songs' illustrates what happens when music is abruptly transplanted from one social context into another. For the authentic sea shanties are in no way concert items; they are not even, in the modern sense of the term, community songs; and they are completely out of place as drawing-room ballads with piano accompaniment. At the risk of anticipating a little—for their demise did not occur until the 1880s or thereabouts—something may here be said on the nature and function of the sea shanties which were to be heard on British ships until almost the end of the nineteenth century.

Shanties are to be distinguished from the folk songs and theatrical tunes which sailors sang when not on duty. They are work songs and as such are out of place among landsmen, who are in any case unlikely to understand the nautical terminology which some of them introduce. In the period we are discussing they were an essential part of life at sea—so much so that most vessels of any size (and certainly those plying between this country and America, India or Africa) included a shantyman among the crew. His duty was to lead the singing, to add to the repertoire of songs and if necessary to improvise new shanties. On sailing ships there were innumerable occasions on which communal labour had to be engaged in, and the shanties—songs shared between a solo singer and a chorus—were sung to lighten the burden of hard and continuous manual labour by bringing in music when rhythmical bodily movements were called for. It is customary to make a rough division between capstan shanties and pulling or hauling shanties. When working the capstan the sailors followed a forward motion, lending their weight to the wooden bars which slotted into the capstan itself. Capstan shanties were often of a fairly free rhythm, as in 'Shenandoah' and 'Lowlands', the music of which is reminiscent of recitative.

The hauling shanties, on the other hand (brought into use when the men were hoisting up ropes or furling sails), employed a more regular rhythm. This was rendered necessary by the fact that at such times there had to be a regular application and relaxation of effort; this was marked by the accentuation of the music. A good example is 'O Boney was a warrior' which consists of a mere eight bars in $\frac{6}{8}$ time; the soloist's part of the shanty gives a potted version of Napoleon's progress, while the chorus chimes in with the reiterated 'Away—ay—ah' and 'Jean François'. An identical structure is followed in other hauling shanties such as 'O Fare-you-well, My Bonny Young Girls', and 'Goodbye, Fare You Well', which was used when taking up anchor in a foreign port. A duple rhythm is common in hauling shanties; but 'Paddy Doyle's Boots', which accompanied the process of 'bunting up' the foresail or mainsail, is in $\frac{3}{4}$ time. For these 'pull-and-haul' shanties the shantyman did not himself take part in the job on hand; he stood by, starting up the music and then contributing the subsequent verses until the task had been completed. Shanties did not, of course, exhaust the seaman's repertory. Sailors picked up melodies which they had heard sung in foreign lands; and in the middle of the nineteenth century there was a period when a great number of American tunes were appropriated by British sailors on ships trading with the southern United States. The sailor's life in general forms the subject of a substantial ballad literature from about 1760 on-wards. In the early nineteenth century such favourites as 'Sling the Flowing Bowl' and 'Come, Loose Every Sail to the Breeze' have much in common with the song material we have already discussed. Authentic shanties, however, seldom dwell (except in mockery or satire) on the kind of sentiment which forms the staple of such songs as 'The Voice of Her I Love', 'Ever of Thee I'm Fondly Dreaming' and 'Her Bright Smile Haunts Me Still', which are occasionally found in collections purporting to be re-presentative of sailors' songs in general.

Reverting to songs and ballads which have no connection with the sea, we find that in addition to those which deal with some aspects of working-class life as seen in its relation to daily em-ployment, there are many songs which describe the sports and pastimes of the proletariat. In ballads like 'The Collier Lads' (from Newcastle) and 'The Girls of Lancashire' (Livesey, Man-chester) the people themselves are celebrated. Street cries are described in ballads from both London and Manchester, and 'Owd'ham Streets at Dinner Time' and 'Victoria Bridge [Man-chester] on a Saturday Night' depict street scenes very vividly. The commonest recreations treated of in the ballads are racing, boxing and poaching. Fox-hunting is the subject of some, and one of the most interesting is 'The Bonny Grey', which describes a cock-fight. In many areas 'cocking' continued long after it was prohibited by law, and versions of 'The Bonny Grey' have been found in Westmorland, Leeds and also Liverpool. It was sung to Cecil Sharp at a folk-song competition at Kendal in 1905 and exists as a broadside printed by Harkness of Preston. Along with these ballads devoted to popular recreations may be classed those which satirized the repressors of amusement—the con-stabulary, the temperance enthusiasts and the politicians. Similar in tone are the sung commentaries on unjust Parliamentary enactments, on the vicissitudes of the Irish immigrants and on great national scandals. 'What will Old England come to?' is a question posed frequently by ballad writers in the period be-tween 1780 and 1850.

III

Urban folk music from this period has several characteristics in addition to those mentioned above. Many of the ballads, for instance, introduced naval themes, and either detail actions in which British vessels have taken part or recall aspects of the sailor's life on shore and afloat. The press gang figures in such songs as 'Rochester Lass', and there are numerous cases of mistaken identity, as in 'Pretty Polly Oliver'. In one song, for instance, the ship's captain engages an attractive 'cabin boy' under the very eyes of his wife, who is also on board. There are many songs which exhibit the manners of one social class to the classes above or below it. The uncouth habits of the countryman up in London, for instance, had comic possibilities which ballad makers quickly seized upon. Taken as a whole, the popular songs current in England—and more particularly urban England—during the reigns of George III and George IV are extremely varied. They cover many aspects of life, and at their best exhibit a spontaneity and charm of a different order from that of the majority of the sentimental effusions sung at Marylebone and Vauxhall.

Before the opening of the Victorian period, however, the ballads had begun to lose their authentic 'folk' quality. It slowly becomes apparent that the men who composed them were less intimately identified with popular feeling than was, say, a working cutler like Joseph Mather. For there is a distinction between songs which *voice* the aspirations of the populace and songs which merely exploit them. The two qualities are sometimes present in the same song; but in the early Victorian period there is a tendency for the latter to predominate. The popularity of bar-parlour concerts led, after the Theatres Act of 1843, to the establishment of music halls in which adaptations of ballad material for quasi-theatrical purposes became common. Many of the broadsides themselves are partly sung and partly spoken; and in this kind of entertainment we have what almost amounts to an 'act' of the kind Charles Dibdin excelled in. Some of the street musicians were, indeed, potential music-hall performers; but the burlesques, the dialect songs and the comic take-offs they concocted made it difficult for the straight ballad to survive in its primitive form. In 1861 a writer in the *National Review* declared: 'The decay of the street ballad singer, which is a fact beyond question, and which we attribute more to the establishment of such places of amusement as Canterbury Hall and the Oxford, and the sale of penny song-books, than to the advance of education or the interference of the police, will probably be followed by the disappearance of the broad-sheet, and may silence the class of authors who write the street ballads.'[1] The broadsheets did not, of course, disappear immediately; but the requirements of the music halls certainly gave rise to a new type of popular song writer—a composer whose expertise enabled him to achieve humorous and satirical touches which the balladmongers were seldom able to rise to.

The great days of the English music hall may be said to date from 1861, when Charles Morton opened the Oxford in Oxford Street; but this type of establishment was a development out of the saloon theatres of an earlier day. Free and easy musical performances in taverns and tea gardens were common enough from the Restoration onwards; in the early part of the nineteenth century, however, they greatly increased in number and variety. In an article called 'Soothing the Savage Breast' in *The Train* for January 1858, Edmund Yates described Easton's Grand Music Hall as much superior to the famous Lord Somerset in Holborn. This converted building behind a public house ('last used as a place of meeting for silly chartists and ungrammatical demagogues') did a roaring trade at sixpence and ninepence for hall and gallery seats respectively: and 'though it is scarcely ten o'clock, we are told there is only standing room, and find, on entering, that we have not been deceived. The hall is very large, and very lofty with a regular stage fitted up with a drawing-room, "flat" and "wings", a grand piano, and an harmonium at one end, and a very spacious gallery at the other.' Eventually the music hall proper emancipated itself from the public house and became in effect another theatre, but specializing in variety turns rather than in the legitimate drama. There were many different types of music hall in London and the provinces, and some of them were little more than extensions to existing tavern property. But the demand for the kind of entertainment they provided signalizes one important fact: the enormous popularity of convivial music-making among the people who habitually went to public houses to obtain some form of diversion.

In this connection, incidentally, we must remember that in thickly populated manufacturing towns and in the dock areas of London and Liverpool men were literally driven to drink because

[1] The *National Review*, XIII (1861), p. 416.

the houses they had to live in were too small to make family life tolerable, so that the public house was the most appropriate place of refuge. After describing the dingy and unwholesome nature of working-class dwellings, Viscount Ingestre, in his lecture 'Social Evils: their Causes and their Cure', explained why the public house exerted such a seductive influence:

> The ample windows, lighted from handsome lustres, pour a brilliant flood into the street. Within, the massive counter, the huge casks, the painted barrels, the shining brasses, and active well-dressed attendants, seem to betoken the height of comfort and prosperity; in the penetralia of the place there is every accommodation, whether for rich or poor—every contrivance to give comfort or pleasure— games, music, attendance, newspapers, company. Alas for our working friend! he thinks one moment of his wretched home; he gazes the next on the brilliant palace: at one instant Conscience tells him to be a man; the next, his companions laugh at his scruples. The stream of temptation proves to be too strong.[1]

The very fact that musical recreation could be obtained at establishments which served liquor was a matter for grave concern to educationalists and reformers; and the association of the music hall with strong drink gave it an evil name in the estimation of the 'unco guid'. 'It is known to your Lordships, and Mr. Mayhew's painfully interesting work on *London Labour and the London Poor* has made it known to all readers of that book,' wrote T. W. M. Marshall in his General Report on Roman Catholic Schools in Great Britain (1852), 'that it is an habitual practice in public houses of an inferior stamp, all over the country, to have frequent musical entertainments of a low and immoral character, for which performers are in great demand.'[2] He goes on to suggest that music as currently taught in schools was only too likely to augment the number of singers who would seek to engage in this sort of entertaining, but at the back of his mind is the conviction that tavern music is reprehensible—at any rate in the form enjoyed by the masses. Yet the music-hall lyrics were the legitimate successors to the ballads we discussed earlier and reflect with considerable accuracy the ways of life of those accustomed to go out of an evening in the 'fustian jackets' to

[1] Viscount Ingestre, ed., *Meliora: or, Better Things to Come* (Second Series, 1853), pp. 92–93.
[2] Minutes of the Committee of Council on Education, 1852–3 (1853), II. 722–3.

which Edmund Yates refers. A song such as 'The Times are very Queer now' (sung by J. A. Hardwick and printed in *Diprose's Comic Music Hall Song Book No. 3*, 1859)

> With competition in each trade,
>   No fortunes now-a-days are gained;
> And these by speculation made,
>   Very few rich men have them retained:
> The only trades that flourish are
>   The Church, Undertaking, and the Bar . . .

establishes continuity with the other urban folk songs we have already mentioned. By this time, however, writers for the music halls had adopted the habit of making the working classes appear slightly comic, and the element of slang finds its way into the music-hall songs for this reason.

One of the main problems which occupied many philanthropists throughout the early nineteenth century was that of how to draw the people away from the pursuits mentioned in Marshall's Report. The considerable literature exposing the evils of factory life illustrates that social welfare work generally failed to forestall the worst consequences of mechanized production. Yet even before the days of effective legislation against long hours and bad working conditions there were some notable attempts to redeem the masses from wholesale mental and spiritual degradation. The period after 1815 brought forth a number of ventures intended to reduce the ignorance of the proletariat, and of these the most ambitious was the Mechanics' Institute. It is customary to date the movement for founding Mechanics' Institutes from 1823, since in that year the London Mechanics' Institution was inaugurated; but societies for the enlightenment of the lower orders were in being long before this. The original intention of the Mechanics' Institutes was to give to artisans a modicum of specialized knowledge which would make them better workers; but as time went on these establishments assumed other functions. In general their organizers overestimated the workers' appetite for culture, and the Institutes gradually became clubs for the lower middle class. Yet these colleges for the artisan have a certain place in the social history of our music. This is to some extent true of the Owenite Halls of Science as well, though in their case political interests were predominant and the outlook was strictly secular—a point which offended their rivals.[1] Under Rule XXVIII of the Huddersfield Choral Society (founded in 1836), for instance, any person who frequented the local Hall of Science 'or any of the "Socialist Meetings" ' was automatically debarred from membership of the Society.

In his study of George Birkbeck, Thomas Kelly writes: 'By the middle of the century the mechanics' institutes had everywhere become a recognized part of the educational scene, not only in the industrial cities but in rural market towns and even in quite small hamlets. There were by this time close on 700 of them, besides a considerable progeny of mutual improvement societies, literary institutes, and similar bodies.'[2] It is convenient to regard the Mechanics' Institute movement as falling into two phases, before and after 1830. Many of the Mechanics' Institutes commenced with grand intentions, but for several reasons the mechanics themselves could not always be induced to retain their membership for very long. 'It has frequently been asserted', said Barnett Blake in 1859, 'that Mechanics' Institutions, so far from realizing the objects for which they were originally established, have been converted into mere literary associations, in which the several advantages of a cheap circulating library, a reading and newsroom, with occasional lectures of a popular character, form an uncertain attraction to the middle classes of our large towns, whilst they have little or no influence on the education or social habits of our mechanics or artisans . . .'[3] Blake denies that this was the case in Yorkshire; but the considerable demand for lyceums, in which light entertainment and social gatherings were an important feature,[4] indicates that the working classes as a whole looked for something less didactic than scientific instruction. All the same, whether presenting the 'middle-class image' or not, the Mechanics' Institutes did achieve something of value from a cultural point of view. A large number of them offered instruction in general subjects as well as in practical and factual ones. Music, both vocal and instrumental, appears in the time-tables of most of the larger Mechanics' Institutes.

[1] See Thomas Kelly, *A History of Adult Education in Great Britain* (Liverpool, 1962), p. 145.

[2] Thomas Kelly, *George Birkbeck* (Liverpool, 1957), p. 148.

[3] Barnett Blake, 'The Mechanics' Institutes of Yorkshire' in *Transactions of the National Association for the Promotion of Social Science, 1859* (1860), p. 335.

[4] On the Lyceums see Kelly, *George Birkbeck*, pp. 246–50.

In a report to the Society for the Diffusion of Useful Knowledge (1841), Thomas Coates stated that 'music is now pretty generally introduced into them (the Mechanics' Institutes) and evening meetings of the members and their families are becoming more frequent'.[1] Coates mentions the music classes at such places as York and Newcastle, and also gives the names of lecturers prepared to speak on musical topics. In the third year of the Miles Platting Mechanics' Institute (founded 1836) a class for instrumental music was started and in 1840 David Winstanley, the secretary, reported that 'Scarcely a quarter has passed over our heads without a Concert or a Tea Party with music and dancing and a variety of other amusements'.[2] Sir Benjamin Heywood, who was closely associated with the Manchester Mechanics' Institution, was warmly appreciative of the good work done there by the music instructor, Mr. Ward, who in turn had expressed his gratification that as a result of his exertions 'several parties (had) been formed amongst the members of the (singing) class, to meet in the evenings to practise Glees or Psalmody'.[3] At Bradford 'a course of weekly concerts for working classes was . . . commenced in the autumn of 1845 by a special committee, acting with the committee of the Mechanics' Institute';[4] while at Leeds in 1849 the Mechanics' Institute arranged a series of lecture-recitals at the first of which 'Mr. Boyes read an address on the advantages to be expected from adding instruction in music to the sciences taught at the Institution'.[5]

This was only one out of many such attempts to recommend rational amusement and innocent entertainment. The procedure adopted in most of the Mechanics' Institutes was to establish a singing class and then work towards a concert which, if successful, would be followed by further communal activities. In this connection an interesting development at Salford is recalled by J. W. Hudson. Writing of the Salford Lyceum (founded in

---

[1] (Thomas Coates) *Report on the State of Literary, Scientific, and Mechanics' Institutions in England* (1841), p. 14.

[2] Edith and Thomas Kelly, eds., *A Schoolmaster's Notebook* (Manchester: Chetham Society, 1957), p. 40.

[3] Benjamin Heywood, *Addresses Delivered at the Manchester Mechanics' Institution* (1843), pp. 77–78.

[4] William Cudworth, *Musical Reminiscences of Bradford* (Bradford, 1885), p. 41.

[5] *Leeds Mercury*, 24 March 1849 (quoted in J. F. C. Harrison, *Learning and Living 1790–1960* (1961), p. 88).

1838), he says: 'The allurements held out to the working-classes at many of the beer-houses by means of organs and other musical entertainments, were found to be great rival attractions. The directors of the Lyceum in 1838, 1839, and 1840, formed their members into vocal and instrumental music classes, elocution and discussion societies, and held frequent coffee parties that the members might derive as much entertainment as instruction.'[1] It was too much to hope that the substitution of a non-alcoholic beverage for more potent liquor would quickly draw habituees of public houses into places of enlightenment; yet the achievements of some Mechanics' Institute choirs and bands were of a high order. At a vocal and instrumental concert consisting mainly of selections from Handel and Haydn given at Pateley Bridge near Harrogate in 1848, 'nearly all the performers were members of the [Mechanics'] Institution and they "attracted an overflowing audience" '. At Wakefield the study of Italian was introduced to meet the demands of concert singers.[2]

It has been argued that the Mechanics' Institutes only attracted a negligible proportion of the working class; and that those workers who did attend for any length of time were indoctrinated with false notions. There is no denying, of course, that numbers of these institutions began enthusiastically and then gradually lost ground. But though the mechanic class was not so well disposed towards them as the promoters had hoped, there were countless individuals who obtained a fair all-round education from attending mechanics' institute classes. One such was Thomas Cooper (1805–92), the noted Chartist and author of *The Purgatory of Suicides*. A Methodist cobbler turned schoolmaster, Cooper was born at Leicester in 1805. After teaching for a time at Gainsborough, he went to Lincoln in 1833 to take charge of a school there. The Lincoln Mechanics' Institution was just then being established, and Cooper joined it; before long he was elected to its first Committee. Teachers were found for the classes in geometry, algebra, botany and drawing; Cooper himself took on a Latin class and afterwards taught French. He had a flair for languages and subsequently learned German and Italian. (He had taught himself Latin by following the example of Dr.

---

[1] J. W. Hudson, *The History of Adult Education* (1851), p. 138.
[2] Mabel Tylecote, *The Mechanics' Institutes of Lancashire and Yorkshire before 1851* (Manchester, 1957), pp. 273–4.

Samuel Lee, who had memorized the whole of Ruddiman's Latin Rudiments.) 'But', he tells us, 'a new attraction arose at last; and all resolves about study, and purposes of intellectual progress, and interests however important, were sacrificed for my new passion. A few young men wished to form a Choral Society, and asked me to allow them the use of my school-room for rehearsals. I consented readily, and became a member of the new society—taking my stand, weekly, as a tenor singer in the choruses. My heart and brain were soon on flame with the worship of Handel's grandeur, and with the love of his sweetness and tenderness. They made me their secretary; and my head went to work to make the music of the Choral Society worth hearing in old cathedralled Lincoln.'[1] Cooper goes on to describe the zeal with which he pursued his objective, remarking that 'A passion for music is something far above the indulgence of feeling'. Admittedly, the Lincoln Choral Society did not come directly under the aegis of the Mechanics' Institute; but Cooper's enthusiasm is typical of the spirit shown by the more advanced class members at such establishments. Cooper was obviously more gifted than the average mechanic, and he had submitted himself to a form of elementary education which enabled him to take more advanced studies in his stride. To this extent the kind of success which Cooper and others like him enjoyed emphasizes the disadvantages under which, in music as well as in other subjects, the ordinary members of Mechanics' Institutes laboured.

IV

'The attempt to establish Mechanics' Institutes throughout the country', wrote John Ella in 1869, 'has proved a signal failure, and instead of being arenas for instruction to the illiterate mechanic, most of them have become places of popular entertainment, in which music, in some form or other, holds a large share. Abstruse theories and technical science, however clearly expounded, must ever fail to enlist the sympathies of the great mass of the lower orders who lack the commonest elements of education.'[2] On the whole, the Mechanics' Institute movement did not succeed in diverting the attention of the populace from

[1] *The Life of Thomas Cooper Written by Himself* (1872), p. 107.
[2] John Ella, *Musical Sketches, Abroad, and at Home* (3rd. ed. 1878), pp. 421-2.

unworthy entertainments—though it must be remembered that few of the Mechanics' Institutes themselves were in a position to put on concerts comparable with those sponsored by John Ella. Reporting on the efforts made in Leeds from 1853 to establish cheap concerts under the auspices of the 'Rational Recreation Society', James Hole recalled that the audience for these had mostly been drawn from the middle class 'and those in social positions immediately above the operative classes; in this respect strikingly corresponding to Mechanics' Institutions'.[1] And *Good Words* in 'A Plea for Music in Common Life' (2 July 1866) contrasted the slight progress made by Mechanics' Institutes with 'the numbers of popular music-halls and concert-rooms that are being opened throughout the kingdom, till now there is scarcely a town of any consideration that has not a place of this kind'.[2]

Yet both the authorities just quoted remark on the latent capacity among all classes for the appreciation of 'good and refined music'. And the very fact that adult education had so far been unable to entice people away from the haunts in which melody was the handmaid of vice was a good enough argument for including music in all schemes of fully *national* education. Or so, at any rate, a good many reformers believed. Their efforts in this direction have an important bearing on music-making during the Victorian period as a whole; and in this connection the decades after 1840 are of particular interest.

[1] James Hole, *The Working Classes of Leeds* (1863), p. 118.
[2] James Valentine, 'A Plea for Music in Common Life', in *Good Words*, 2 July 1866, p. 474.

V

<><><><><><><><><><><><><><><><><><><><><><><><><>

The Victorian Era:
National Education and Musical Progress

<><><><><><><><><><><><><><><><><><><><><><><><><>

Soon after the death of William IV in 1837 the Rev. Sydney
Smith preached a sermon in St. Paul's Cathedral on 'The Duties
of the Queen'. 'First and foremost,' he said, 'I think the new
Queen should bend her mind to the very serious consideration of
educating the people. Of the importance of this I think no reasonable doubt can exist; it does not in its effects keep pace with the
exaggerated expectations of its injudicious advocates; but it
presents the best chance of national improvement.'[1] On these
grounds reform in education was potentially of greater consequence than the extension of the franchise; and even if Sydney
Smith's advice was not acted upon immediately by the young
monarch it was not lost on others. For Sydney Smith was by no
means alone in offering comments of this kind. From the first
years of Queen Victoria's reign the question of national education occupied the minds of practically all responsible English
people. It was the subject of impassioned newspaper articles; it
kept parliamentary committees engaged for years; it led to acri-
monious contention among people of all shades of opinion. The
musical side of national education was obviously bound up with
the growth of this and other mass movements. The social history
of English music in the nineteenth century is largely a history of
the manner in which a vastly increased demand for music of all
kinds was met.

[1] Sydney Smith, *The New Reign: the Duties of Queen Victoria* (2nd ed., 1837),
p. 11.

I

During the 1830s and 1840s a number of educationalists urged that more serious attention should be given to the teaching of vocal music in junior and infant schools. In this they were actuated by several motives, mostly of a moral or disciplinary nature. In a lecture delivered before the London Mechanics' Institute in 1837, for instance, W. E. Hickson, the 'father of English school music', voiced his ambition to have music taught even to the youngest children as a means of improving their general taste and happiness. The moral influence of music, he believed, was of two kinds: 'it has a tendency to wean the mind from vicious and sensual indulgences; and, if properly directed, it has a tendency to incline the heart to kindly feelings, and just and generous emotions'.[1] Sentiments such as these were expressed over and over again in the next few decades. They were given a classic and official formulation in the Minutes of the Committee of Council on Education for 1840–1, in which the Inspectors of Schools are quoted as saying that 'vocal music has been successfully cultivated in comparatively few of the elementary schools of Great Britain'. In Sunday schools there had been a certain amount of musical instruction, chiefly by poorly equipped teachers who encouraged the children to imitate them in singing hymns and psalms by ear; but what was really needed was a successful method of instruction which would enable singing 'by note' to be widely practised. The greater part of the Prefatory Minute is devoted to an explanation of the systems of musical pedagogy used in France by Wilhem and Hubert, but one or two passages are relevant here. 'In the northern counties of England', we are informed, 'choral singing has long formed the chief rational amusement of the manufacturing population. The weavers of Lancashire and Yorkshire have been famed for their acquaintance with the great works of Handel and Haydn, with the part-music of the old English school, and those admirable old English songs, the music of which it is desirable to restore to common use.'[2] The last point shows that the revival of folk song had begun years before the foundation of the English Folk Song Society. The Minute goes on: 'The manufacturing

---

[1] Quoted in *Central Society of Education, First Publication* (1837), p. 307.
[2] Minutes of the Committee of Council on Education 1840–1 (1841), p. 46.

population of Norfolk, in like manner, has shown taste in the cultivation of vocal music. . . . Similar evidences of the native genius of the people are scattered over different parts of England. Among the lower portion of the middle classes the formation and rapid success of choral and harmonic societies is one of the most pleasing characteristics of the recent improvement of the class of apprentices, foremen, and attendants in shops, who a century ago were (especially in the metropolis) privileged outlaws in society.'[1] It is clear that the desire to 'wean the people from vicious indulgences' lay behind the general anxiety to improve the musical sensibility of the young.

John Hullah's great work for English musical education—following closely on the Wilhem system of teaching, which had been such a great success in France—has been much discussed.[2] Encouraged by the secretary to the Committee of the Privy Council on Education, Dr. James Kay, Hullah had a twofold aim: to perfect a form of class instruction in music which would not confuse the learner, and to see that his methods were thoroughly understood by training college students before they went out to teach in schools. In Hullah's edition of *Wilhem's Method of Teaching Singing* (1841), issued by authority of the Committee of Council, the teacher is given full instructions as to how to conduct the graded lessons and the 'examination' by which the scholar's progress is tested. Hullah always insisted that those who professed to teach the 'Hullah method' must be thoroughly competent before trying to impart their knowledge to others. His influence among the training colleges was the outcome of his association with the College of St. John, Battersea. In the demonstration lessons which he gave at Exeter Hall, Hullah was assisted by students from this College. He also taught at other establishments such as St. Mark's, Chelsea, Whitelands College and King's College, London, and in 1872 he was appointed a Government inspector for musical subjects. On the whole, Hullah's system of class instruction surmounts very well the major difficulties encountered by all who attempt to learn sight-singing. It names the degrees of the scale according to the old gamut terminology and adopts a simple set of rules for recognizing intervals and progressions. But it has one serious drawback:

[1] *Ibid.*
[2] See H. M. Pollard, *Pioneers of Popular Education* (1956), pp. 103–7.

it insists on retaining the 'fixed *do*' (i.e. the note *do* is always identical with C natural), which is hard on singers without perfect pitch who find correct intonation difficult. In other respects the Hullah method is precise and comprehensive. Its success convinced many of the sceptics that class tuition in music had a glorious future. Of Hullah's classes in London, W. H. Husk wrote in Grove's *Dictionary* that 'Not only schoolmasters but the general public flocked to obtain instruction, and country professors came to London to learn the system and obtain certificates of being qualified to teach it'.

Hullah was not, of course, the only experimenter in the field of class-singing instruction. About the same time as he was carrying all before him with his classes at Exeter Hall, an exile from Germany by the name of Joseph Mainzer (1801–51) was attempting to propagate *Singing for the Million*. In many places Mainzer's classes were extremely popular; he himself claimed that they were 'attended by an assembly of between *two* and *three hundred* persons, of both sexes, and of all ages'. His usual procedure was a public lecture to arouse enthusiasm for his aims, followed by classes conducted either by himself or by a devotee of the Mainzer methods. In 'Some Recollections', for example, Joseph Bennett told of the manner in which one James Watts, organist of Wotton-sub-Edge, Gloucestershire, started Mainzer classes 'under the Patronage of the Worshipful the Mayor' in the little town of Berkeley during the 1840s.[1] Mainzer himself was very much preoccupied with the status of music in education, but he thought that the Government had gone the wrong way to work, after giving their half-consent that music should form a recognized subject in the curriculum. 'If you really wish that music should lay hold of the young population, and penetrate into the very heart of the British islands,' he wrote, 'throw widely open the gates of instruction; surround yourself with a whole army of different teachers and different systems: efface the narrow line of demarcation, and let the stream of competition carry on its waves, life and animation, through the schools, into the people.'[2] This is a pointed reference to the monopoly enjoyed, as it seemed, by the Hullah system of class teaching. But in spite of his popularity (especially in Scotland), Mainzer was

[1] *Musical Times*, 1 July 1898, p. 451.
[2] Mainzer, *Music and Education* (1848), pp. 94–95.

not the most serious rival to Hullah: his really formidable competitor was the Rev. John Curwen (1816–80).

Curwen was the leading advocate of the Tonic Sol-Fa method, so called from its use of the gamut together with a system of signs to denote time values. Tonic Sol-Fa has much in common with the Hullah method, since the degrees of the scale are called by the same names (*do*, *re*, *mi*, etc.). Where Curwen differed completely from Hullah was in permitting the use of the 'movable *do*', this particular syllable representing the tonic note, whatever key the music happened to be in. This distinction, incidentally, was the cause of much bitter comment from supporters of the two systems; for both Hullah and Curwen stuck to the belief that his own attitude to *do* was the correct one (though at a later stage John Hullah did acknowledge that the Sol-faists showed great ingenuity in surmounting the difficulties caused in ordinary staff notation by the irregular structure of major and minor scales). The great feature of the Tonic Sol-Fa method is the importance which it places on the correct aural relationships between sounds. 'The methods of teaching which are truest to the nature of the thing taught, and are the least artificial, are always the most successful,' Curwen said on one occasion, and this might well be taken as the theoretical foundation of his work. After all, many musicians read orthodox notation as a matter of course and still remain quite indifferent to the harmonic implications of the sounds represented. Tonic Sol-Fa aimed, among other things, at eradicating this anomaly: furthermore, it attempted to make the student attribute extra-musical qualities to the various degrees of the scale so as to fix them firmly in his mind.

The Tonic Sol-Fa method of instruction was in use long before Curwen's time. But it had been brought to a high level of practical applicability by Miss Sarah Ann Glover of Norwich, from whom Curwen learned it. That was in 1840. Up to 1834 Curwen knew absolutely nothing of music. He was a Congregational minister, and being deputed in 1841 to discover a suitable method for teaching music simply to Sunday-school choirs, he heard of Miss Glover's work and went to Norwich to discuss the principles of Sol-Fa with her. Her efforts, incidentally, have much in common with those of several writers mentioned in the last chapter; she compiled a *Scheme for Rendering Psalmody*

Congregational (1835), though she was by no means the first to propagate a knowledge of 'Old English Sol-Fa'. The results of Curwen's investigations into Miss Glover's musical teaching were published in articles in *The Independent Magazine* during 1842. These were followed by Curwen's first major expository work, the *Grammar of Vocal Music* (1843). From these writings it is obvious that Curwen had a flair for methodizing and simplifying knowledge. He understood the manner in which young people assimilate and retain what they have learned, and this was put to good use in the various Tonic Sol-Fa textbooks. For its success, Tonic Sol-Fa largely depends upon the way in which the singer—recalling the 'mental effects' of the various tones—works his way from one interval to another. For unison singing it is practically foolproof, as it greatly reduces the difficulties caused by the presence of accidentals. But Curwen also taught Sol-Fa singing in many parts, in which, obviously, true intonation is a *sine qua non*. Some idea of the acceptability of his method —and also of the seeming thirst for musical instruction among the masses—can be gained from a manuscript 'Journal of a Singing Class' which Curwen kept during October 1843. Notice had been given in four Sunday schools of a singing meeting for children to be held on the Monday and Tuesday evenings following, 'to which those children would be admitted who were fond of music'. About seventy young people assembled soon after eight o'clock: 'an earlier hour could not be chosen, as many of the children do not leave work till eight'.

Originally intended for the purpose of promoting musical instruction in Sunday schools, Tonic Sol-Fa soon came to be used by teachers in other institutions such as day schools and Mechanics' Institutes. Some idea of the state of vocal music in schools during the period 1840–70 may be derived from the reports of Government inspectors covering many parts of the country. In general, John Hullah's methods brought excellent results, and most of the inspectors were biased in his favour. But there was a division of opinion for some years on the subject of singing by ear and singing by note. In the Eastern District in 1846, for instance, the Rev. F. C. Cook commented favourably on the 'sweet and accurate singing by ear' which he had heard from the children in Essex, Middlesex, Huntingdonshire, and Cambridgeshire; and the Rev. Henry Moseley eulogized the excellent music so taught at King's Somborne (Dorset). Visiting the South Western District in 1848, the Rev. E. D. Tinling reported that 'Music from notes is very general; the children and teachers both appear very fond of it, and its effect upon a school is certainly advantageous, it gives a softness to the children, and spreads a calm and pleasing tone throughout a school'. Some inspectors were anxious that only good tunes and wholesome words should be taught to the children; but masters and mistresses were left to their own devices so far as the instruction itself went. In parts of East Anglia, for example, Miss Glover's system was in use; those teachers who had been trained at Battersea or at one of the other recognized colleges used Hullah's method with success; in more remote parts different methods were introduced, the teachers sometimes making the children follow the music as played on an instrument. Not all Her Majesty's inspectors were equally enthusiastic about musical instruction; some thought it a waste of precious time, and before Hullah came to be appointed inspector in 1872 it was claimed that some of the reports betrayed a woeful ignorance on the inspectors' part. Nevertheless, most educationalists of the time were astute enough to urge that teaching by note was a more effective discipline than teaching by ear alone; and when music was no longer taught 'in (an) offhand, or perfunctory, but in a deliberate and systematic manner' (to quote the Rev. J. S. Laurie in his report on the British Schools of Cornwall, Devon and Wiltshire in 1861) the influence on morale and general alertness was very noticeable. Some inspectors were insistent that intending teachers ought to be able to play an instrument, and in 1853 T. W. M. Marshall made the interesting suggestion that teachers should be vigilant in excluding from the repertory of songs taught anything profane and corrupting, while at the same time admitting that a fair number of good songs are 'handed on among the poor chiefly by oral tradition, and . . . exist wholly independently of the *musical profession*'.

Amongst the numerous references to music made in Government publications in this period one calls for particular mention. This is the Minute of 1867 which laid down the conditions under which music might become a grant-gaining subject. It induced many teachers to take music far more seriously than before (several of the inspectors' reports, of course, reveal that in a great many schools no attention whatever was paid to musical instruction). By 1867 the Tonic Sol-Fa method had gained a firm entry into a large number of schools, and the inspectors' reports indicate quite clearly that it had, in fact, prevailed over the Wilhem-Hullah method. Speaking of the excellent work being done in Welsh (British) schools as a consequence of the 1867 Minute, W. Williams reported in 1871 that 'the Tonic Sol-Fa notation has been adopted in all the schools that I have examined in music, and some of the advocates of this system speak of it as a kind of "royal road" to reading music'.[1] Testimonies to the efficacy of Tonic Sol-Fa teaching are ubiquitous in reports drawn up during the 1870s. An independent observer, the Rev. William Howard, wrote in 1875: 'The less scientific system of Wilhem, once so much in vogue, is evidently losing ground in the estimation of teachers' (in Devon); and Horace Waddington, speaking of the Monmouth area in 1876, said: 'It may or may not be a quack method, but of its practical results in elementary schools I have had a very pleasant experience.' The decision—under the Code of 1872—to make vocal music a compulsory subject in schools gave additional impetus to the spread of Tonic Sol-Fa principles. 'After careful observation,' wrote the Rev. Capel Sewell in reference to Nottinghamshire and Lincolnshire schools in 1873–4, 'I have come to the conclusion that the real secret of the advance lately made in school singing lies in the immense skill and care, with which the art of teaching to sing is handled by Tonic Sol-Fa professors.'

At a meeting of the National Association for the Promotion of Social Science held at Nottingham in 1882, John Spencer Curwen (son of the Rev. John Curwen) informed his audience that 80 per cent of music teaching in elementary schools was then carried on by teachers using the Tonic Sol-Fa system. With the assistance of thirty boys from a Nottingham board school he demonstrated how easily musical knowledge might be imparted by this method. He emphasized, however, that Tonic Sol-Fa ought to be considered not as an end in itself but as a short cut to a knowledge of staff notation. John Hullah died in 1884, surviving John Curwen by four years; long before the 1880s the success of Tonic Sol-Fa had become a considerable embarrassment to him. Yet as Chief Inspector he was magnanimous enough to request

[1] Report of the Committee of Council, 1870–1 (1871), p. 279.

that no compulsion should be used to force schoolteachers to adopt his own system. Though occasionally harried by the 'sol-faists', he remained faithful to his conception of the fixed *do*, and until the end of his connection with the Board of Education he carried on a serious campaign for singing by note. In the sphere of instrumental music Tonic Sol-Fa was less widely used, but in that of vocal performance this method of notation—an 'exploded system of tablature', as William Chappell called it—unquestionably lived up to all the claims made on its behalf. But of equal importance with the technical aspects of Tonic Sol-Fa were the social consequences of the movement. As the system became widely known, Tonic Sol-Fa choirs were formed in nearly every part of Britain, as well as in certain quarters of the British Empire, and these organizations were very effective in encouraging unity among men and women who were keen on self-improvement. Curwen's methods and aspirations made a particular appeal among lower- and middle-class nonconformists. It is estimated that whereas in 1853 there were two thousand pupils learning to sing from the Tonic Sol-Fa notation, by 1863 this had increased to a hundred and eighty thousand. In *Music in the Five Towns*, Reginald Nettel has shown how powerful the Tonic Sol-Fa influence was in the Potteries during the 1850s and 1860s.[1] It was just as strong in other industrial areas. The career of Henry Coward, the great Sheffield choral conductor, is an outstanding memorial to, among other things, the virtues of a thorough Tonic Sol-Fa training.

Coward's life span (1849–1944) stretched from the early days of the Tonic Sol-Fa movement to the Second World War. He was a highly intelligent man and by almost any standard a remarkable musician. He is particularly interesting, however, because his personality resembles that of John Curwen himself. Like Curwen, Coward was a strict dissenter and an ardent temperance enthusiast. He made his way in life solely by his own efforts and evinced an unusually strong talent for mastering whatever he set his mind to and then explaining it helpfully to others less gifted than himself. Originally a cutler in Sheffield, Coward sought to advance himself by becoming an elementary-school teacher. This enabled him to develop his interest in music. He had already grasped the principles of Tonic Sol-Fa by attending

[1] Nettel, *Music in the Five Towns* (1944), pp. 8–9.

classes conducted by Samuel Hadfield, a well-known Sheffield musician. Having established himself as a schoolmaster, Coward engaged in a very active musical life. He ran Tonic Sol-Fa classes at the Church Institute and the Mechanics' Institute, taught music privately, served as choirmaster in several connections, and was appointed conductor of the Sheffield Band of Hope Festivals at which three thousand children sang at the annual demonstration in the Botanical Gardens. These are only a few of Coward's musical activities, the increasing number of which eventually induced him to give up teaching and become a professional musician. His greatest work was achieved after he had assumed responsibility for training the Sheffield Choral Union. In studying for academic degrees Coward had, of course, derived a comprehensive knowledge of musical form and counterpoint. Though his own compositions are of very little consequence, he is a representative figure because he appreciated the sense of solidarity which choral singing gave rise to among members of the social classes he was familiar with. His career as a trainer of choirs was thus productive of something more than purely musical results.

Henry Coward was merely one outstanding example of a musician who came to prominence by way of an early enthusiasm for Tonic Sol-Fa. There were scores of others, most of whom shared the ethical aspirations of John Curwen and his circle. These, along with other technicalities, were propagated in the *Tonic Sol-Fa Reporter*. The strength of Curwen's radical dissenting personality, which comes out clearly in his lectures and in the prefaces to several of his books, is frequently reflected in the *Reporter*. The paper did not withhold social comment and moral injunction; it was particularly severe against people who though unsympathetic to Tonic Sol-Fa ethics yet took advantage of this method, as when the Theatre Royal, Glasgow, offering auditions to female singers, announced that preference would be given 'to those accustomed to the Tonic Sol-Fa system'! Time and again the *Reporter* warned against the temptation—at concerts, soirées and musical parties—to flirt with sin and neglect the calls of moral duty. Thus in December 1866 appeared the following homily on 'Low Dresses in Public', which on the face of it seems out of place in a musical journal, but shows how strong was the interest taken by women in this movement. 'The dreadful tide of this fashion', says the writer, 'comes from France. We have heard the proverb "French Morals". Shall the Tonic Sol-faists fall into the vortex and so go off into the *fashionable* world (who will be glad enough of them and their music) or shall they stand by the Christian Church and have everything done "purely" and decently? Shall our Tonic Sol-fa teachers lead the young people (for their influence on whom they will have to give account before God), shall they lead them in new untried paths of *pure* unalloyed music, or as near to the vain sinful world as they can get for shame? We watch with *intense anxiety* to see the answer which our *Christian Sol-fa ladies* will give to this question.'

After Curwen's death, John Spencer Curwen wrote of his father's work: 'The Tonic Sol-Fa movement touched almost all efforts for the elevation of mankind. By simplifying musical notation, the art in its domestic and religious aspects entered thousands of homes which had before been without music. Thus the method was the indirect means of aiding worship, temperance, and culture, of holding young men and women among good influences, of reforming character, of spreading Christianity. The artistic aspect of the work done by the Tonic Sol-fa method is indeed less prominent than its moral and religious influence.'[1] Be this as it may, the purely musical effects of Curwen's work must not be underestimated. He addressed himself to clergymen, teachers, temperance and mission workers—in fact, to all in charge of groups capable of singing. He helped to extend the taste for religious (and religiose) music which was such an important feature of our cultural life throughout the nineteenth century. The Tonic Sol-Fa notation made works like *The Messiah* and *Elijah* accessible to hundreds of people who could not follow the intricacies of a full score. It also facilitated home music-making. Curwen admitted that he had reservations about Protestants singing the 'Ave Maria'. He also disliked the idea of respectable folk rendering the bibulous words which are found in so many of the English glees. Yet he claimed that the Tonic Sol-Fa method gave people an active interest in music, and the value of this to the poorer classes was expressed by William Harrison, a Bradford composer whose prize essay on 'Recreation for the People' was printed in the *Tonic Sol-Fa Reporter* for January 1859: 'By spending your spare evenings at the singing

[1] *Memorials of John Curwen* (1882), pp. 73–74.

class, instead of at the public house, you not only have an hour of pleasant social intercourse, but the pleasure is followed by no morning headache. Your heart is lighter, but not your purse.'

II

By the latter half of the nineteenth century the singing-class movement had created a great enthusiasm for music among the middle and lower classes. As we have seen, those who were active in fostering this were also anxious that music should exert a moral influence. From the reports quoted above it can be inferred that the school inspectors were just as anxious as the disciples of John Curwen to 'preserve many from the dangers of the theatre, the snares of the dancing saloons, and the dissipations of drinking shops' (*Tonic Sol-Fa Reporter*, May 1857). But the question of music's moral qualities was canvassed by a number of critics and philosophers who were not themselves associated directly with education. The problem is not, of course, a simple one, because so much depends on what is understood at any given time by the word 'moral'; and the issue is frequently confused by people who—like many of the Sol-faists—fail to make a distinction between music itself and the words to which it is set. The Rev. H. R. Haweis's book, *Music and Morals*, which had a certain vogue at one time, advances the theory (with reference to actual melodic shapes) that certain musical forms have the power of inducing in us a preference for wholesome rather than unworthy attitudes, and of encouraging balanced and reasonable judgements. The main objection to this notion is that a series of sounds may have a very different effect on us if we happen to hear it under unfavourable conditions (e.g. a delicate melody by Schubert arranged as a euphonium solo).

There is, however, one obvious sense in which music may be said to exert a good moral influence, and this was certainly appreciated in Haweis's time. Any sort of genuinely co-operative action is likely to have a beneficial effect on the men and women who take part in it; and even if (as was unquestionably the case) the innumerable choral groups which were formed as a result of the Hullah and Tonic Sol-Fa propaganda did not always turn their attention to music of the very highest quality, it can hardly be denied that the practice of vocal music induced habits of forbearance and 'give-and-take' which are in some degree 'moral'. Visitors to England from foreign countries were sometimes surprised to observe that in English choral concerts there were both male and female voices. 'It augurs well for our social system', wrote Joseph Proudman in the *Musical Standard* for 8 February 1868, 'that there is no hindrance to the union of the sexes in the pursuit of pleasant and healthful recreation, as found in our choral societies and classes.' In this respect, at any rate, we had a decided 'moral' advantage over our neighbours the French, for when a group of Orpheanist singers (the French counterpart of the Hullah school) arrived in England in 1860 it was revealed that they did not permit the sexes to intermingle on the concert platform.

The thirst for music which had been aroused by men like Hullah, Mainzer and Curwen was partly appeased by choral and competitive festivals—though the full development of competitive music-making took place in the choral sphere nearer the end of the century. In response to the prevailing belief that oratorio choruses should comprise hundreds (sometimes thousands) of voices, new halls had to be built, as at Leeds and Liverpool. To later writers the grand array of musicians over which Joah Bates presided at Westminster Abbey in 1784 seemed a comparatively unimpressive gathering. Nothing less ambitious than the throng of 3,625 performers packed into the Crystal Palace for the Sacred Harmonic Society's monster festival of 1862 seemed worthy of composers such as Handel and Mendelssohn. Among the rank-and-file performers who took part in the mammoth choral events which became such a common feature of English musical life after 1850, there arose a decided feeling that such occasions were the means best suited to the best and noblest music. There may have been a lack of discrimination about the way in which works like Costa's *Eli* (1855) and Spohr's *Fall of Babylon* (1842) were accepted as outstanding masterpieces, but at least those who took part in them under a conductor of national repute did so in an honest kind of good faith.

The brass-band contests, which called into play musical gifts of a rather different order, also had their own *rationale*, but in this instance the sporting element was slightly more prominent, the music being on the whole less solemn. The occasional 'horse-play' which, we are told, went on when some band objected to the judgement against it, would have been quite out of place at a choral festival; and from their commencement the brass-band contests had a kind of masculine gaiety which was not diminished by the necessity for discipline in actual performances.

Bands made up entirely of wind instruments have been known for centuries, but until the nineteenth century such ensembles—except, of course, for the waits in certain towns and the church instrumentalists mentioned above—were more common in military than in civilian life. During the eighteenth century a number of regimental bands had been formed, although some of the more famous British military bands are considerably older than this. The Horse Grenadiers had a wind band in Charles II's time, but it was the more settled conditions of the later eighteenth century which encouraged the recruitment of musicians for service with the army. They frequently retained their civilian status, and were often trained by foreign bandmasters; German musicians, in particular, were very keen to secure such appointments, and it was as director of the Duke of Brunswick's regimental band that Sir William Herschel, the great astronomer, began his career in this country. When, in 1783, some musicians engaged to play for the Coldstream Guards objected to performing on the occasion of a water excursion to Greenwich, they were dismissed from their posts and replaced by a band of German instrumentalists.

But brass bands as we know them were not a direct offshoot of these military bands, though sometimes a man with military experience might be called upon to train them. In the first instance, some of the most famous of nineteenth-century bands were very humble ensembles. We have already noticed that some early factory-owners encouraged music-making among their employees; as time went on, encouragement came from other quarters. And it might almost be said that the nation-wide brass-band movement, which was such an important feature of working-class life after about 1840, was made possible by two main developments: the rapid growth of railways (which brought down the cost of passenger travel and led to the granting of concessions for those going on 'excursions'), and a series of ingenious improvements in the manufacture of brass instruments. In particular the invention of the cornet-à-pistons made it possible for a moderately persistent player to master a melodic

1. Medieval musicians: illumination from the Bromholm Psalter in
the Bodleian Library, Oxford.

THE SUNDAY BANDS.

Little Jemmy Jackson (taking a light) :—" Yes, I LIKE THIS HERE PLACE VERY WELL, BUT THERE'S SICH A LOT O' SNOBS,
DON'T YER KNOW."

2. Music in the parks: a mid nineteenth-century comment (from 'Fun', 1862)
on Sunday performances in public places (see page 185).

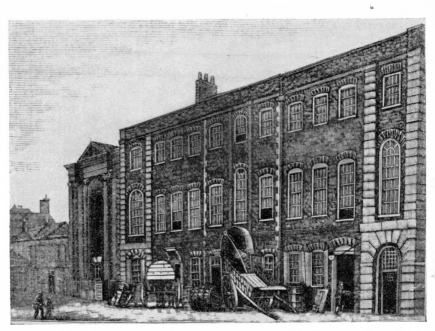

3. *The Beggar's Opera:* site of the Lincoln's Inn Fields theatre, where Gay's ballad opera was first produced (see page 99).

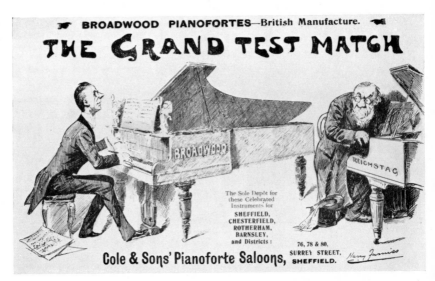

4. Anglo-German trade competition: an advertisement from the souvenir programme of the Sheffield Musical Festival of 1902 (see page 221).

line without the years of application called for by the more delicate woodwind instruments. The stages by which the cornet-à-
pistons came to be perfected need not concern us;[1] suffice it to
say that many inventors in several countries were working
simultaneously to produce simplified devices which would make
possible a large range of notes on brass instruments generally.
By the time a number of bands had been established in the north
of England the instruments patented and sold by Adolph Sax
(1814–94) had become famous and were in great demand. Their
popularity is explained by Enderby Jackson, himself perhaps the
most distinguished of all brass-band conductors: instruments
made by the Sax family, he says, 'rapidly became favourites with
the public for their tune and equality; and also with the players,
not merely for their full and free power and good intonation but
more especially for their ease in blowing and simple fingering.
The latter quality was an inestimable boon, for . . . most of the
members of this class of band were then . . . drawn from the
weekly wage earning classes. . . . Their hands, horned and
often malformed by their daily toil, were well served in these
new instruments by the short easy manipulation, three fingers
sufficing to work the mechanism of the three equi-distant
pistons.'[2] The piston principle was, of course, applied to instruments other than the cornet; its great advantage, so far as the
average player was concerned, lay in the fact that it took a great
deal of strain from the lips and throat and placed it on the hands
and fingers.

Musical contests of one sort or another have been held from
time immemorial. A writer in *Eliza Cook's Journal* for 23 March
1850 recalled that bell-ringing was one of the oldest amusements
among the village musicians in the north of England, and added
that 'Matches in bell-ringing are still often played for high
stakes; the greatest number of changes correctly rung on the
peal of bells within the shortest time, giving victory to the party
that achieves it'. But so far as wind bands were concerned,
France was ahead of England. This was pointed out in the
Musical World for 24 March 1837, where it was stated that

[1] See R. Morley Pegge, 'The Horn, and the Later Brass' in Anthony Baines, ed.,
Musical Instruments Through the Ages (1961), pp. 309–11.
[2] Jackson, 'Origin and Promotion of Brass Band Contests' in *Musical Opinion*,
1 March 1896, p. 392.

competitive festivals ought to be held here, as in France, in order to encourage a higher standard of playing. Small-scale contests had, as it happened, taken place before this, but the first one of any great consequence was held at Burton Constable, near Hull, in 1845. This event is of interest for several reasons. In the first place it enjoyed the patronage of Lady Chichester, who was familiar with the band festivals in France and believed that something of the same kind might be attempted in Yorkshire; secondly, each band entering was to be restricted to twelve players; and thirdly, among those taking part was Enderby Jackson, who in later years was to have charge of the ambitious Crystal Palace band contests.

Enderby Jackson's career has been sadly neglected by musical historians, perhaps because it is of a kind that can be paralleled in most branches of English musical life during this period. The son of a tallow chandler in Hull, Jackson was born in 1827 and educated at the Hull Grammar School. As a child he was taught to play the chromatic trumpet, and at eight years of age was taken to hear Paganini perform at the Theatre Royal, Hull, which fired him with an enthusiasm to become a musician. But meeting with no encouragement from his father, he left home and worked as a theatre musician in York and elsewhere. Seeing that brass bands had a great future, Jackson devoted much of his time to rehearsing such ensembles, and in 1856 arranged a large-scale contest in the Zoological Gardens at Hull. Twelve thousand people paid for admission, the first prize being won by the Leeds Railway Band. Other contests followed, and a few years later Jackson was put in charge of the musical arrangements for the opening of Pearson Park, Hull. In 1860 he entered into negotiations with the managers of the Crystal Palace with a view to holding brass band contests there, and as a result of this the Crystal Palace became virtually the home of English brass-band festivals until it was destroyed by fire in the later 1930s.

These grand meetings at Sydenham commenced in 1860. But before this date a pattern of procedure had been set at Belle Vue, Manchester, where contests were started in 1853. Sheffield held a contest in 1858 at which twenty-six bands were present, though only six were permitted to play. In all these activities a very important part was assumed by Enderby Jackson, who, among other things, persuaded the railway companies to issue cheap fares to bandsmen and their families—so that at one time it was possible to obtain a ticket from Leeds to London for as little as four shillings and sixpence. Describing some effects of this form of recreation on those who enjoyed it, Jackson writes: 'In a few years almost every village and group of mills in these districts (i.e. Lancashire and Yorkshire east and west of the Pennine Hills) possessed its own band. It mattered not to them how the bands were constituted, or what classification of instruments was in use; each man made his own choice, and the teacher found music suitably arranged for their proficiency. If these things were cleverly managed, music was the result; and music was the love and pride of these people and their ever abiding pastime.'[1] The village of Queensbury, near Bradford, is a case in point. Records of a band there go back to 1816; another reed band was established in 1833; but it was in the 1850s that the Foster family established the ensemble which has ever since been known as the Black Dyke Mills Band. In the later part of the nineteenth century the formation of works bands was a means of improving the relationships between capital and labour.

III

English musicians have had to endure a good many jibes about the alleged inferiority of this country to Germany in the sphere of music. 'There is no country', wrote George Hogarth, 'in which the moral and social agency of music is so remarkable as in Germany. In the various countries which compose that wide region, the national character has been much refined and softened in the course of a few generations; and, in this progress, the operation of music can be palpably traced.'[2] Admittedly, since the time of Handel we had been inclined to look to Germany for well-trained composers and disciplined executants. But in the nineteenth century (and especially after 1815) English musical custom was also influenced by what was being done in France. As we have seen, the French excelled as manufacturers of orchestral wind instruments; they also made excellent pianos. This encouraged French composers to produce large quantities of light and attractive keyboard music suitable for private

[1] *Ibid.*

[2] Hogarth, *Chambers's Information for the People* No. 99 (1842), II. 769, col. 2.

drawing-rooms. But before going on to speak about other aspects of the French influence on English musical habits and tastes, something must be said about domestic music itself in this period.

During the early nineteenth century both home music-making and public performances were greatly affected by various mechanical inventions. Improvements in machine tooling and in the production of accessories such as springs and keys made possible acoustic refinements which earlier composers had not envisaged. It is not in place to follow up such developments in detail; but it may be noted that whereas the violin family had virtually reached perfection by the beginning of the eighteenth century, wind and keyboard instruments were to undergo a variety of metamorphoses between 1700 and 1850. In 1800 it could be claimed that the best violins and violas then available would never be superseded; but the same could not be said of the flute or the oboe. Indeed, the thorough application of processes and skills which only the evolution of industry could bring about was necessary before the orchestra such as, say, Berlioz demanded, could take shape. During the nineteenth century the engineer came to the aid of the musician, extending the range of 'effects' obtainable from musical instruments and constructing buildings in which music might be heard to best advantage. It is not entirely a coincidence that some of the most notable personalities in the English musical world between 1800 and 1900—among them men like Henry Smart, Sir George Grove, Dr. William Pole and Sir Charles Wheatstone—either began life as engineers or had a very considerable interest in mechanical contrivances.

Although, as has been said, the best brass instruments used in the early days of the brass-band movement originated in France and Belgium, English horns and cornets can claim some distinction. Credit for the introduction of several ingenious devices— sometimes adapted by foreign makers—must go to men such as Charles Claggett, who produced a chromatic trumpet, and James Halliday, whose improved key bugle won the praise of the Duke of Kent for its potentialities as a military band instrument. But special mention must be made of James Shaw, the Glossop farmer and brass worker, whose 'transverse spring slides for trumpets, trombones, French horns, bugles, and every other musical instrument of the like nature' was entered as Patent No.

5013 in 1824. Instruments using this device were made in Sheffield in the 1820s, and Shaw's invention was imitated, with or without acknowledgement, in many other places. Indeed, mechanical improvements to musical instruments were so numerous in this period that it was difficult to avoid plagiarism, conscious or unconscious.

This is well illustrated in the case of the pianoforte, an instrument which invited adjustment and refinement of the keyboard action, the stringing, provision for pedal mechanisms and general appearance. In some quarters a prejudice against the pianoforte persisted. William Gardiner, for instance, speaks of his friend Mrs. Alexander, the wife of a Leicester doctor, as spurning the piano in favour of the harpsichord;[1] but by 1800 it had, among the wealthy at any rate, become the leading domestic musical instrument. As a result, a sharp distinction arose in the minds of composers and performers between concert music and salon music.[2] There were, of course, a host of makers of pianofortes in London and the provinces from 1750 onwards. These applied themselves to two main problems: how to perfect the tone of concert instruments and how to bring down the price of pianos intended for private use. Mention has already been made of John Isaac Hawkins, a civil engineer who experimented with the use of iron and wood in the making of pianoforte frames. Hawkins was no more distinguished than dozens of other inventors whose work has since been forgotten, but in 1800 he assembled a 'Portable Grand Piano' which was virtually the ancestor of the modern upright instrument. It was left to others to perfect the action and obtain from a comparatively small instrument a full and satisfying tone.

By the middle of the nineteenth century the firm of Broadwood was dealing in five main types of pianoforte—the grand, the semi-grand, the cabinet, the cottage and the square piano. 'Those who can carry their recollection back over a period of thirty or forty years', wrote George Dodd, 'will remember the pianoforte as an instrument for the noble and the wealthy, sparingly seen in the houses of the middle classes; they will remember the gradual steps by which it has reached the domestic

[1] Gardiner, *Music and Friends*, I. 427.
[2] Salon music, of course, took countless forms: descriptive pieces, song variations, dance movements, and so on.

firesides of the bulk of the class just alluded to; and they will be prepared to expect that such an extension in the use must have brought along with it extensive plans of improvement, and equally extensive manufacturing arrangements.'[1] In 1849 Robert Cocks and Co. (the firm responsible for publishing the works of Carl Czerny in England) sold semi-cottage or 'piccolo' pianos for thirty guineas, and a slightly more elegant model for thirty-eight guineas. As items of furniture neither of these appears, from the illustration given in *Cocks's Musical Almanac*, to be particularly impressive. They could not be as elaborate as the finely veneered and handsomely decorated models available from other makers at prices up to eighty or a hundred and twenty guineas.

It is a commonplace that no Victorian drawing-room was supposed to be complete without its pianoforte. What is less often appreciated is the fact that the domestic instrument which became so common after 1850 is the end-product of countless mechanical improvements. So much so that the affluent classes were led (as in the case of motor-cars a hundred years later) 'to reject the pianos they possess, not because time and use have impaired them, but because the genius and invention of makers have placed before them instruments with better touch and more powerful tone. The old instruments are sold and resold until pianos that have graced mansions are found in the humblest cottages.'[2] The year of the Great Exhibition, 1851, may perhaps be marked out as the *annus mirabilis* of pianoforte manufacture. The numerous instruments submitted by exhibitors showed many subtle refinements; there were many kinds of grand pianos, mechanical pianos, transposing pianos, expanding pianos for use on board ship, and ingeniously overstrung pianos. The way in which mechanical developments kept pace with the technical demands of composers like Thalberg, Clementi, Liszt and Chopin (and, on the other hand, the effect which inventions had on their individual styles of writing) is in itself a fascinating study. But the gradual evolution of moderately priced instruments proved a stimulus to composers of studies, salon pieces and, in particular, dance music which was poured out to suit the demands of the season. Here French as well as German and Austrian composers made a determined entry into the British

---

[1] Dodd, *Days at the Factories* (1843), p. 388.

[2] Edgar Brinsmead, *History of the Pianoforte* (1889 ed.), p. 142.

market. Their marches, waltzes, and quadrilles displaced the sonata in common esteem—this was, in fact, the age of the short, showy piece, either strongly rhythmical or attractively melodic. Arrangements of operatic selections were current in every publisher's lists, and most of the really great pianists of the time earned their reputation (apart, that is, from their skill at improvisation and variation) for their ability to simulate vocal effects at the keyboard.

Indeed, the enormous popularity of the pianoforte is partly to be accounted for by its imitative powers. Unlike the organ, it cannot sustain sounds; yet it can *suggest* a range of effects (e.g. pizzicato, drum points, flute-like arpeggiations) which are produced by other instruments. It is no exaggeration to call a piano, as John Hullah did in *Music in the House* (1877), a 'family orchestra'; for two performers on one instrument can give a very full rendering of almost any Beethoven symphony. But pianoplaying in the age of Mendelssohn came to be regarded as a valuable social accomplishment for two particular reasons: on the one hand, the pianoforte is an excellent accompanying instrument; on the other, it is a first-rate vehicle for social display. A writer in *Eliza Cook's Journal* for 4 May 1850 complained that, 'female children are too ordinarily set to music whether they have an ear for it or not, because, forsooth, it is a fashionable branch of education'. Since Jane Austen's youth it had been customary in middle-class establishments to encourage young girls to sit 'for hours together on a music-stool, drumming at a pianoforte', because this was a sphere in which personal rivalry between parents could be vicariously exercised, and prowess at the keyboard might well improve a girl's chances of matrimony. The persistence of such motives for 'learning music' is reflected in a Report of the Commissioners issued in connection with the Schools Inquiry Commission of 1868. 'Music (which appears not always to be taught in the cheapest schools)', says the Report, 'is equally demanded of all girls, however little taste they may have for it . . . one of the considerations which mainly influence parents of the middle class in selecting a school for their daughters is that instrumental music is to be the leading subject of instruction for women except in the lowest ranks of life. It is said to be seldom more than the acquisition of manual skill, to be taught without intelligence, and too much confined to instrumental music to the neglect of singing.' One of the Commissioners, a Mr. Bumpus, gave a summary of the reasons *against* including pianoforte tuition in the curricula of middle-class girls' schools. These were, its 'undue consumption of time, the impossibility of simultaneous teaching, its expensiveness, (and) the embarrassment it causes in the school arrangements'.

On one point Mr. Bumpus was misinformed. It had been demonstrated, earlier in the century, that class teaching of pianoforte-playing *was* possible. The chief exponent of this system was a German by the name of Logier (1777–1846) who aimed to promote Logierian academies in which, in the words of George Hogarth, 'a dozen or twenty pianos, under the fingers often of twice the number of young ladies, kept up an incessant discord, to the edification of delighted mammas, who each thought that her own darling was the chief performer in the concert, and who were moreover tempted by the comparatively cheap rate at which the power of doing such wonders was imparted'.[1] Logier's methods brought him into serious controversy with the Philharmonic Society, whose members called at one of his establishments and were divided amongst themselves as to the validity of his plan. But when Ludwig Spohr visited Logier in London in 1820 he was convinced, after testing the children under Logier's care, that this method of instruction, which embraced harmony as well as keyboard skill, was sound. William Gardiner saw the Logier system demonstrated and thought that the Lancasterian method of teaching might just as well be used in this connection as in any other. He noted that the opposition to Logier arose from the jealousy of certain professors who imagined that if Logierian academies became too numerous the private teachers might suffer.[2] Logier died in 1846. And his influence died with him, except that since his time some teachers have continued to use the chiroplast device which he employed to develop the hand muscles. He is mentioned here because of the astuteness with which he anticipated a growing demand. Knowing that parents wanted their children to learn pianoforte-playing, Logier tried to eliminate some of the drawbacks associated with private tuition. His method may or may not have been a piece of impudent quackery, but unfortunately he minis-

[1] Hogarth, *The Philharmonic Society of London* (2nd. ed. 1862), p. 19.
[2] Gardiner, *Music and Friends*, II. 649.

tered to an unworthy aspiration. A writer in *The Cornhill* for July 1863 pointed out that modern musical education invariably begins from the wrong premises: 'How to perform a certain number of pieces glibly is made to be the sole ambition of most young persons; which is not unlike teaching a child the *Whole Duty of Man* by heart, before he has learnt to spell.' Systems such as Logier's had this effect, and merited the scorn which George Hogarth and others poured upon them. Perhaps no musical instrument (except the Spanish guitar) is more susceptible to insensitive usage than the pianoforte. This is reflected in the great mass of meretricious piano music produced throughout the nineteenth century.

IV

The musical journals—of which there were many in the nineteenth century—contained advertisements for low-priced pianos. In 1865, for instance, the *Tonic Sol-Fa Reporter* announced a special arrangement by means of which the Tonic Sol-Fa agency was able to market the Pianette at from twenty-two to twenty-seven guineas and the Drawing-Room model at from thirty-eight to forty-two guineas, both manufactured by Cramer, Wood and Co. Frequently novel instruments, such as the Aeolian piano and the pianoforte-harmonium, appeared on the market. Inevitably, of course, the principle of mass production was applied to the manufacture of stringed instruments as well as to that of woodwind and brass. But really cheap editions of music did not become numerous until the 1840s. In a previous chapter reference was made to the publishing ventures of James Harrison and his serial publication of *The Messiah* at six and sixpence. Writing in 1838, William Gardiner gave it as his opinion that 'one reason why music is less studied in this country than abroad is the very high charge for music-books; when they are so reduced in price as to come within the reach of the middle ranks, we may have some chance of becoming a musical country'.[1] The anonymous publishers of the *Musical Library* of vocal and instrumental music, which was in circulation in 1837 and after, claimed that their volumes had 'placed the first overtures of any age or country within the reach of nearly all, whether as relates to

[1] *Ibid.*, I. 211.

expense in obtaining or facility in executing'. But the votaries of Hullah and Curwen needed something which was more convenient to handle than the sizeable tomes of the *Musical Library*, and credit for meeting their needs must go mainly to the house of Novello, founded in 1811 by one of the most versatile of nineteenth-century musicians, William Vincent Novello.

Novello's *Choral Hand Book*—consisting of a collection of anthems issued at threepence per page—may well have been the cheapest music ever published in England. It came out in the early 1840s, and was undertaken 'in obedience to the demand created by the revival of Church feeling in and about the year 1840'.[1] The musical consequences of the High-Church movement will be dealt with at a later stage; but Alfred Novello knew that the demand was wider than this phrase implies. He was faced, however, with the obstacle which beset all attempts to bring about cheap publications at this time—the so-called taxes on knowledge, and the use of restrictive practices among printers. These latter could only be overcome by Novello's setting up as his own printer, which he did in 1847; but the Advertisement Duty and the Tax on Newspapers (which particularly affected the *Musical Times*, published by Novello's since 1844) were not removed until 1862. By this time, Novello and Co. had brought out their 'Octavo' editions of oratorios, the size being uniform with the *Musical Times* (this journal itself, incidentally, being a continuation of Mainzer's *Singing Class Circular* and therefore a product of the movement discussed earlier in this chapter).

While it may be said that the foundations of Novello's concern rested mainly on the dissemination of sacred music (its first big 'catch' was Mendelssohn's *St. Paul* in 1836), the Novello catalogue also contained a large quantity of secular music. Later came instructional books and standard textbooks, of which the 1852 edition of Hawkins's *History of Music* is one notable example. In due course other publishers adopted the octavo format; and although large and elaborate editions were still very much in evidence, the tendency was to reduce the size of music type and thus bring more manageable musical books within the range of modest music-lovers. By the middle of the century most of the major London publishers had their own special lines of business.

[1] *A Short History of Cheap Music* (1887), p. 30.

In the 'fifties, for example, Chappell and Co. did a very big trade in dance music, and Robert Cocks acted as agent for composers such as Johann Strauss, Phillipe Musard and Carl Schubert. The enormous sale of songs and duets (for which the firm of Boosey was to become so well known) increased the stocks of 'sheet' music which publishers kept on hand, and there were cases of slow-selling classical works being subsidized from the profits brought in by some quite ephemeral novelty. Brass-band music was in constant demand, and it is surprising to find solo music for the harp and guitar being advertised on almost the same scale as pianoforte pieces quite late in the century.

A full account of nineteenth-century music publishing (which was not, of course, confined to London) would reveal some curious changes of fashion and would show the extent to which composers and publishers used to capitalize on events of the day. At some time in the 1840s Frank Musgrave published an 'Excursion Train Galop', the cover of which showed a train-load of excursionists passing under Shakespeare Cliff, Dover, on a South Eastern Railway train; at various other times political, military and national events were celebrated by the production of specially named waltzes, quadrilles, marches and polkas. The design of covers for songs and instrumental pieces developed as a lucrative branch of commercial art, especially after the introduction of chromolithography in the early 1840s. But one feature of nineteenth-century music publishing which should be particularly noticed is the readiness with which certain firms undertook to popularize music further by sponsoring concerts. Novello's oratorio concerts were a great success. Of a different kind were the Monday Popular Concerts instituted by Chappell and Co. and the famous Boosey Ballad Concerts. Obviously, such ventures were not embarked upon from wholly disinterested motives. At the same time they were not organized entirely for the sake of boosting the sales of music published by particular houses.

In the sphere of concert promotion itself the tendency was to move away from the principle of subscription and to introduce the selling of tickets more liberally at reasonable prices. This, obviously, became possible where larger halls were available. The London Philharmonic Society (founded in 1813) was about as 'exclusive' as such a concern could be. It was originally intended for professional musicians, though members of the general public could become 'Fellows', the subscription being a guinea for concerts and half a guinea for rehearsals. When the New Philharmonic Society was commenced in 1852 its promoters announced that they would not tolerate the 'baneful hindrance to all progress of Art' which kept admission prices so high. The Society therefore introduced standard prices from half a crown to ten shillings. This reduction of costs dates from about 1848. One of the most famous and successful organizations which from the first aimed to meet the requirements of the amateur with only moderate means was the Sacred Harmonic Society (1832), which gave oratorio performances in Exeter Hall. The older principle of subscription persisted in the case of John Ella's Musical Union chamber concerts (1845); from Ella's *Musical Sketches* it is quite clear that Ella himself regarded the Ancient Concerts 'with their compact band, professional chorus, and choice variety of English and Foreign standard works sung by the best native and foreign vocalists'[1] as a type of desirable excellence. But such concerts were for an *élite*, not for the general public. And while Ella's own concerts catered for such a clientele, the Monday Popular Concerts aimed from the first to attract a less highly privileged audience.

The Monday 'Pops' (later alternated with some Saturday Popular Concerts) commenced in 1858 and lasted for forty years. Their main attraction was their high standard of performance and their freedom from formality. Although the greatest artists of the time appeared in them, it was generally understood that music which was simply exhibitionistic would be ruled out; the programmes were therefore of an essentially serious nature, though by no means stolid and unadventurous. Commenting upon these concerts in their heyday, H. Sutherland Edwards wrote: 'There are liberals in art as in politics; and it is part of the liberal artistic creed that the people have a greater capacity for the enjoyment of works of a higher class than they are generally credited with.'[2] This creed, as we shall see later, was responsible for the provision of many series of concerts apart from the Monday Popular performances. But philanthropic attempts to induce 'the people' to accept good music simply

[1] Ella, *Musical Sketches* (1878), p. 72.
[2] Edwards, *The Lyrical Drama* (1881), II. 230.

because it was good for them did not always succeed; and in any case the Tonic Sol-Fa movement proved that in general moderately capable musicians seem to prefer co-operative performance to passive listening—or at least did so in this period. All the same, during the 'sixties and 'seventies attendances at concerts of all kinds increased greatly. This brought into play a great deal more musical journalism that had been current in the earlier years of the century.

The musical press was well established in this country by 1840. We have noted the appearance of some periodical criticism of music during the eighteenth century, and the publication of magazines containing musical supplements; but until the nineteenth century no specifically musical periodical managed to establish itself for long. The first important musical journal was *The Quarterly Musical Magazine and Review* (1818), inaugurated by Richard Mackenzie Bacon. This continued publication for ten years, as also did *The Harmonicon* (from 1823). These were followed by a great many other such journals, some of which, like *The Musical World* (1836–91) and *The Musical Standard* (1862–1933) enjoyed a very long life. Serious journals like A. F. C. Kollmann's short-lived *Quarterly Musical Register* (1812) and E. F. Rimbault's *Musical Journal* (1840) aspired to a high standard of scholarly writing, but there were countless ephemeral productions which simply retailed information and superficial comment. Yet such papers as *The Atlas* and *The Examiner*, though mainly literary in character, published musical criticism of a high order, and music held an important place in the estimation of editors like Dickens and Charles Knight, the musical commentary in *Household Words* and *All the Year Round* being particularly illuminating. With such representative figures as J. W. Davison of *The Times* and H. F. Chorley of *The Athenaeum* the office of music critic assumed a new importance. Both these writers appealed to standards of judgement which were largely ignored by the purveyors of the musical and dramatic gossip found in the columns of the less intellectual journals of the time. Certain musical periodicals—the *Musical Times*, for instance, and (later) *Musical Opinion*—had close affiliations with the music trade, but they performed a necessary service in bringing news of forthcoming publications and developments at home and abroad to large numbers of people. They were thus effective in establishing some of the conventions current in English musical life even now.

V

The French influence on English music during the period under discussion had wide ramifications. French musical customs, although they had much in common with our own, differed markedly in certain respects. The French, for example, did not share the English passion for oratorio. They preferred dramatic music of another sort, and idolized composers of opera and ballet music. For reasons to be considered presently, the stage productions of Auber, Halévy and others, though successful enough when performed in the London opera houses, were not *widely* popular in this country. Admittedly, a writer in *Sharpe's London Magazine* for 1870 named Offenbach as 'The Composer of the Period', but he hinted why for a great many enthusiasts this composer's music had to be enjoyed in arrangements and selections rather than 'in the flesh': 'Somebody once said that Offenbach's music was "so delightfully wicked" and I am afraid that somebody was right. There is a sort of gaiety and liveliness in the music of Offenbach's operas that has never been equalled before.'[1] Lightness and vivacity—in the form offered by French operettas—was not the kind of thing the habitués of Exeter Hall expected from music. But one French musical institution did prove acceptable to the general musical public from the earliest days of Queen Victoria's reign: this was the promenade concert.

During the winter of 1840–1 there were no fewer than three series of promenade concerts taking place simultaneously in London theatres. Announcing an earlier series in its issue for 6 December 1838, the *Musical World*, sarcastically remarking on the complacency of the average attender at the Philharmonic concerts, suggested that to a promenade audience the music was really a secondary concern: 'The chief interest lies in the elegant perambulators themselves, who wander in pairs, finished by Stultz and the St. James's Street milliners, and arranged to orchestral accompaniments by Strauss and Musard.' The promoters of promenade concerts, however, were careful to see that the public, while being allowed the opportunity to promenade, did

---

[1] John Churchill Brenan, 'The Music of the Period' in *Sharpe's London Magazine*, XXXVI (1870), p. 266.

not have a chance of ignoring the music completely. This was particularly true of the programmes put on by Louis Jullien (1812–60), whose appearances were intended to create a sensation. 'It was his proud boast', writes A. W. Ganz of Jullien, 'that he first taught the masses to appreciate what was best in music, by offering elaborate dance numbers as an inducement to listen to serious works. In truth they came to watch *him*, but certainly did stay to hear the symphonies.'[1] This claim is exaggerated, perhaps, but it was not entirely without foundation.

Louis Antoine Jullien was the son of a military bandmaster. After an irregular pupilage at the Paris Conservatoire and a short career as a composer and conductor of dance music, he fled to England in 1839.[2] He wrote countless marches, waltzes and quadrilles; but his feverish activity as musical director, publisher and impresario failed to free him from debt, in spite of the considerable sums of money he must have made in the course of his tragic career (he died in a lunatic asylum at the age of forty-eight). Jullien's concerts were characterized by an extraordinary *bravura*, the conductor himself engaging in a histrionic display designed to keep the audience amused and attentive. Apart from the music itself, which was cleverly varied, Jullien introduced a range of 'effects' which in New York included an outbreak of artificial fire to accompany the 'Fireman's Quadrille'. As a conductor Jullien was a good disciplinarian. He was dynamic without being slapdash and his concerts set a high standard of instrumental ensemble. He also gave renderings of major choral works. And by intermingling movements from symphonies with a miscellaneous collection of lighter pieces, he persuaded his audiences to accept a good deal of serious music while at the same time acquainting them with attractive *bonnes bouches.*

Jullien and his orchestra appeared at Covent Garden, Her Majesty's Theatre and at the ill-fated Surrey Zoological Gardens (Kennington Park Road); but he did not confine his appearances to London. He made repeated tours of the provinces, showing off his ensemble in many places which had not previously heard what a full-scale professional orchestra could do. 'The good effected by M. Jullien', writes Enderby Jackson, 'can never be overestimated: unparalleled success always attended his Yorkshire

[1] Ganz, *Berlioz in London* (1950), p. 17.
[2] See Adam Carse, *The Life of Jullien* (Cambridge, 1951), pp. 36–37.

and Lancashire tours. The "Jullien" concerts proved in the north the opening of a new era in advance of general musical art. Never before had such perfection been held up to our homely toilers as models for their guidance and imitative power. New readings of works supposed well known, new forms of phrasing, new colourings of extremes in light and shade, peculiar rendering of uncommon harmonies, and beautiful clear rendering of novel contrapuntal devices, rendered by the very highest procurable artists on their respective instruments. Herr Koenig, on the cornet-à-piston, M. Vivier, with his full chords on the French horn; M. Prospère, unrivalled on the ophicleide; with magnificent players always on the trombones, instruments ever admired and loved in the north of England. . . . These all proved sources of wonder and emulation to our music loving workmen, and educational to our local professors and band teachers.'[1] Jackson speaks of the ardour with which Jullien's marvellous performances were discussed in mills, foundries and factory workshops in the areas where brass bands were so popular. The following is the first part of a Jullien concert given in the Theatre Royal, Bradford, on 30 March 1848:

Overture	Zampa	Hérold
Quadrille	The Standard Bearer	Jullien
Symphony	The Allegro of Symphony in F	Beethoven
Grand Scene from Ernani		Verdi
Valse	Ravenswood	Jullien
Aria	Non più andrai	Mozart
Sacred Music from Elijah		Mendelssohn
Romanza	Dulcet Music	Balfe
Quadrille	The Swiss	Jullien

The second part, which contains further items by Jullien himself, consisted mainly of solos, both vocal and instrumental, some more operatic selections and a concluding Schottische by Jullien.[2]

To some critics Jullien was simply a charlatan. He was an easy target for satire and is represented in many caricatures. *Punch*, however, treated him indulgently and in 1851 declared that 'The Jullien era of music must always form an important epoch in the Calendar'.[3] Despite his eccentricities, Jullien's aims

---

[1] Jackson in *Musical Opinion*, 1 April 1896, p. 455.
[2] Given in G. Haddock, *Some Early Musical Reminiscences* (1906), pp. 76–77.
[3] *Punch*, XXI (1851), p. 233.

6. Music in wartime: Anglo-American co-operation in a concert, London, 1944.

5. Music and commerce: manufacturing company commemorates the Coronation of Edward VII.

7. A modern orchestra: the Hallé at Cheltenham, 1956.

were worthy ones; many of those familiar with him spoke highly of his musical sensibility. In a notable essay published in *The Musical World* for 17 March 1860, J. W. Davison wrote: 'Jullien was essentially and before all a man for the people. He loved to entertain the people; he loved to instruct the people; and the people were just as fond of being taught as of being amused by Jullien.' To the last he remained a showman, exhibiting many of the features of a competent ringmaster. But he had a wide knowledge of the musical repertoire, and it is much to his credit that he attempted (with complete lack of success) to put on a season devoted entirely to English opera. After his time the custom of presenting promenade concerts every year was kept up, and ever since (though especially since 1895) it has formed an essential element in English musical life. But Jullien rendered another service to English music: he was instrumental in persuading Hector Berlioz to visit this country and conduct his own music here.

Berlioz shared with Jullien a love of the grandiose (not to say monstrous), but he was cautious about undertaking the kind of concerts for which Jullien was famous. Yet whatever may be said about the miscellaneous programmes presented by Jullien, it cannot be denied that by his example he urged upon English musicians the necessity for improved standards of performance. This responsibility he shared with other notable conductors, such as Spohr, Mendelssohn, Berlioz himself and Michael Costa. The latter abolished the system whereby orchestra players might absent themselves from rehearsals on payment of a fine, laying down the rule that permission from the conductor himself was required for non-attendance. The immediate effect of this was to reduce the number of rehearsals necessary for each performance. The arrival of musicians from France and Germany—the number of them increased after the Revolutions of 1848—caused English musicians to look to their laurels. But in any case the era of the Great Exhibition was a period in which the spirit of competition was intense. This, after all, was the first major attempt to hold an international exhibition in England. The presence of men like Berlioz, Sigismund Thalberg and the Chevalier Neukomm as adjudicators on the instruments submitted was a serious challenge to English craftsmen and professors alike.

But for English music as a whole the 'Philosophical Instruments and their Dependent Processes' which the Jury were called upon to examine did not constitute the most important aspect of the Exhibition. Far more impressive was the feeling that such glorious achievement called for vocal expression. The gigantic building in Hyde Park invited a choral demonstration of unprecedented magnitude. It was felt, in the words of R. K. Bowley, historian of the Sacred Harmonic Society, 'that the vast edifice . . . ought to have, as a valuable adjunct, such an exhibition of choral and orchestral music as would adequately display to the representatives of the invited nations the real state of executive music in England'.[1] Unfortunately, the musical accompaniment of the opening ceremony disappointed a great many of those taking part. The original Crystal Palace was not congenial to the type of performance attempted—and the less said about it the better. But when Paxton's ingenious structure was rebuilt at Sydenham, the accoustics proved to be very suitable indeed for large-scale musical events. The available floor space of 16,016 sq. ft. (as compared with 2,656 in Birmingham Town Hall and 2,400 at Leeds Town Hall) allowed choirs and orchestras to perform in comfort. The Crystal Palace, it was clear, was going to be a valuable centre for concerts. In actual fact it became very much more than that. It became the scene of monster choral festivals and band contests. And in a relatively short time it was noted for regular orchestral concerts of a high standard. If the good example of Jullien cannot be overestimated, that of August Manns must be mentioned in the same breath, for the tradition of concert management established at the Crystal Palace when Manns was conductor and Sir George Grove secretary outlived the Victorian era altogether. At a later stage the Alexandra Palace in North London was something of a rival to the Crystal Palace in this respect.

VI

So far very little has been said in this chapter about operatic performances in nineteenth-century England. The main reason for this is that during the early decades the pattern of opera production in this country showed very little change and was hardly affected by the influences so far discussed. A writer in The Corn-

[1] Bowley, *The Sacred Harmonic Society* (1867), p. 32.

hill for September 1863 claimed that by this date 'the opera (had) ceased to be an aristocratic luxury, and (had) become a public entertainment', but this was only partly true. Grand opera still enjoyed the patronage of the wealthy, and it could not have continued without their heavy financial backing. In the absence of state subsidies, such as were provided in France, managements relied on the support of opulent noblemen. And opera generally remained a costly entertainment. But although the habit of opera-going was never so widespread as in France, Germany and Italy, operettas and musical sketches—to say nothing of pantomimes—maintained the ballad-opera tradition until late in the century. In this connection a special importance attaches to the popular family entertainments put on at the Gallery of Illustration, Regent Street, by Thomas and Priscilla German Reed.

In a sketch of 'Dullborough Town' from *The Uncommercial Traveller* (1860) Dickens imagines a concert at a provincial Mechanics' Institute at which 'one very agreeable professional singer, who travelled with two professional ladies, knew better than to introduce either of those ladies to sing the ballad "Comin' through the Rye" without prefacing it himself with some general remarks on wheat and clover; and even then, he dared not for his life call the song, a song, but disguised it in the bill as an "Illustration".'[1] The German Reed's Illustrations were dramatic sketches with music designed to accommodate the tastes of parents who had doubts about the propriety of taking young people to the theatre. John Parry's monologues at the piano and Corney Grain's one-man shows were witty, inoffensive and not without considerable dramatic point; they were in any case of native origin and thoroughly wholesome. But opera, which commanded the services of foreign musicians, had to contend with a number of prejudices which do not now seem at all reasonable, though we must take into account the extreme conscientiousness which gave rise to the Sabbatarian controversy.

Those who lamented the desecration of the Sabbath argued that to make Sunday a day of amusement would bring this country down to the level of France. It would also mean an increase in Sunday trading. In the 1850s, when Sir Benjamin

---

[1] Dickens, *The Uncommercial Traveller* (New Oxford Illustrated Dickens, 1958), p. 122.

Hall, as Chief Commissioner of Works, had allowed refreshments to be sold in certain London parks at the same time as military bands were playing, his action gave rise to protests similar to those made against the Sunday opening of the Crystal Palace. One of the ablest opponents of Sir Benjamin Hall's schemes was Edward Baines, who in a pamphlet 'On the Performance of Military Bands in the Parks of London on Sundays' (1856) contended that by providing such musical treats the authorities were inviting civil disturbance and also nullifying the original purpose of the first day of the week. 'The love of music', he wrote, 'is all but universal: in itself it is innocent and lawful, but it may be used for the worst purposes, as well as for the best. The strains of martial music cause the pulse to bound, and fire the imagination, and they are wholly out of accordance with the sacred repose of the Sabbath.' Unhappily, the Queen herself had created a precedent by permitting Sunday band performances at Windsor Castle—as Lord Palmerston quickly pointed out to the Sabbatarians. But this was deplored by religious men, who saw it as the thin end of the wedge. A little music might be all very well in private, but to admit a concourse of 90,000 people into Regent's Park on a Sunday afternoon was nothing less than an open defiance of God's word—especially as this example was capable of being followed in other parts of the country.

The position *vis-à-vis* opera is well put by John Ella: 'The prevalent religious sentiment of the English middle-classes', he writes, 'conduces much to the increase of vocal societies and choral performances in London, supported by a numerous class of persons who never enter a theatre.'[1] A few years later Mrs. Florence Marshall commented: 'In the country especially . . . there are numbers of people, the inheritors of puritanical principles, who cherish a distrust and dislike of anything theatrical, to whom an opera-house is *terra incognita*, and who have an uncomfortable feeling about any art pursuit when it is quite dissociated from their own form of religious service. All the artistic and musical aspirations of this class are resumed and expressed in the oratorio.'[2] The view of the lyrical drama alluded to here is closely related to a more general antipathy towards drama as a

[1] Ella, *Musical Sketches*, p. 149.
[2] Marshall, 'Music and the People' in *The Nineteenth Century*, VIII (December 1880), p. 926.

whole which many clerical figures of the time maintained. Among the stoutest opponents of the theatre in all its forms was Thomas Best, Vicar of St. James's, Sheffield, who for over forty years delivered an annual sermon against plays; according to the editor of his *Sermons on Theatrical Amusements* (1865), Thomas Best's diatribes were not only disseminated widely through the Press in England but 'have even been found in the backwoods of America'. A typical spokesman for the Dissenting communities was Dr. Cumming, who identified opera with idolatry and likened theatrical pleasures to deadly nightshade. A more reasonable view was expressed by the Broad Church minister, H. R. Haweis, who was a musician of catholic tastes and maintained that if respectable people deliberately stayed away from theatres and opera houses these places would become the haunt of undesirables and would thus deserve a bad name.

The widespread distrust of opera derived from a certain amount of anti-Romanist feeling as well as from a largely unformulated xenophobia. It was also associated with a recurrent zeal for purity. One reason for Mendelssohn's enormous popularity in England lay in the fact that his life was entirely free from moral taint. His dealings with the public were exemplary; his career gave no evidence of anything remotely resembling impropriety; the father of five children, he showed a consistent reverence for family life, and his personal manner charmed all those who knew him. Moreover, Mendelssohn never applied his talents to unworthy objects. Significantly, an opera on the theme of *The Tempest* which he was to have produced in collaboration with Augustin Eugène Scribe (who had produced the libretti for *La Muette de Portici*, *Robert le Diable* and *Les Huguenots*) did not materialize because of 'temperamental' differences between the two men. And the extent to which Mendelssohn was accepted as a symbol of purity in life finding its expression through religious —and divinely inspired—music is revealed in Elizabeth Sara Sheppard's *roman-à-clef*, *Charles Auchester* (1853), the hero of which is Mendelssohn himself. Miss Sheppard's rapturous enthusiasm for the noble artist who had triumphed so gloriously over the 'Baal-worship of corrupted art' and then descended to an early grave was reflected in countless obituary notices of the composer. Another of the *personae* depicted in *Charles Auchester* is Jenny Lind, whose engagement to Captain Claudius Harrison was broken off because Harrison, who had been brought up in a stern evangelical home, disapproved of Jenny Lind's appearing in opera.[1]

The fact that grand opera so frequently dealt with violent and erotic passions inhibited the pious from tolerating it. Incidentally, it is worth noting—as a mark of sectarian diversities— that many orthodox protestants still clung to the view that sacred themes should not form the subject of *any* musical works. The Rev. John Newton's fulminations against *The Messiah* can be paralleled in the utterances of several nineteenth-century divines. When Ludwig Spohr came to England in 1839, for example, he found that opinion in Norwich (where he had been engaged to conduct) was sharply divided about the propriety of allowing his *Calvary* to be performed in the Cathedral. And on the occasion of a musical festival held at St. Thomas's Chapel, Newcastle upon Tyne, on 18 September 1842, the Rev. Richard Clayton preached a sermon called 'Oratorios Unsuited to the House of Prayer, and Inconsistent with a Christian Profession', in which he dwelt on the inappropriateness of inviting opera singers and other theatrical people to take part in sacred music; such individuals, he contended, were not in the habit of giving serious thought to the awful subject of salvation, and it was therefore wrong to make use of their musical gifts. To those who held such extreme views, and who regarded most amusements as likely to result in a decline of moral standards, operas which presented scenes from Bohemian life and drew on other sources of Continental intrigue came directly under suspicion. H. Sutherland Edwards contended that Violetta in Verdi's *La Traviata* is 'no more offensive than Cleopatra . . . in Shakspere's tragedy'.[2] But the fact that Mendelssohn himself had declared, in reference to Auber's *Fra Diavolo*, that 'if the present epoch exacts this style and considers it indispensable, then I will write oratorios', told strongly in favour of those who, like Ruskin, Carlyle and F. W. Farrar, condemned the luxury and sensuality of opera as a whole.

None of the great Victorians believed more fervently in the

[1] The matter is not quite so simple as this. Jenny Lind had for some years been intending to dissociate herself from opera; but at the time of her engagement to Captain Harrison she was under a contract to appear at Her Majesty's Theatre. She felt bound to honour this obligation.

[2] Edwards, *The Lyrical Drama*, I. 310.

essential purity of music than Arthur Sullivan. 'Music', he told an audience at Birmingham in 1888, 'can suggest no improper thought, and herein may be claimed its superiority over painting and sculpture.' But while he admitted that unwholesome words could ruin a composer's best intentions, Sullivan never engaged in the priggish detraction of opera. He knew that the specifically English tradition of lyrical drama did not exploit the possibilities of suggestive situations and illicit love. Indeed, English opera of the nineteenth century counts for very little in European music simply because it is so innocuous and lacking in verve. The works of composers like Bishop, Loder, Macfarren and Frederick Clay are all lightweight affairs; yet they could not be accused of ministering to what Dean Farrar described as 'the worst and lowest passions'.[1] The one English composer of romantic operas whose music still holds the stage, Michael Balfe, was declared by his biographer, W. A. Barrett, to have been 'by predilection a moral teacher. There is no sensuous swim in his music, no association with doubtful actions, or connection with words of equivocation, to carry the soul to regions of impurity.'[2] In an address to the Dean of Westminster, dated 4 May 1882, thirty-six eminent English musicians testified to Balfe's distinction and added that 'In the colonies and in the United States, the name of Balfe is as much a household word as in the heart of London, equal, as a Musician, to Dickens, as a novelist, if the widest popularity counts as a test'.

This association of Dickens's name with that of an operatic composer is, for other reasons, not entirely fortuitous. Dickens was himself interested in the possibilities of comic opera and had contributed the libretto of John Hullah's *The Village Coquettes* (1836). The element of burlesque is prominent in much of his fiction, and the desire to promote an innocent kind of cheerfulness (which is found in many of the English operas produced in his lifetime) is perceptible throughout Dickens's work. Dickens's much-maligned 'sentimentality' is also akin to that found in the libretti of the comic operas written in this period. It is a quality which does not make a strong appeal today, but in its

---

[1] F. W. Farrar, *Music: in Religion and in Life, A Sermon preached in Westminster Abbey* (1882), p. 11.
[2] Barrett, quoted in Eric Walter White, *The Rise of English Opera* (1951), p. 106.

context it represents an attempt to divert the audience's mind from strong emotions and unworthy desires. The humorous element of mid-nineteenth-century comic opera does not always, at this time of day, seem to merit that description. It lacked one quality in particular—pungency. And this, in the fullness of time, was supplied by 'Gilbert and Sullivan'. The partnership between the two men need not be recounted; but its appropriateness to the situation to which the German Reeds, Corney Grain and their colleagues directed their attention is indicated in an address delivered by Gilbert some years after Sullivan's death. 'When Sullivan and I began to collaborate', said Gilbert, 'English Comic Opera had practically ceased to exist. Such musical entertainments as held the stage were adaptations of the plots of the Operas of Offenbach, Audran, and Lecoq. The plots had generally been so "Bowdlerized" as to be almost unintelligible. When they had not been subjected to this treatment, they were frankly improper . . . Sullivan and I set out with the determination to prove that these elements were not essential to the success of humorous opera. We resolved that our plots, however ridiculous, should be coherent; that the dialogue should be void of offence; that on artistic principles no man should play a woman's part, and no woman a man's. Finally, we agreed that no lady of the company should be required to wear a dress that she could not wear with perfect propriety at a private fancy ball.'[1] *Cox and Box* (1867) and *The Contrabandista* (1867) (though the libretti in both cases were not by Gilbert) were ideal German Reed pieces, and it was at one of their rehearsals that Sullivan first met Gilbert in 1869. The popularity of the Gilbert and Sullivan operas in the years that followed, however, was not simply due to their propriety; Gilbert's wit has an 'edge' which finds many parallels in Sullivan's music, and his habit of 'taking off' the conventions of the day is matched by Sullivan's very considerable gift for parody. On the purely musical side the Savoy operas bespeak an expert knowledge on Sullivan's part of many different musical styles, as well as an impressive technical accomplishment, but 'Gilbert and Sullivan' as a national institution stands or falls by the success with which it applied the *finesse* of Continental operatic writers to a specifically English kind of subject-matter.

---

[1] W. S. Gilbert in a speech to the O.P. Club in 1906; quoted in Malcolm Sterling Mackinlay, *The Origin and Development of Light Opera* (1927), p. 227.

VII

'It was hoped', wrote *The World*, in its notice of *The Sorcerer*, (1877), 'that he would soar with Mendelssohn, whereas he is, it seems, content to sink with Offenbach'.[1] The composer of 'My name is John Wellington Wells' can hardly be said to have sunk. Yet when, in the mid-1870s, Sullivan's collaboration with Gilbert showed unmistakable signs of success, many of his friends entertained misgivings. They thought that his career had taken the wrong course, and that he would not now become the founder of a great national school of composers equipped to produce successors to *The Prodigal Son* (1869) and *The Light of the World* (1873). Addressing the National Association for the Promotion of Social Science at Manchester in 1879, Sir Coutts Lindsay gave a grudging recognition to the prodigious success of *H.M.S. Pinafore* (1878), but he added: 'I think it much to be deplored, however, if it seduces him from the nobler type of music that made his reputation. In the sister arts we may view with equanimity one or other artist fall to a lower level, but in music masters are scarce, and such a loss is irreparable.'[2] Sullivan's reputation had not, as it happens, been made on one type of music alone. His incidental music for *The Tempest* (Leipzig, April 1861) had been followed by a Symphony (1866) several overtures, ballads, part-songs and other pieces. But Sir Coutts Lindsay's remark is an instance of the manner in which Sullivan's contemporaries assumed that serious music must have religious associations. This is partly attributable to the continued popularity of oratorios and sacred cantatas; it is also linked to developments in church life and changes of attitude towards music in the service of religion.

The 'revival of church feeling' about 1840 (referred to earlier in connection with Novello's publishing ventures) had a profound effect on English church music. Before that time, the performance of music in Anglican establishments was either perfunctory or, at least, eccentric. The cathedrals maintained choirs, but these were seldom well instructed or adequately disciplined. Parish churches relied on the services of the parish

---

[1] Quoted in Arthur Jacobs's 'Sullivan, Gilbert, and the Victorians', *Music Review*, XII (1951), p. 123.

[2] *Trans. Nat. Ass. for Prom. Soc. Science*, 1879 (1880), p. 116.

clerk and had to make do with such musical accompaniment as could be found among the congregation. 'At St. Paul's Cathedral, fifty years ago,' wrote E. J. Hopkins in 1886, 'it was no uncommon thing for the organist to be absent from eleven out of the fourteen services held every week, his place of course being supplied by a deputy. Nor was it by any means a rare exhibition for two or three of the vicars-choral to be late in their attendance at service. They would sometimes arrive just before the commencement of the psalms, and would sidle their way into their places, buttoning on their surplices at the collar as they proceeded; occasionally they would be away altogether.'[1] The author of *An Apology for Cathedral Services* (quoted in *The Harmonicon* for 1831) mentions the custom of singers doing duty in several choirs; and Miss Maria Hackett, the noted advocate of the rights of choristers, complained bitterly about the nonchalance with which organists and choirmasters employed the choir boys to sing at soirées and concerts. Parish churches either did without music altogether or sought 'a full accompaniment of violin, violoncello, clarionet, and flute (and well if there be not some noisier instrument of music) from the village band, sufficient to banish every idea of melody from the minds of those who might otherwise take a part in the singing'.[2] In this period the west-gallery parish orchestras were subjected to more and more abuse; it is, indeed, remarkable that so many of them survived as long as they did.[3]

It was noted in a previous chapter that during the later eighteenth century a great deal of dissatisfaction was expressed about the state of church music in general. But it was not until the 1840s that movements were set on foot for the express purpose of improving this aspect of Anglican worship. The formation of the Society for Promoting Church Music was paralleled by the establishment of diocesan choral associations in various parts of the country. The aims of all these organizations are briefly summed up in the foreword to Charles Steggall's *Church Psalmody* (1849): 'While all means are employed to render the Music of the Concert Room, and of the Opera as perfect and

[1] Hopkins, 'Professional and Personal Recollections'; read to the National Society of Professional Musicians at Clifton on 15 October 1886 (quoted in William Spark, *Musical Memories* (1888), p. 351).
[2] *Church of England Review* (1841), p. 468.
[3] There was a determined crusade against church bands at this period.

attractive as possible,' he writes, 'that which more peculiarly appertains to the "habitation of the Lord's House", to the "place where His honour dwelleth" has, for more than a century, been suffered to remain uncultivated, and therefore unimproved.' Steggall's work is only one of many similar publications. Practically all of them have the same end in view: the banishment of secular melodies from church (in some cases the leaders of the west-gallery bands had adapted ballad tunes and opera airs more fervently than any of Wesley's associates), the provision of truly sacred music in their place, and the recruitment of reliable church choirs to lead the singing and to maintain a spirit of reverence. This in time led to a dispute as to whether women's voices should be admitted in church choirs, but few were prepared to deny that all choir members ought to be able to read music well and be amenable to instruction. At this point the singing-class movement came in aid of church reform, but the clergy themselves also did a great deal to foster an interest in good religious music among the laity. The Rev. W. H. Cope, for example, gave lectures on the subject at many centres, and other scholars took the same course. On a less ambitious scale we hear of vicars exhorting their congregations to develop a serious interest in the matter. Typical of this concern is a circular distributed to the parishioners of Gleadless Church, Sheffield, in 1847, which read: 'Sermons will be preached, on Sunday next, the 20th of August instant, after which Collections will be made for the purpose of raising Funds for carrying on the Instruction in Church Music, which has for some time past been in operation with the view of rendering the Singing and Responsive Parts of the Services in this Church generally Congregational and more Devotional.'[1] In many cases an appeal was made for a return to the music in use before the Reformation. A leading figure in the so-called 'Gregorian Revival' was Arthur Sullivan's teacher and John Hullah's colleague at St. Mark's College, Chelsea, the Rev. Thomas Helmore (1811–90).

The publication of Helmore's *The Psalter Noted* (1849) marks a reaction against the formal ecclesiastical style employed by eighteenth-century church composers; from the ritualistic point of view it denotes an attempt to follow principles similar to those which inspired the founders of the Camden Society. From

[1] Quoted in *The Parish Choir*, October 1847, p. 95.

1840 onwards there was a great deal of discussion among church musicians about the true nature of chanting, the proper use of the organ and the most suitable types of vestment to be worn in church. But, as Sir John Stainer explained, 'the forward movement did not stop [there]. Urged by a desire to make the public services as ornate and beautiful as possible, anthems and elaborate canticles were rapidly introduced into many parish churches, and also artistic settings (English or foreign) of the Nicene Creed, Sanctus, and Gloria in Excelsis; in short, in many churches, especially in those where some little antipathy was felt towards the archaisms of Gregorian music, a cathedral form of service, pure and simple, was adopted.'[1] In some places the 'artistic settings' here spoken of roused the anger of those who opposed High Church practices and refused to countenance 'Papistical abominations'. At Brighton in 1863, for instance, the Rev. Arthur Wagner was openly insulted by parishioners because he introduced what was referred to as 'the morning Opera at St. Paul's'—though in due course the full musical service made St. Paul's Church, Brighton, one of the best-attended on the south coast. We need not enter into the question of Gregorianism and anti-Gregorianism during this period; but it is important to observe that as a result of ritualistic fervour the metrical psalter fell into disrepute and there were repeated demands for more and better hymns. A number of modern hymn books appeared during the 1840s and 1850s. In 1858 an advertisement was inserted in the *Guardian* inviting the co-operation of clergymen who desired to bring about the compilation of a 'national' hymn book. This resulted in the formation of a committee which was responsible for the first (1860) edition of *Hymns Ancient and Modern*. The first edition with music appeared in the following year, the musical editor being W. H. Monk, a close associate of John Hullah and a versatile ecclesiastical musician.

From the middle of the century, church building and church restoration proceeded rapidly, and this had many musical consequences. In the first place, organs were now becoming much more common in English churches than ever before. The organ,

---

[1] Stainer, 'Music Considered in its effect upon, and connection with, the Worship of the Church' (a paper read at the Church Congress at Exeter, October 1864), p. 2.

like the piano, had been greatly improved by the application of mechanical devices, and from the 1850s the trade in organ-building flourished exceedingly. The most famous English organ-maker of the period was Henry Willis, whose success as an exhibitor at the Crystal Palace in 1851 led to his being commissioned to construct organs at St. George's Hall, Liverpool, the Albert Hall, London, and (most famous of all in its day) the Alexandra Palace. There were, however, excellent organ-builders in the provinces. 'The days are happily numbered', declared the *Church of England Review* in 1857, 'in which a fiddle and a bassoon were looked upon as the appropriate accompaniments to a church choir. . . . Few churches are now without an organ, and the wives and sisters of the clergy form an excellent staff of organists, where there are no funds to secure professional help.' But where such funds *were* available the office of organist and choirmaster took on a new and more serious significance. As time went by, the status of ecclesiastical musicians was enormously improved. The standard of knowledge and performance demanded from potential organists gradually rose; at Rochester Cathedral in 1855, for example, the competitive interview for the position of organist constituted 'a very searching trial, for not only did the candidates play the organ, but they actually had to work a paper containing a chorale to harmonize, and a short subject on which to write a fugue!'[1] Applicants for posts in cathedrals and large town churches were numerous, and the proposal (first canvassed in the pages of the *Musical Standard*) that there should be a recognized institution for the training of church musicians resulted in the foundation of the Royal College of Organists in 1864. The first examination was held in 1866 and the F.R.C.O. diploma (notoriously difficult to obtain) tested the candidate's ability with a thoroughness that would have startled cathedral organists in John Wesley's day. To a very large extent the Royal College of Organists met a demand made in Samuel Sebastian Wesley's trenchant discourse of 1849, *A Few Words On Cathedral Music with a Plan of Reform*, that 'THE CATHE-DRAL ORGANIST should, in every instance, be a professor of the highest ability,—a master in the most elevated departments of composition,—and efficient in the conducting and superintendance of a Choral body'.

[1] Sir Frederick Bridge, *A Westminster Pilgrimage* (1918), p. 25.

VIII

But church music was not the only field in which there were reiterated demands for training schools. In 1850 England had nothing quite comparable with the Paris Conservatoire. The Royal Academy of Music (founded in 1822) had never really carried much weight in the national musical life. In 1867, in fact, its management committee investigated the possibility of surrendering their Charter, though they were told they could not do this except through the Court of Chancery. Various other schemes for establishing training colleges exclusively for musicians were proposed during the 1860s and 1870s. The Trinity College (1875) originally had a decided ecclesiastical bias, while the National Training School for Music (1876) was more general in its curriculum. For a short period there was a Crystal Palace School of Music, and a similar establishment attached to Alexandra Palace functioned for several years. Two other London institutions, the Guildhall School of Music (1880) and the Royal College of Music (1883), commenced their activities with rather better financial backing than some of the earlier academies had enjoyed. In due course, colleges of music were set up in Manchester (where Sir Charles Hallé had long agitated for such facilities) and at Birmingham; here an 'Elementary Instruction in Singing' class commenced at the Midland Institute in 1859, though it was not until twenty years later that anything like full-scale professional music teaching was firmly established. But in the last quarter of the nineteenth century the demand for teachers of music was intense, and the possession of 'letters after one's name' gave the diploma a kind of authority which did not seem to attach to some more palpable distinctions.

By the end of the nineteenth century the musical profession held out excellent prospects for organists, teachers, orchestral players, theatre musicians and solo singers. Further aspects of this situation will be considered in the next chapter. Meanwhile two features of our social life call for some attention: the increasing importance of the annual family holiday, and the great faith which invalids and the elderly had in a 'change of air' at a spa or some other watering-place. Relatively cheap railway travel had opened up the seaside resorts, and had made such places as Malvern, Leamington and Matlock as easy of access as Tunbridge

Wells or Epsom had been a century earlier, and the extension of third-class fares had enabled the middle and lower classes to get away from the cities at least once a year. The entertainments provided at seaside places during the later half of the nineteenth century had a serious as well as a frivolous side, and in many cases the music offered was quite ambitious. The record of Bournemouth is particularly notable, though good orchestras also came to be established at places like Scarborough, Eastbourne and Brighton. In 1876 Bournemouth's musical fare was provided by a band of Italians who had previously been engaged at Bath. For a decade after this no very exciting developments took place, but from 1892 the Corporation employed a military band of twenty-one players. The following year Dan Godfrey was commissioned to form a band of thirty instrumentalists, which made up the nucleus of what became the Bournemouth Municipal Orchestra. In due course other towns such as Eastbourne, Torquay and Buxton saw the desirability of providing regular musical programmes as an extra attraction. During the 'season' of 1890 the Concert Hall at Harrogate boasted an orchestra which gave concerts twice daily under the baton of A. E. Bartle, and the *Harrogate Pictorial* added that 'Yorkshire is a music-loving country. . . . In the heart of such a shire, the musical catering must be of the highest to find acceptance'. The larger resorts received frequent visits from foreign vocalists and instrumentalists, and it was a matter of national pride that the orchestras engaged to accompany them should be capable of something better than *ad hoc* renderings of the standard classics.

IX

'It is no exaggeration', wrote Francis Hueffer in 1887, 'to say that with the exception perhaps of natural science . . . there is no branch of human knowledge, or of human art, in which the change that the half-century of the Queen's reign has wrought, is so marked as it is in love of music'.[1] And in a lecture to the Musical Association on 8 June 1897, W. H. Cummings declared that 'We have, in the year of jubilee, great cause for congratulation as to the advance of music, not only in the estimation of the

[1] Francis Hueffer, 'English Music During the Queen's Reign' in *The Fortnightly Review*, New Series, XLI (1887), p. 899.

lettered class, but also as an art which has come within the grasp of the horny-handed sons of toil'.[1] Those who rejoiced in the diffusion of musical knowledge among the various strata, of society since about 1830 did so in proud awareness that during the century as a whole an enormous range of opportunities had opened up for both amateur and professional musicians. But these opportunities were commercial as well as purely cultural and, as has been suggested, publishing, instrument manufacture and concert organization all benefited from the various movements for musical education which are so characteristic of Queen Victoria's reign. By the end of the century music had itself become an important national industry and a field for financial speculation on the same terms as the theatre, book production and interior decoration. The further ramifications of this fact concern the twentieth century as well as the transition period leading into it.

[1] W. H. Cummings, 'Music during the Queen's Reign' in *Proc. Mus. Ass.*, XXIII (1897), p. 148.

VI

'Fin de Siècle':
The Ethos of Competitive Enterprise

THE period covered in the present chapter—1870 to 1914—
overlaps with that just discussed. It is of interest to the social
historian of music for many reasons, but chiefly because in it
music-making was so much influenced and determined by economic and political phenomena which at the time had great
national significance. These include the movements for social
amelioration which characterized the decades after 1867, the
'imperialist' phase of public sentiment from about 1870 onwards, and the increasing power of foreign competition, particularly from Germany and America. There are two subsidiary
topics indirectly connected with these—the consolidation of the
musical profession, and the growth of suburbanism in the later
nineteenth and early twentieth centuries. These various subjects
are all, of course, interrelated; but the last two are treated in a
separate section because they anticipate issues which arose in the
period following the First World War.

I

During the eighteenth century, as we have seen, a great deal
of musical activity was carried on for the purpose of giving assistance to charitable concerns. This practice was continued
throughout the nineteenth century, when charity concerts were
very common and a number of large choral festivals devoted
some part of their profits to the relief of sickness or destitution.

Music also entered into the schemes of social betterment which were an important feature of English life from 1832 onwards. A typical example of this is the Early Closing Association (founded in 1842), which organized a musical society in order to bring to public notice the fact that even shop assistants knew how to utilize their leisure profitably. Reporting a concert which this choral and orchestral group gave in London during July 1884 (the instrumental side being contributed by wind bands made up from amateur players in the employment of Messrs Shoolbred and Marshall and Snellgrove), the *Musical Times* wrote: 'If the members remain together and rehearse with regularity, the body may eventually take an honourable position among metropolitan choral societies.'[1] Other instances could be cited of such ensembles combining for similarly demonstrative purposes. The 'Music for the People' campaign, which had a considerable success in the last three decades of the nineteenth century, was prompted by the desire to show that the underprivileged had the ability to appreciate good music if only it were offered to them.

This impulse resembles that which led to the creation of middle-class settlements in large cities. 'All settlements', said Sir John Gorst in 1894, '. . . seem to be begun upon one uniform principle. The first object, to which every other is subsidiary, is to make friends with the neighbourhood—to become part of its common life; to associate with the people on equal terms, without either patronage on the one hand or subserviency on the other; to share in the joys and sorrows, the occupations and amusements of the people; to bring them to regard the members of the settlement as their friends.'[2] To extend this ideal into the realm of culture was not, as some of those responsible for musical entertainments at the Mechanics' Institutes and Lyceums discovered, a simple matter. But in many cases the difficulties were gradually overcome. And in London such organizations as the Kyrle Society, the People's Entertainment Society and the National Sunday League were formed to break down the barriers which seemingly existed between the lower classes and the full enjoyment of music.

The Kyrle Society (1877) was not devoted entirely to music.

[1] *Musical Times*, 1 May 1884, p. 270.
[2] Sir John Gorst, ' "Settlements" in England and America' in John M. Knapp, ed., *The Universities and the Social Problem* (1895), p. 10.

It was founded by Miranda Hill (sister of Octavia Hill) for the purpose of 'bringing beauty home to the people'; it ran art exhibitions with this in mind, arranged social gatherings and assisted Octavia Hill in her campaign for obtaining access to open spaces. Speaking of the Kyrle Society's aims, William Thomson Hill remarks: 'There were no "pictures" in those days. The cheapest theatre seat cost a shilling. Apart from music halls of a type more or less vulgar—avoided in any case by respectable women—there was no amusement for the people of poor streets beyond the gin-palace at the corner.'[1] At Toynbee Hall, Whitechapel (1884), one man responsible for introducing musical performance was J. M. Dent, the publisher. Dent's association with Toynbee Hall began in 1886; with some difficulty he managed to persuade the Warden, Canon Barnett, to let him arrange some Sunday-afternoon concerts, given at first by amateurs, but later with the help of professional singers and players. These concerts were a great success and ran until the beginning of the First World War. Outside London, excellent work was done by the Birmingham Musical Association, which began a notable series of concerts on 8 November 1879 under the auspices of Jesse Collings. At about the same time the Working Men's Concerts in Manchester were commenced. In the first place these were run on a voluntary basis, but later the Council of the Working Men's Clubs Association (under whose auspices the concerts were given) agreed to the appointment of a paid director. Admission cost 4d, though there were more expensive seats; the average attendance was about 3,400. On a slightly different scale and with more miscellaneous programmes, the Ancoats Recreation Committee provided free Sunday-afternoon concerts during the winter months, with open-air choral performances and band concerts in the summer.

Cheap concerts were given elsewhere in the provinces, as at Norwich in the 1880s and in Liverpool during the same period. But some of the most notable achievements in this field were the 'Sunday Evenings for the People' presented during the 1870s by the National Sunday League. These were held at the South Place Institute, London; the South Place People's Concert Society (1878) was started in order to disprove the notion that working people had no taste for high-class music. 'Any person who was

[1] W. T. Hill, *Octavia Hill* (1956), p. 166.

present at South Place Institute last Sunday evening', wrote the *Pall Mall Gazette* for 3 April 1888, 'could testify that such is not the case. It was the last concert of the present season, and long before the advertized time the doors were besieged by an eager throng, who, on the doors being opened, quickly crowded the building to its utmost capacity.' At the South Place concerts there was no charge for admission, though a collection was taken.

Such ventures as the South Place and National Sunday League concerts represent an attempt to provide the people with good music at reasonable prices. In the same period a number of schemes were devised for the purpose of encouraging active music-making among those who had not yet been caught up in the Tonic Sol-Fa movement. One of the most interesting of these was the outcome of Emma Cons's enterprise at the Royal Victoria Coffee Hall, Waterloo Road. In 1884 this attempt to provide South London with a temperance music hall, at which serious evening programmes of an instructional nature were intermingled with ballad concerts and variety shows, was in some financial difficulty. But at a meeting in June of that year it was announced that £4,000 had been subscribed towards future costs. 'At one point,' we are told, 'after Lord Mount Temple had stressed the importance of music as a civilizing influence to which the "lower classes" were particularly responsive, Sir Julius Benedict [by this time—like Arthur Sullivan—a member of the Council] said, "I should like to see an orchestra of working men playing in the Victoria Hall." Interruptions from well-bred women at meetings were unusual in those days, but at this Emma Cons could not resist calling out, "There is one!" '[1] A substantial part of the £4,000 had been donated by Samuel Morley; and although Morley College, as it was later to become, did not attain eminence in the musical sphere until after the turn of the century, its musical tradition was more or less guaranteed from then on.

Music in the working men's colleges varied in strength from one place to another, but in this connection may be mentioned the Musical Guilds for working people which existed in theory if not extensively in practice. Music was, of course, to take its place in the activities of Ruskin's Guild of St. George. 'I have

[1] Denis Richards, *Offspring of the Vic* (1958), p. 67.

stated, in the first sketch of the design of our St. George's education,' wrote Ruskin in *Rock Honeycomb*, 'that music is to be its earliest element.' Far from being inconsistent with manual labour, music was to be performed and enjoyed because of its power to refine and modify civilized life.[1] A Guild run under the guidance of an experienced musician was that established at Nottingham in the 1880s. It was directed by Mrs. Mary Bowman-Hart, whose primary aim was to elevate the standard of musical literature available to the people. In 1886 the Guild had 400 members, mostly working men and women. It organized singing classes, and one of its professed objects was to provide solo singers, choruses and instrumental music for Saturday-evening entertainments in Mission Halls, Girls' Homes, and Young Men's Institutes at Nottingham. The 'Nottingham Bowman-Hart Musical Guild' did excellent work in showing uneducated people how to entertain themselves; it even produced a Quarterly Magazine, edited by a working man. More fruitful than the Musical Guild idea, however, was the competitive festival movement which if not exactly begun in the 1880s at least received an initial stimulus which far outlived the careers of its inaugurators.

It is commonly held that the competitive festival movement owed its inception to the initiative of Mary Wakefield (1853–1910). In fairness to others it should be said that Mary Wakefield herself claimed no originality in this connection, and her efforts had been anticipated by several musicians before her. In her own generation, for example, an eisteddfod had been held at Workington (1872) under the guidance of Ivander Griffiths, and in 1882 John Spencer Curwen arranged a similar festival at Stratford, Essex. Musical competitions of one sort or another had been well known in England for a long time, but the choral festival for which Mary Wakefield made herself responsible in 1885 may be taken as marking the commencement of what was to become an ambitious and well-patronized national institution. One of Mary Wakefield's aspirations was to make effective a proposition of Ruskin's that 'Music fulfils its most attractive and beneficial mission when the masses of the people enjoy it as a recreation and a solace'.

Quite apart from her work in connection with the festivals

---

[1] Ruskin, *Works* (ed. Cook and Wedderburn), XXXI, p. 107.

held year by year at Kendal, Mary Wakefield was a remarkable woman. The daughter of wealthy parents, she was born in Westmorland and studied music with Alberto Randegger. In physique and personality the 'robust and tuneful Miss Wakefield', as Dr. John Brown called her, bore some resemblance to Florence Nightingale, and like the Nightingale sisters she was anxious to put her talents to use. She became a highly accomplished vocalist and composed many drawing-room songs which were quite popular. She was also a successful lecturer on musical topics. Several of her essays were published, and her most notable literary work is a volume of selections called *Ruskin on Music*. Among Mary Wakefield's close friends were Maud Valerie White, Lady Folkestone, Rosa Newmarch and Henry Leslie, the choral conductor. It was through her association with the latter that she came to know something about the musical side of the Welsh eisteddfodau; she disapproved, however, of the mercenary spirit which had crept into a great deal of competitive music-making. This led her to envisage a kind of musical festival which while not completely dispensing with the element of prize-winning did not exist for that alone.

In 1885 the idea of a competitive festival was a complete novelty in the Lake District; as a consequence only three vocal quartets entered. But next year there were twenty-one entrants, and in 1887 a hundred and forty performers appeared. In 1890 over six hundred competitors performed at Kendal, and the increasing magnitude of the festival made it necessary for the number of classes to be increased. The great success of the Kendal Festival gave rise to many similar ventures in the north of England, of which the Morecambe Festival is perhaps the most famous, though there were several in the north-east as well. By about 1890 the pattern followed by most competitive festivals since Mary Wakefield's time was firmly established: a large number of classes for vocal and instrumental performers were held, with additional classes in drama and elocution. An innovation at Kendal was the inclusion of a folk-song class. Competitors were asked to perform a genuine folk melody which they had learned in their own locality; this produced several hitherto unknown songs.

The competitive festival movement attracted amateur musicians from long distances. It cannot be said to have attached itself to the promotion of any particular 'cause', but Mary Wakefield held that it had a distinct rationale. 'I believe the highest attainable object', she wrote, 'is to "create the love and in consequence the demand for the greatest music, by the greatest number". There is, today, no lack of splendid education for those who intend to make music the business and profession of their lives : neither are there any difficulties of instruction for those whom I will call cultured pleasure seekers in the paths of music. But the object of this movement, as I have already said, is to reach the "greatest number", which must represent the great general public, whose life is mainly spent in earning its livelihood.'[1] Mary Wakefield maintained that the stimulus of competition leading to a final combined concert performance was something which could improve the state of musical culture and help to provide an intelligent form of enjoyment. The mere expenditure of energy was not enough, however : 'If music as a serious art is ever to be appreciated and understood here, as it is in Germany,' she wrote on another occasion, 'the formation of an educated, enlightened public is the first requisite.'[2] The educational side of the competitive festival movement may not always have been as effective as Mary Wakefield and her circle hoped it would be. These gatherings did, however, constitute a step towards more comprehensive instruction in 'musical appreciation'.

The Kendal festivals aroused the interest of many imitators and disciples. Among these perhaps the best known on account of his philanthropic work in other directions was the Duke of Westminster. At Eaton Hall, his seat in Cheshire, he started a competitive festival identical with the Westmorland one. Among the other influential people who used their good offices to arouse interest in corporate musical activity of this kind were Mary Egerton of York, Canon Gorton of Morecambe and Mrs. Mansel of Wincanton, Somerset. The 'Choral Competitions' started in Suffolk by the Hon. Alice Henniker in 1897, though slightly different in intention from Mary Wakefield's (they aimed in the first place at improving the standard of church music), produced much the same results. By 1904 there were

[1] A. M. Wakefield, 'The Aims and Objects of Musical Competition Festivals and How to Form Them' (reprinted from *The Commonwealth*, Kendal, n.d.).
[2] 'Amateur Music as it should be', *Musical Times*, 1 March 1884, p. 144.

forty-nine offshoots from the Kendal Festival, and it was resolved to form an Association of Competitive Festivals, which held its first Conference in June 1905 under the guidance of William McNaught, J. A. Fuller-Maitland and Lady Mary Forbes-Trefusis. All these ventures point to one significant fact —the willingness of a large body of well-to-do and musically enlightened people to assist the underprivileged in their efforts towards self-realization. Such propensities on the part of the rich often led to a suspicion of meddling paternalism. In the case of those named above, however, anything of that kind was over-ridden by a disinterested desire to bring out the musical talents of ordinary people.

II

It would be impossible to exaggerate the variety and profusion of English musical life from, say, 1897 to 1914. Throughout the country amateur music-making was extremely vigorous: choirs and small orchestras were numerous, and it was at this period that some of the best-known brass bands, such as the Creswell Colliery Band and the Barrow Shipyard Band, were formed. The scope of professional music was also extending. In London private recitals were a common feature of upper-class social life. Public concerts followed one another in quick succession during most of the year. A typical enterprise of this period was the formation of the London Symphony. This was made up of players from the Queen's Hall Orchestra who were not prepared to abide by Sir Henry Wood's decision not to allow the deputy system to continue. Under this arrangement (which was common in musical circles for years before 1914) a player who had signed a contract to perform at the Promenade Concerts might secure what he considered to be a better engagement elsewhere, and then send a colleague along to deputize for him at Queen's Hall. The effect of this on standards of performance may be imagined. But the original London Symphony Orchestra considered Sir Henry Wood's endeavours to curb the deputy system rather high-handed, so they set up a rival organization and began giving concerts on their own account.

Two other features of English musical life in this period were the proliferation of concert agencies and the formation of opera companies. The distinction of being the oldest concert agency in the world was claimed by the firm of Vert, of Cork Street, London. In the 1890s W. Norman Neruda and Co. managed the professional affairs of Lady Hallé and Leonard Borwick, while Cecil Barth found engagements for Jules Rivière's Grand Orchestra. In the decades before 1914 such concerns as Mitchell and Ashbrooke, Schultz-Curtis and Powell, and Ibbs and Tillett supplied artists to London and provincial concerts. The Carl Rosa Opera Company (1875) achieved a very high standard of performance throughout this period, but it had to face competition from a number of other ventures, such as the Moody-Manners Company (1897), the Rousby Opera Company, the Burns-Crotty Company, the Quinlan Company, and several others which did not survive the First World War. Opera-going was an important part of the lavish entertaining that was *de rigueur* among the wealthy in Edwardian England. Musical comedy enjoyed an enormous vogue. At a different level there was the music hall, which was then in its heyday, and in the 'straight' theatres the incidental music (frequently of a very high order) was expertly played under the direction of such men as Edward German, Norman O'Neill, Herman Finck and James Glover. Outside London, cities like Liverpool, Manchester and Birmingham enjoyed a number of first-rate concerts every season. These, too, were the palmy days of the concert orchestras at the seaside and inland resorts, at Llandudno, Colwyn Bay, Southport, St. Anne's, Bath, Buxton and elsewhere; at these places, ensembles of anything up to fifty players were to be heard regularly through the summer months, and smaller bands in winter. Public music-making benefited greatly from the growth of a *rentier* population at such towns as Bournemouth and Eastbourne. Municipal sponsorship of concerts was carried on successfully in many watering-places, as, for instance, at Margate, where a profit of £2,085 was made on concerts given during the 1906 season.

Amid all this activity there was one feature which even at the time excited a great deal of comment; this was the continued presence in England of a large number of foreign musicians. When the Crystal Palace Orchestra was disbanded in April 1900 it contained upwards of two dozen foreign players. Not that there was a shortage of rank-and-file performers born and bred in England: their work was, indeed, frequently praised by singers and instrumentalists from abroad, but they seemed to lack the *finesse* which belonged to those accustomed to Continental traditions of performance. In some circles it was regarded as deplorable that so much dependence should be placed on French, German and Italian musicians, but the public revealed a curious preference for foreign names rather than British ones—in the higher reaches of the art, at any rate. So much so that many English performers assumed appropriate *noms de guerre* before appearing on the concert platform. Up to the First World War even so distinguished a musician as Basil Cameron thought fit to adopt for professional purposes the name of Basil Hindenburg.

Yet in one sphere, that of large-scale choral performance, English musicians were doing some fine work. During this period there was a vast extension and improvement of the great provincial festivals, some of which have already been discussed. Apart from the Three Choirs Festival, there were also privately sponsored festivals at Bridlington and Hovingham (Yorks.). The more important festivals date from the later part of the eighteenth century. In some cases, however, there seems to have been a decline of interest during the early Victorian period, followed by a resumption of activities thirty or forty years later. This was the case at Chester, where the festivals, begun in 1772, continued until 1829, after which there was break in continuity until 1879. The Chester festival of 1897 may be taken as a typical instance of the sort of thing attempted at these great choral gatherings. It began with a special service in the Cathedral, at which Mendelssohn's *Hymn of Praise* was performed. The following Wednesday, Thursday and Friday (21–23 July) a programme was presented which included *Judas Maccabeus*, *Zadok the Priest*, Sullivan's *Festival Te Deum*, Dvorak's *Stabat Mater*, Gounod's *Messe Solenelle*, J. C. Bridge's *Resurgam*, Schubert's Mass in E, Part I of Haydn's *Creation* and orchestral works by Tschaikovski, Max Bruch, Adolf Jensen, Spohr, A. C. Mackenzie and Granville Bantock. 'There was no difficulty in obtaining a splendidly efficient chorus from Chester, Yorkshire, and Lancashire,' wrote the *Musical Times* for August 1897, 'and other centres were drawn upon for an excellent orchestra, with Mr. Willy Hess, of Cologne, as principal first violin.' Among the solo vocalists were Anna Williams, Muriel Foster, Daniel

Price and Watkin Mills, but the outstanding success of the festival was gained by the Italian contralto Giulia Ravogli. The Chester Festival is characteristic of other festivals at Leeds, Birmingham, Bristol, Norwich. For many years the provincial festivals gave rise to a great deal of non-musical festivity. They brought a temporary stimulus to trade, since the railway companies allowed concessions to travellers attending them, and visitors needed amenities of a rather higher standard than those usually provided for day-trippers. In a subtle way the festivals did something to boost national morale, and this was very much in keeping with the spirit of the times. For in many cases the festival committees were encouraged to commission new works —the novelties were, in fact, one of the main attractions. This gave rise to a large body of festival music (both sacred and secular), all too frequently characterized by what George Bernard Shaw once described as 'the extra-special dullness supposed to be proper to such solemn occasions'. The solemnity, it must be admitted, frequently concealed poverty of invention, for which reason many works of this kind have completely fallen out of the repertory; Bridge's *Resurgam* is a case in point. But among these items—especially after the Diamond Jubilee of 1897— were compositions which had a patriotic or semi-patriotic theme. Elgar's *Banner of St. George* (1897) is a work of this kind; so is Sir Frederick Bridge's *The Flag of England* (1897), Stanford's *The Revenge* (1886) and *Songs of the Fleet* (1910). Indirectly these choral pieces ministered to the national pride which was expressed in countless political speeches and in the poetry of Henley and Kipling.

A festival at which this sentiment was felt with particular keenness was given at Sheffield in 1902. In the middle of the nineteenth century Sheffield, like Chester, had gone through a comparatively slack period musically. An attempt to revive the festivals of an earlier day had been made when the Albert Hall was opened in 1873; but it was not until 1895 that the movement to start a triennial festival received much support. For the 1902 Festival, as for the previous one of 1899, the chorus-master was Henry Coward; this time a work of his own composition, the cantata *Gareth and Linet*, was included in the programme. Henry J. Wood was the conductor, and major works by composers of the so-called 'English Renaissance', Elgar and Hubert Parry, were performed. At this festival there was a fairly even distribution of works between English and foreign composers, Handel being represented only by a selection from *Israel in Egypt*. Ysaye was the soloist in Beethoven's Violin Concerto and Fritz Volbach took part in his own *Easter* for organ and orchestra. As Henry Wood was an advocate of a lower pitch for all concert performances, it was decided (at great expense) to make an alteration to the pitch of the Albert Hall organ. Of the performance on the Thursday, when Elgar was to conduct his Coronation Ode and the *Dream of Gerontius*, the *Sheffield Daily Telegraph* reported: 'Weeks ago all the seats in the hall had been allotted for this concert, and every day since has brought fresh demands for tickets. Yesterday a gentleman telegraphed stating that he would pay a guinea if he could only stand.'

There was one slight hitch in the Sheffield Festival of 1902, when the chorus began the Kyrie of the *Dream of Gerontius* slightly out of tune. Elgar was unruffled, but it did not escape the Berlin representative of the *Allgemeine Musikzeitung*, Otto Lessman, who gave an otherwise favourable report of the Festival. For the rest, the other works—*Elijah*, the *Hymn of Praise*, the *Triumphlied* of Brahms, Parry's *Blest Pair of Sirens*, Cowen's *Ode to the Passions*, *Gareth and Linet* and Coleridge Taylor's *Meg Blane*—brought effusive praise from the *Telegraph*. 'The Press', wrote the same paper on 30 September 1902, 'indicates the throbbing of the pulse of the public, and it is a sign of the times when thirty-five leading papers in various parts of the kingdom send special representatives to report on Sheffield music. Sheffield sentiment is no longer considered to be embodied in steel.' And the Festival itself would 'be famous for giving birth to fresh conceptions of musical genius, and also for imparting new life to old inventions'.

The Sheffield Festival of 1902 was a brilliant success socially as well as musically, but it was hardly within the reach of the ordinary music-lover, since the cheapest seats cost six shillings. After it was over, the *Sheffield Telegraph*'s critic justified the holding of such a grand affair on the grounds that 'if there are some hundreds of thousands of people in the city who have never heard a note, it must be remembered that the influence of all this is not limited to the four walls of the Albert Hall. The educational value, the enthusiasm created, the moral force of it all will inevitably permeate the musical life of the city.' No doubt there was a modicum of truth in this, but the fact remains that some of the festivals held throughout the country as a whole were far too costly. In a letter to the *Sheffield Daily Telegraph* on 6 October 1902, S. Dixon complained that the prices for this Festival were 'prohibitive to the plebeians of our city' and suggested that seats should be in the shilling to three-and-sixpence range (with, if necessary, less eminent vocalists). But this would partly have ruined the effect of such occasions. The famous names and foreign artists were there to create the festive atmosphere: for a matter of three days or so the provincial towns rose to a splendour that was missing for the rest of the year. The voluntary chorus were well rewarded by the enjoyment of a certain excitement which did not arise in other circumstances; this, in turn was necessary to the rendering of the music.

In spite of the acclaim which the Sheffield, Leeds, Birmingham and other festivals enjoyed, the provincial festival *ethos* itself was not without its adverse critics. George Bernard Shaw, for instance, was characteristically derogatory, and Rutland Boughton in a pamphlet published in 1913 deplored these 'gatherings of such wealthy folk as are too kind, or too lazy, to pot grouse';[1] yet even he admitted that they did occasionally bring interesting new works to general notice. Their importance so far as we are concerned lies in the fact that they were frequently the means by which English achievement in music was publicized in countries abroad. As far back as 1873, Henry Leslie after a visit to Paris at which his choir won a coveted prize in an international competition, declared that this success was 'a vindication of English musicianship . . .' Others shared Henry Leslie's feeling that English music needed some kind of championship in foreign parts—and none more so than Henry Coward, in whose nature there was a strongly chauvinistic strain. Yet Coward went even farther than Henry Leslie. Having trained famous choirs at Leeds, Newcastle, Huddersfield and Glasgow, he determined to make British choral singing appreciated in other countries by taking his Sheffield choir farther afield. The first visit, arranged with the help of W. L. Lindlar, a German national residing in Sheffield, took place in the autumn of 1906 when the choir

[1] Rutland Boughton, *The Death and Resurrection of the Musical Festivals* (1913), p. 1.

performed at Cologne, Düsseldorf and Frankfurt. This was a carefully planned expedition, and Coward was far from indifferent to the reception the choir obtained. In his *Reminiscences* he quotes from the *Kölnische Volkszeitung* the only 'tempered praise' which he met with in the German Press reports: 'We could recognise the fine training of the magnificent material of the voices. Its delicacy of representation is not often reached by even the very best German choruses.'[1] Other journals, such as the *Kölner Tageblatt* and the *Anzeiger für Elberfeld*, expressed enthusiasm and even 'envy and astonishment' that the three hundred Yorkshire voices should exhibit such fine attack, volume and balance.

The Sheffield Musical Union undertook a second and more extensive tour of Germany in 1910. Coward had already made what he called a 'choral invasion of Canada' during October and November 1908. This was a mere preliminary to a much more prolonged tour three years later; but before touching on the significance of that, a word must be said about some of the musical manifestations of the imperialist spirit. In May of each year the *Musical Times* advertised suitable music for Empire Day. Schools and colleges performed appropriate songs (the 'action song' was then popular), and public concerts were held as a gesture of friendliness towards the various British Dominions. Trafalgar Day (October 21st) was the occasion for further celebration by the performance of such works as *1812*, Mackenzie's *Britannia Overture*, Frederick Godfrey's *Reminiscences of England* and ballads like 'The Bay of Biscay' (John Davy), 'The Death of Nelson' (John Braham) and 'Rocked in the Cradle of the Deep' (J. P. Knight). The Jubilee of 1897 inspired many commemorative choral and orchestral works as well as patriotic songs for drawing-room performance. Broadly speaking, patriotic music of this period falls into two classes: the light and romantic kind written by composers like Sullivan and German, and the more ponderous ceremonial type of Elgar and Parry.

For their world tour of 1911 the Sheffield Musical Union was joined by a number of other choral groups. The proposal for this strenuous undertaking had come from Dr. Charles Harriss, a London organist who had settled in Canada in 1883 and pursued a distinguished career as choirmaster in Montreal. The company sailed from Liverpool on 17 March 1911; from Halifax they

[1] Henry Coward, *Reminiscences* (1919), p. 195.

travelled throughout Canada, into parts of the United States, then across the Pacific to Australia, New Zealand and South Africa, arriving back in Plymouth on 30 September. The primary object of the tour was, of course, to give concerts in cities of the Dominions, collaborating as far as possible with local symphony orchestras. But Coward had an ulterior motive: he wanted not only to show off British musical talent in the Empire but also to make the Mother Country more Empire-conscious. 'The British Governments in the past', he wrote in his account of the tour, 'did not set very much store on the Colonies beyond a materialistic view. So long as they were a source of income there was no call for further thought. If they gave any passing trouble or expense, they were regarded as a burden to the State. Neither was the British Empire visualized by the people at large.'[1] There is a certain naïvety in Coward's view that solidarity might easily be brought about by means of choral union. But his confidence in the power of music to soften political differences was to some extent justified by the reception he and his colleagues received in South Africa. Even after nine years, bitter memories of the Boer War still lingered in this 'new and naked land'. When recollecting the concerts which his choir gave in the Bloemfontein area, Coward wrote: 'That an English choir should be received with such cordiality and enthusiasm in the "war area" after so short a time seemed to us to border on the marvellous. The more we think about it, the more wonderful it seems.'[2]

The Dominion Tour of the Sheffield Musical Union was, of course, made unofficially, though it attracted the favourable attention of Whitehall and was launched with the encouragement of the British Government. The financial risk involved was borne by Dr. Harriss, who had married the wealthy widow of an iron magnate. All the participants were unpaid amateurs, many of them products of the competitive festival movement. Not all of Dr. Coward's well-wishers shared his extreme view that 'Choralism is possibly the most socialistic—using the term in its proper anti-Bolshevist sense—of all the amenities of life',[3] but from several quarters the civic and political importance of music received strong endorsement during the Edwardian and early

---

[1] Henry Coward, *Round the World on Wings of Song* (1933), p. 1.
[2] *Ibid.*, p. 177.
[3] *Ibid.*, p. 13.

Georgian periods. Nineteen-eleven, the year of King George V's Coronation (itself a notable musical event), witnessed many great public celebrations. The Conference of Imperial Prime Ministers took place in June; the Musical Festival of the British Empire dominated English music-making; the London Music Festival and the Pageant of London held the attention of overseas visitors. And music also played some part in improving our relationships with countries outside the Empire. King Edward VII's fondness for French operas and operettas is well known; throughout his reign works by Gounod, Massenet and Bizet were heard frequently in London. During the summer season of 1906, for instance, *Faust* was staged six times at Covent Garden and *Carmen* twice. Earlier in 1906 the Band of the Garde Républicaine had paid a visit to England. A few weeks beforehand the London Symphony Orchestra received an enthusiastic welcome in Paris; musically speaking there was a perfect *entente* between the two countries which has been of long duration. Unfortunately, the same could hardly be said of our relationship with Germany in the same period.

III

In an article published in *The Musician* for 25 August 1897 Nicholas Kilburn raised the question, 'Is Germany the Leading Musical Nation?' This was a subject canvassed very frequently in the first quarter of the twentieth century. Our debt to German musicians over the centuries has been so great that for many people a negative answer was unthinkable; and yet there was some speculation as to whether Germany really merited the esteem in which her musicians were held. Admirers of English attainments in the field of 'choralism' contended that in this sphere England outshone Germany. Yet there had been no English Mendelssohn or Beethoven and certainly no English Wagner. Even Handel, to whom the choral tradition in England owes so much, was not a native of this country. The matter is confusing and controversial, but so far as our period is concerned it can be considered in relation to three main topics, composition, performance and the music trades.

During the early part of the nineteenth century many English musicians went to Germany to finish their professional education. They knew that they would find good teachers there and would have the opportunity of attending operas and concerts of a high standard. In 1836, for instance, William Sterndale Bennett was sent to Leipzig for a year at the expense of the firm of Broadwood, and when Arthur Sullivan arrived in the same city in 1858 he found a small group of English students in residence there. Germany also attracted the patrons of music, musical scholars and *littérateurs*. Sir George Grove, for example, was a confirmed admirer of the German classical school: for upwards of fifty years he contributed programme notes on the symphonies of Mozart, Haydn and Beethoven for the Crystal Palace concerts. Grove was not himself a composer, but as secretary of the Crystal Palace he was in a very favourable position to encourage the efforts of the rising generation. Yet the work of English musicians, though occasionally given a hearing, did not arouse much enthusiasm in German critical circles. It is one thing, of course, for a composer to receive a few favourable Press notices, quite another for him to be remembered and distinguished from his colleagues. After Sterndale Bennett, the first English composer to be taken with complete seriousness in Germany was Elgar, and German teachers can perhaps be excused for showing some dismay at the fact that over the years no indisputably major talent seemed to have been produced by any of the English musical academies. They could not foresee that when a genuine 'renaissance' occurred among English composers it would be influenced by two features of English musical life which did not at the time secure widespread publicity in Germany: the English folk-song revival and the development of musical antiquarianism.

These two things are closely related, but as the second is of greater academic than social interest it will not be discussed in detail. It must be noted, however, that from about 1840 scholars began to bring out modern editions of early English music, principally from the sixteenth and seventeenth centuries. Something was said in the last chapter about the place of this in the 'religious revival' of the 1840s and 1850s. It had a secular side also and was the means by which younger composers came to know at first hand the airs, madrigals and fantasies from the Elizabethan collections, the operas of Purcell and a great many more compositions written in the pre-Handelian idiom. To this was added an acquaintance with the unsophisticated airs and dances which had been 'lost' over the centuries. Here the folk-song movement is of the first importance: it combined antiquarian interests with musico-sociological pursuits and those who believed in it most strongly were convinced that they were helping to wrest from oblivion the remnants of a way of life that had passed away for ever.

The English Folk Song Society was founded in 1898, but over the previous fifty years or more many collections of English folk songs had been published. They were derived from various sources and localities, and often caused embarrassment to collectors because of the frequent indelicacy of the words. But so far as the original singers were concerned, it was essential that these should be recalled in order that the tune could be brought fully to mind. Some critics have deplored the squeamishness of Victorian editors who suppressed the original words of many racy English folk songs. It should be pointed out, however, that coarseness does not of itself necessarily make a good song, as some of the inanities in *Pills to Purge Melancholy* (1719–20) go to show; and the better editors made a practice of depositing literal transcriptions of what they had discovered in libraries, while publishing emasculated versions for more general use. In this connection the name of the Rev. Sabine Baring-Gould (1834–1924) is a particularly distinguished one. For about fifteen years Baring-Gould noted down the songs sung by elderly people in remote parts of Devon and Cornwall. 'The hunt after this expiring strain of music', he writes in his *Further Reminiscences* (1925), 'was very delightful, and what was of advantage to me was that it brought me into touch with a class of men hitherto quite apart from the influence of the parson; and it afforded these men genuine delight to yield up their treasures of song that had been scouted and despised by the generation that could read and write. It was touching to note the affection and confidence we inspired when the ice was broken, and they discovered that we really valued what they had once so prized, but which the present and rising generation regarded with scorn.'[1] The tendency for increased literacy and the spread of urban habits of life into rural districts to weaken the common people's attachment to folk songs is commented upon by other collectors of the time, in particular the Rev. C. L. Marson, who was closely associated

[1] Sabine Baring-Gould, *Further Reminiscences* (1925), p. 212.

with Cecil Sharp for a number of years. Baring-Gould also collaborated with Sharp, who had a great respect for his work in the West of England. Sharp was, of course, the main protagonist for the cause of folk song in England and also one of the agencies by which its idiom came to be known to composers.

Baring-Gould's comments on the nature and quality of folk song are worthy of further comment. In their collections Baring-Gould and his colleague the Rev. H. Fleetwood Sheppard included ballads, soldiers' songs, and songs about rural occupations. They tried as far as possible to dissociate themselves from the 'composed' melodies which could be found in such collections as Chappell's *Popular Music of the Olden Time* (1855–9) and also from 'professional' compositions of more recent date. They despised the 'sawny-sentimental stuff that is poured forth in floods today from the music-printers'; as an alternative they recommended the fresh and robust tunes still alive in the consciousness of the people. The fundamental justification for their efforts is stated unequivocally by Baring-Gould himself: 'It may be asked, Is our English folk music worth preservation? I assert with confidence that it is quite as good and more genuine than the German Volkslied. The Volkslieder Schatz is made up to a vast extent of compositions by cultured musicians of the end of last century and the beginning of the nineteenth, as Kreutzer, Nageli, Reichardt, Silcher, Weber, &c., and only a small percentage are really spontaneous productions of the people themselves.'[1]

This raises provocative issues; and in any case it is extremely doubtful whether folk song is ever the 'spontaneous production of the people'. But the position adopted by Baring-Gould helps us to appreciate the appeal of folk song in this period. For generations men's conceptions of musical idiom had been based upon their knowledge of German and Austrian (and to a less extent French and Italian) music. But now it appeared that there was close at hand a large mass of thematic material which was entirely native in origin, quite 'unscientific' in its modes of presentation, and possessing an aesthetic quality of its own. In reality, the existence of English folk song had always been known to some interested people, but the late nineteenth-century editors pressed their claim for its widespread recognition because

[1] S. Baring-Gould and H. Fleetwood Sheppard, *A Garland of Country Song* (1895), p. x.

they believed it to have a rare musical quality and to be capable of assisting in the formation of a healthier public taste. There was an educational opportunity here, to which members of the Folk Song Society quickly addressed themselves. But so far as composers are concerned, the texture of folk music suggested possibilities which had not struck the 'cultured musicians' of an earlier day. Parry and Stanford, and to a certain extent Elgar, were influenced by folk song, but members of the generation next to theirs—Vaughan Williams, Holst and in part George Butterworth—evolved a kind of musical speech which is nearer to the language of folk song than to that of conventional 'art' music. For them the craft of composition consisted not in emulating the formal procedures of Brahms and Schumann, but in following impulses which led in directions not so far explored. To make this clear would require some technical discussion of their works; suffice it to say that at their best these composers are recognizably English throughout, but are never 'folksy' in a slavishly imitative way. Both Holst and Vaughan Williams in their early years were active in amateur music circles, and both composed distinguished 'utility' music for such groups.

As regards performance, Germany had some claim to be regarded as the leading musical nation because the systems of training in use there were so thorough. For many generations German musicians had regarded this country as a place in which they could exhibit their talent, and the number of German professors who settled in England was very considerable. In church music, for instance, the Kollman family were famous during the first half of the nineteenth century; as orchestral players the Ganzes of Mainz achieved great repute; among pianists Ernst Pauer and Oscar Beringer enjoyed much esteem in their time. A characteristic figure of this period was Wilhelm Lutz (1822–1903). The son of an organist, Lutz studied music at Würzburg; he came to England in 1848, and after serving as organist at several important churches in Leeds, Birmingham and London conducted operas and operettas (some being of his own composition) at the Surrey and Gaiety Theatres. To the Germans the art of coaching musical ensembles seemed to make a special appeal; which largely accounts for their presence in English seaside resorts as directors of military bands. During the 1890s Gustav Holst played the trombone in the White Viennese Band on Brighton Pier under Stanislaus Wurm, whose rhythm in conducting Strauss waltzes was electrifying. The German bands which were once a common feature of London street life were humble groups often made up from the members of one family who had decided to try their luck abroad; their playing sometimes exhibited an attack and *esprit de corps* to which English players could not rise. In 1861 a German street musician told Henry Mayhew that at dances and other functions the German bands played 'cheaper than the English', and an English one observed : 'The German bands have now possession of the whole coast of Kent and Sussex, and wherever there are watering-places.'[1]

Certain artists like Charles Hallé and Joseph Joachim—the cream of the musical profession—made for themselves a special place in English musical life by sheer force of character and expert musicianship, but there were many lesser men whose presence was not so congenial. Throughout the later nineteenth century, in fact, English musicians were disconcerted by signs that German singers and instrumentalists regarded themselves as superior. In 1879, for instance, the pianist and conductor Hans von Bülow wrote some disparaging letters to a German paper implying that the orchestra at the Liverpool Philharmonic Society's concerts was well below standard, and sneering at Sterndale Bennett as the 'miniature Mendelssohn'. Some remarks made by Eduard Hanslick on the occasion of his second visit to England in 1886 are much more thoroughgoing than von Bülow's gibes. These appeared in some articles Hanslick contributed to the *Neue Freie Presse* of Vienna. In them he slated Sterndale Bennett's slack and unenergetic conducting : Sullivan he declared to be an even worse orchestral leader, and Cusins (Bennett's successor at the Philharmonic Society in London) practically useless. It did not escape Hanslick's notice that English critics were not slow to complain about the invasion of foreign (and especially German) musicians, but in his view there was nothing extraordinary in this. 'I have already mentioned', he said, 'that, besides Richter [Hanslick's trump card] two Germans—Hallé and Manns—are considered the best conductors in London. Is it likely that they would be entrusted with important orchestral Concerts if the English conductors were

[1] Henry Mayhew, *London Labour and the London Poor* (1861 ed.), III. 163.

more, or even equally, competent? Would the Cologne Heck-
mann Quartet be engaged every year if four Englishmen could
show as much excellence? The same may be said of the German
pianoforte teachers in London—Ernest Pauer, Wilhelm Ganz,
Wilhelm Kuhe; of the German *impresario*, Karl Rosa; of the
German musical critic of the almighty *Times*, Franz Hueffer.'[1]

The position was made slightly difficult for English musicians
by the fact that right up to the outbreak of the First World War
liberal opinion was biased in favour of the large number of
Germans who had settled in England and made positive contributions to English cultural life. These included Carl Engel,
author of the monumental *Descriptive Catalogue of the Musical
Instruments in the South Kensington Museum* (1874); Franz
Rodewald, the distinguished Liverpool conductor; Alfred Jaeger,
Novellos' highly valued adviser, and many more. Among them a
rather special place is held by Edward Dannreuther (1844–
1905), who founded the English Wagner Society in 1872. The
aim of this was not only to spread a knowledge of Wagner's
music but to expound his political and aesthetic ideas and thus to
create a union between the master-minds of Germany and
England. In this connection *The Meister*, the journal of the
Wagner Society, invoked in 1888 the name of Thomas Carlyle,
and went on to proclaim that 'as the English discovered to the
Germans the genius of Arthur Schopenhauer, whose philosophy
was either neglected or completely forgotten in his own father-
land, so is there open to our English comrades a wider possibility, in the assimilation of the culture-creating thoughts of
Richard Wagner, and in their future elaboration'. Wagner's
genius as a composer is sufficiently obvious, but the claim that
his prose works rank him 'among the foremost thinkers of the
day' seems an exaggeration. Yet some idea of the hold which
Wagner had on advanced progressives in this period may be
gathered from an essay by William Ashton Ellis. In the course
of a discussion of Wagner's *Opera and Drama* and *The Art-Work
of the Future* Ellis draws up the following summary: 'In the
present case the one great principle to which Wagner comes
ever back, as the foundation and the governor of all Art, is that
of Communism, against Egoism; it is the *"common urgence of
every art* towards the most direct appeal to a *common public"*. It is

[1] See *Musical Times*, 1 September 1886, p. 520.

from this standpoint, and this alone, that he holds up the united Drama above the works of Absolute Music.'[1] Generalizations of this kind persuaded many people to confide in the inscrutable German intellect. In musical circles resentment arose when composers and performers took advantage of this, but nothing could be done to safeguard against the possibility of German musicians being favoured by their own temperamental peculiarities and the power of the musical traditions which lay behind them.

In the musical trade as distinct from the musical profession the position was more serious. England could hardly hope to remain the workshop of the world indefinitely, and towards the end of the century she was being overtaken by other countries in the production of some manufactured goods. Organ-makers in this country managed to maintain a high quality of work in supplying the export market; but by the 1870s pianoforte manufacturers had begun to feel the effect of foreign competition. 'There are at this moment in Germany', said *Musical Opinion* on 1 September 1884, '424 pianoforte manufactories, employing 7,834 workmen. . . . In one year the Germans turn out nearly 73,000 instruments. . . .'[2] German factories were also developing an extensive trade in accessories such as stands, tuning forks, metronomes, cases, etc.; they made large numbers of small portable instruments (concertinas, harmonicas) and several types of mechanical instruments. Throughout this period German music-printing remained the finest in the world: the great Bach and Palestrina editions from the house of Breitkopf and Härtel were as yet unrivalled by British firms, some of which indeed—as, for example, Novello's in the case of the Purcell Society publications —were obliged to call on the services of German workmen. Whereas in 1886 the value of pianos exported from Germany stood at £740,000, in 1896 this had risen to £1,054,000, and by 1912 to £2,314,000. In these years German manufacturers had succeeded in finding markets for musical products in practically all European countries and also in Australia, New Zealand, South America and the United States. 'In '91,' wrote E. E. Williams, 'when the whole population of West Australia numbered only 55,000, the colony imported musical instruments to

[1] William Ashton Ellis, 'Richard Wagner's Prose', *Proc. Mus. Ass. XIX.* (1892), pp. 25–26.
[2] *Musical Opinion*, 1 September 1884, p. 563.

the value of £6,639. These were mostly German: the British contribution being so small that it is ignored by the Board of Trade returns.'[1]

A feature of this period was the relative frequency of trade and industrial exhibitions. The Germans were quick to take advantage of these, and free trade told in favour of those engaged in exporting goods to this country. A practice which German makers exployed extensively in this period was that of exporting instruments in sections to be assembled on arrival in the importing country. As a result of this, many instruments which bore the name of English makers were, in fact, manufactured in German workshops. The Germans also produced larger quantities of factory-made violins; and for many years a substantial traffic was carried on in cheap brass instruments originating in Saxony. The village of Markneukirchen was notorious for turning out the valves, spindles, keys, bells and other parts of trumpets and trombones—these being made by men, women and children under conditions of sweated labour, or at any rate for extremely low wages. The Germans were constantly being accused of 'dumping' such commodities.

With the other great commercial rival in this period our relationship was different. America had, after all, no important tradition of musical composition, and as yet she was hardly in a position to supply the concert platforms of the world with an unending succession of celebrated virtuosi. This must not be taken to mean that in musical affairs the traffic between the two countries was negligible. On the contrary: by 1870 a great deal of American music was known in England, though it was mainly confined to two classes of composition—sacred music and light entertainment. The song literature of the period included a number of refined drawing-room ballads ('My Rosary' by Ethelbert Nevin, 'Absent' by J. W. Metcalf and 'Thy Beaming Eyes' by Edward MacDowell, for example) and the nigger-minstrel pieces which were popular from the 1840s onwards.

Nigger minstrels were a curious phenomenon. In the first place they owed much of their popularity to the fact that anti-slavery sentiment was strong in England during the middle of the nineteenth century. They also provided a wholesome kind of family entertainment of some slight educational interest. But the

[1] E. E. Williams, *Made in Germany* (1896), p. 125.

image of the negro which they evoked was a bogus one, for most of the minstrels were of the 'burnt cork' variety and thus hardly fair samples of a cruelly downtrodden people. After the visit of Edwin P. Christy's troupe in 1857, scores of minstrel concert parties came to this country; the songs they sang were not so much genuine negro melodies as cleverly composed tunes interspersed with snatches of Afro-American harmony. To say this is not to belittle the talent of composers like Stephen Foster (1826–64), but the feelings to which many of his songs give utterance are necessarily those of the white man enjoying a strain of melancholy he has himself attributed to the unfortunate Jim Crow.

Negro minstrels did, of course, introduce into their shows a good many of the rhythmic and melodic devices which occur in the folk songs heard in the deep South. The performers themselves are not to be blamed if the audience brought away from their entertainment an impression of the negro which was at variance with actual life. According to the Rev. H. R. Haweis, 'it is not too much to presume that the lasting popularity and deep appreciation of negro fun and pathos in England is mainly due to the genius of *Uncle Tom's Cabin*'.[1] As for the religious music which emanated from the United States, this is well represented by the hymns of Lowell Mason, some of which are included in the Methodist Hymn Book, and the *Gospel Hymns* of Moody and Sankey, which were published in the 1870s and had a great popularity in England. These 'Sacred Songs and Solos' are the result of an attempt to reach the hearts of the masses at a level of response much lower than that to which most English congregations were accustomed, but there were many other American hymn writers whose work soon came into common use among nonconformist denominations in this country.

In the last three decades of the nineteenth century American competition in world markets was very keen. American manufacturers had made great progress in the development of light machinery and automatic devices. 'By 1876', writes R. H. Heindel, 'our machine-made boots had reached Birmingham; American shoemaking machinery which followed revolutionized technique. Competition by American shoes which were characterized by lightness, elegance, finish, and quarter and half sizes,

---

[1] H. R. Haweis, *Music and Morals* (6th ed., 1875), pp. 551–2.

had been steadily increasing, and was to be stopped only by using American methods and machinery or imitations. One of the features of the Shoe and Leather Fair in 1901 was American machinery in motion.'[1] This is only one example of transatlantic encroachment; others might be added from the trades of food processing and garment manufacture. English musicians and music dealers did not regard the Americans as predatory in their general attitude; indeed, with the possible exception of music publishing, it might be said that a genuine reciprocity was maintained without serious interruption. Publications were affected by the uncertainty of the copyright laws, which made it possible for piracy to take place on a considerable scale. In the 1870s Gilbert and Sullivan were forced to visit New York in person in order to mount a performance of *The Pirates of Penzance*—a move undertaken largely to draw the crowds away from *H.M.S. Pinafore*, which was then being played in a pirated version and making large profits for unscrupulous plagiarists. Anomalies of this kind were to some extent offset by the fact that in the same period it was clear that the United States could supply commodities in the musical sphere for which the British were clamouring.

This was the 'heroic age of invention' in America and technologists were perfecting devices which, it was assumed, would extend the possibilities of life immeasurably. America did not produce a notable school of violin-makers, but her piano and organ manufacturers attained international prominence after about 1850. In 1910 American factories were placing on the market no fewer than 370,000 pianos a year, of which 366,000 were upright instruments. The manufacture of organs in the States was encouraged by the mushroom growth of urban communities all containing large numbers of churches and chapels. Comparable developments in England were on a smaller scale, but though the more ambitious Anglican churches (built as a consequence of High Church movements) invariably needed full-size pipe organs, many Nonconformist chapels required nothing more elaborate than a harmonium or American organ. The free-reed organ works on the suction principle and has a sweeter tone than the harmonium; it is easy to move about and has always

[1] R. H. Heindel, *The American Impact on Great Britain, 1898–1914* (1940), p. 143.

been in demand for schoolrooms, rectories, and mission halls. The Americans also developed 'lap' organs for private use; but the general result of American experiments with reed organs was to make organ tone familiar in non-religious buildings. From the early 1870s onwards the demand for American organs was so considerable that many American firms advertized regularly in the English musical Press. In the 1890s Walter Redmond's *American Organ and Harmonium Tutor* enjoyed a popularity comparable with that of Smallwood's *Pianoforte Tutor* which was also sold by Francis, Day and Hunter, the English agents for Harms and Co. of New York.

The number of patents taken out by American organ- and piano-makers covered nearly every aspect of keyboard structure, registration, arrangement of pedals and stops, and so forth. One particularly significant development was the improvement of pneumatic action. The bellows principle has been in use for centuries in connection with musical instruments, but the great achievement of American technicians was that they connected it with other mechanical equipment to produce the player-piano. Though not originally devised by an American, the principle on which the player-piano works was exploited by practically every pianoforte-maker in the States. A small 'Organette' was on sale in New York in 1878, and in 1897 E. S. Votey patented the instrument now known as the pianola. This was merely a trade name for the player-piano sold by the Aeolian company; there were many others—the Symphonola, the Antola, the Harmonola, etc. In 1899 the Aeolian Company opened a shop in Regent Street, London, for the sale of pianolas, and a factory was set up at Hayes, Middlesex, to supply the English market. In the United States the trade in player-pianos was so large that the Aeolian Company eventually bought up seven other companies; in Britain, too, business was fairly brisk, and in due course the company purchased much larger premises in New Bond Street.

In the player-piano the sound is produced by the action of the hammers on the strings, as in an ordinary piano. This action, however, is not made by the player himself striking the keys, but by the force of compressed air directed on to the hammers from a bellows system that is worked either by the feet or by an electric motor. The choice of notes to be struck is dictated by a slow-moving punched paper roll which runs over the 'tracker-bar' of the instrument and in doing so causes to be released or withheld the jets of air responsible for motivating the hammers. The music roll is operated by the power which keeps the bellows at work, and the two actions are carefully synchronized. Levers on the keyboard of the pianola control the speed at which the roll is to pass over the tracker-bar and also give the player some opportunity to observe the expression marks called for by the music.

The punched-roll principle could, of course, be applied to other instruments: it was used in connection with organ mechanisms, most notably on fair-grounds, where the 'Calliope' or great fair-ground organ was heard by countless thousands of people. Its relevance to serious music is at once apparent. The player-piano allowed a person without a keyboard technique to give satisfactory 'performances' of standard works; and it enabled a moderately gifted pianist to learn how particular pieces ought to sound when well played. The pianola manufacturers recorded performances given by well-known virtuosi which were simultaneously transcribed on master-rolls from which copies were duplicated for general sale. Thus the pianola enthusiast could compare his own efforts with those of Cortot or Paderewski. But the pianola was especially useful because it made possible repeated hearings of music which was either too difficult for the amateur, or seldom heard in the concert hall. The possessor of a pianola had at his command, in fact, the most revolutionary piano music of the day. He could (in theory at any rate) sample the whole of Chopin, the complete piano works of Brahms, all the Beethoven Sonatas and the 'Well-Tempered Clavier'. The scope of the pianola was unlimited, since arrangements of symphonies and concertos could be placed on the music roll just as easily as works originally written as piano solos. Its main weakness as a form of home entertainment lay in the fact that it could not easily be used as an accompanying instrument. Yet before the First World War it had a considerable vogue in this country, though new models were quite expensive. In the hands of an experienced player the pianola afforded a kind of gratification such as is described by C. E. M. Joad in *The Pleasure of Being Oneself* (1951). In this Joad recalls that at one time the Orchestrelle Company ran a library of pianola rolls. He explains the steps by which he gradually learned to master the pianola, and the kind of insight into great classical music which this gave him. Pianola technique was not attained all at once: carelessly handled, the instrument could make a dreadful hash of even straightforward piano compositions. The pianola represents an intermediate stage between performance 'in the flesh' and wholly mechanical reproduction.

The next step was taken by Thomas Alva Edison, whose work made the phonograph and the disc gramophone possible. Of 'the newest Edison phonograph' the *Musical Times* for 1 November 1898 remarked: 'There is naturally a ventriloquistic character about the reproductions, but by no means sufficient to be offensive to the ear. There will probably be improvements in the construction of the instrument, whereby the most delicate effects will be absolutely reproducible, though it is almost too much to expect that the results obtainable will be equal to the original sounds.' The price for this machine is given as six guineas with another fifty shillings for the amplifier. Like the pianola, the phonograph was taken up in England soon after it made its début in the United States, and an English Gramophone Company was established in 1898. Wonderful though the phonograph and the disc gramophone were in their early stages, they could not yet hope to meet with the unreserved approval of music-lovers. For though many phonograph records produced before the war are, even by modern standards, remarkably faithful to the sounds actually produced, their playing time was too short. For ballads and novelty numbers the phonograph was excellent; but few musicians could really thrill to a 'Zampa' Overture that was over and done with in three minutes. Moreover, the early records gave a seriously distorted idea of certain types of tone; voices came over fairly well (except for occasional booming) and brass bands were tolerable, but strings were barely recognizable and pianos a hopeless failure. It is true, of course, that Caruso and other notabilities made highly successful discs (from the commercial point of view). But taking the phonograph and the disc gramophone together as influences on musical taste, one must conclude that as yet they served light music far better than any other kind. They were thus agencies by which light entertainment was transplanted from its place of origin and diffused in England on a larger scale than ever before.

The two-way traffic between England and America increased in volume after 1900. For several decades before 1914 English musical plays were taken on tour in the United States, and Gilbert and Sullivan had a prodigious success there. At the same time a vogue for American musical comedy began in England about the time that *The Belle of New York* appeared. When presented at the Shaftesbury Theatre, London, in 1898 the *Belle* created a sensation. It ran for three years and left its mark on subsequent productions of the same kind. The score, by Gustave Kerker (1857–1923), had much in common with conventional mid-European musical comedy, but such numbers as 'Teach me how to kiss' and 'Take me down to Coney Island' exhibited a verve and swagger which is not found in, say, Monckton and Talbot. It is said that George Edwardes, the famous theatrical manager of the period 'sent his Gaiety and Daly's chorus girls to the Shaftesbury, six at a time, that they might acquire the American "pep", and English musical comedy has never lost the bias it received from *The Belle of New York'*.[1] This quality appears to some extent in the music of Leslie Stuart, but few English composers could meet the Americans on their own ground. Thus it was that music by composers like Irving Berlin, Victor Herbert and Jerome Kern was heard on the London stage —either in straight theatrical productions or revue—well before 1914.

In the numerous autobiographies and reminiscences of the Edwardian period frequent allusion is made to the *Merry Widow* (1907). This was an outstanding example of a type of musical production which suited the 'era of the stock exchange'. But though Edwardian society delighted in the romance and nostalgia of such musical comedies as *A Waltz Dream* (1907) and *The Balkan Princess* (1910), it also had a weakness for the buoyancy and witty nonchalance that is caught so well in the music of John Philip Sousa. So far as national prestige is concerned, the success which Sousa's band enjoyed on the occasions when it visited England may be regarded as some compensation for the colossal failure sustained by Oscar Hammerstein in 1911. Flushed with his success as an impresario in New York, Hammerstein constructed the London Opera House with a view to establishing an equivalent of the Metropolitan Opera in the West End of London. But after a time the audiences dwindled. It was, in fact, a serious error of judgement on Hammerstein's part to think

[1] Ernest Short, *Sixty Years of Theatre* (1951), p. 156.

that he could capture overnight the favourable support of the London opera-going public. His London Opera House closed after one season and London, already overstocked with musical drama, disdained the blandishments of a cigar manufacturer intent on making capital out of her most precious pleasures.

IV

'Thanks to the modern Genius of Speed, and the Science of the Rail,' wrote Thomas Morris in 1870, 'a wholesome future is in store for us. . . . Our bankers from Lombard Street, now reach the sea-coast by the time they used to arrive at Clapham; and Brighton, fifty miles away, is virtually a suburb not wrongly called "London super mare".'[1] By 1914 places almost as distant from the City as Brighton had developed into dormitory towns and the phenomenon of suburbanism had become a commonplace. Suburban life was to some extent dependent on the application to domestic needs of techniques and processes akin to those alluded to in the last section. The vacuum-cleaner, after all, has a great deal in common with the American organ, and labour-saving devices are as appropriate to music-making as to housework. But the consequences which followed from the dispersal of population after about 1880 are more interesting, since these inevitably had a considerable effect on our music.

The establishment of satellite towns and the opening out of what had previously been small self-contained communities led, among other things, to the construction of churches and chapels which all required organists and choirmasters. Migration into suburban areas cut people off from theatres and music halls. Up till about 1910 there were few cinemas. But during the decades before 1914 life in Greater London—and we may add, in the environs of Birmingham, Manchester and Leeds—had a certain piquancy for members of the lower-middle and middle classes. Among those above the poverty level the spirit of mutual betterment took many practical forms. The pleasure-loving rich may have been attracted away from serious pursuits by such things as motoring, golf, bridge and foreign travel, but for the shopkeepers, local government servants, and minor professional people there were evening institutes, literary societies, Pleasant

[1] Thomas Morris, *A House for the Suburbs* (1870), p. 1.

Sunday Afternoons and similar organizations which combined recreational activities with inexpensive enlightenment. As James Buchanan explained in the *New Quarterly Musical Review* for November 1895: 'The progress of invention and discovery during the last fifty years, especially since 1870, and the application of the results to our arts and industries have gained for the entire community an increased and an increasing amount of leisure. . . . The time and energy thus obtained is spent too often in trifling, and, it must be confessed, in gross and degrading pursuits, but it is a gratifying reflection that a large portion is being devoted to those recreations and studies that appeal to the higher nature of man. Among these Music now holds an important place.'[1] Thanks in part to some of the movements discussed earlier, such localities as Highbury, Edgbaston, Wallasey and Westcliff began to develop musical societies with a character of their own.

The activities of such groups can be followed up in the musical Press of the time. In the May 1907 issue of the *Musical Times*, for instance, a whole column is devoted to concerts given by the Dulwich Philharmonic Society, the Ealing Choral and Orchestral Society, the West Ham Choral Society, the Lewisham (Algernon Road) Choral Society, and so forth. There was as yet no radio to broadcast the major choral festivals, so these smaller societies did little more, by and large, than produce replicas of the programmes given either at the principal London concerts or at the provincial festivals. The only significant difference—apart from the standard of performance—was that works were included (by composers such as Romberg, Hofman, Tolhurst and Gaul) which would have been scorned at Norwich Cathedral or at the Albert Hall, Sheffield. But behind these smaller choral enterprises there was an active and integrated social organization and a vast amount of teaching activity.

As a mode of day-to-day living, suburban existence is characterized by the fact that for most people it enforces an abrupt separation between work and leisure. In *The Metropolitan Railway* John Betjeman writes of the commuter:

> all that day in murky London Wall
> The thought of RUISLIP kept him warm inside . . .

---

[1] James Buchanan, 'The Education of Audiences' in the *New Quarterly Musical Review*, November 1895, p. 105.

The concept of home took on a new significance towards the end of the nineteenth century, when thousands of people were moving farther away from the place of their employment. And with the advent of large-scale town planning there was an increased interest in gardens and interior decoration. These things may seem to have very little connection with music, but they are reflected in the musical compositions of the period intended for performance at home in the family environment. The importance of the pianoforte in the Victorian domestic scene was discussed in the last chapter. Here we must note the stress later placed on the ability to accompany at the piano. The widespread existence of amateur choral societies and the close connection which churches and chapels still maintained with the cultural life of ordinary people meant that there were large numbers of aspiring solo vocalists. The drawing-room ballad of this period therefore deserves a brief examination.

This was an age in which the so-called 'royalty' song flourished profusely. Hundreds of thousands of these were sold, and publishers thought it worth their while to pay singers to include them in ballad-concert programmes. The themes they treated and the conventional layout of their accompaniment suggest that for the most part they were intended for home consumption. They were, incidentally, the subject of controversy between those who, like C. L. Graves in the *Musical Times* for 1 February 1885, saw them as nothing but money-catchers, and artistes such as Madam Norledge, who in a paper to the North-Midland section of the Incorporated Society of Musicians defended royalty ballads as providing an honourable form of advertising. With such a large variety to choose from it is difficult to illustrate adequately the manner in which royalty-ballad composers worked and the kind of musical sensibility they hoped to engage. There are royalty songs on many topics—patriotic, religious and general—but the majority are escapist in feeling and inclined to ratify a simple optimism or to touch the tender emotions. As Fred E. Weatherley, one of the most prolific of 'lyric' writers, put it in his autobiography, 'the heart of the people is still simple and healthy and sound'.[1] The notion of restrained contentment, warm affection, freedom from *angst*, the loveliness of common objects and familiar scenes occurs again

---

[1] F. E. Weatherley, *Piano and Gown* (1926), p. 142.

and again; the sanctity of Home is repeatedly insisted on. 'Pleading', a typical royalty ballad, begins:

> Will you come homeward
> From the hills of dreamland,

the words being by Arthur Salmon, and the music by no less a composer than Elgar, who seemed to have no compunction about writing in this idiom. This ballad makes use of the cheapest harmonic and melodic clichés, and is in only slightly better taste than the same composer's 'After' (words by Philip Bourke Marston):

> A little time for laughter,
> A little time to sing:
> A little time to kiss and cling,
> And no more kissing after . . .

Ballads of this order were the production of composers and 'lyric' writers with an instinct for commonplace sentiments. Along with the duets produced on much the same principles, they were the chief standby of the musical evenings which formed an important part of home entertainment before the days of wireless. 'The world', wrote Fred Weatherley, 'is not going to forget "The Promise of Life" and "Love's Old Sweet Song", or "Because" and "I Know a Lovely Garden", or "Down in a Forest" and "The Little Winding Road", or "I Passed by Your Window" and the "Wayfarer's Night Song", or "The Little Grey Home in the West". . . .' The world has not indeed forgotten them; but for the majority of people the royalty ballads represent a mode of experiencing that is now considered completely fey.

How did the conditions we have been discussing affect the music-teaching profession? The existence of a large royalty-ballad public with its taste ranging from sacred songs on the one hand to musical comedy on the other stimulated the demand for elementary instruction in music. And the system of examination under the auspices of the Associated Board of the Royal Schools of Music (from 1880 onwards) made it possible for teachers to work a publicity-by-results scheme which could not fail to attract parents who regarded music as an additional social qualification for their children. By 1900 the musical academies were training and examining hundreds of candidates yearly, most of whom either set up as private teachers or found posts in schools. One development of suburban growth in our period was the establishment of music schools away from the centre of cities, such as the Watford School of Music (1880), the Blackheath Conservatoire (1883), the Croydon Conservatoire (1883) and the Hampstead Conservatoire. In the provinces schools of music were founded at Brighton, at Leeds and at Manchester in the 1890s; and this does not take into account the smaller private schools, or 'the many semi-public musical academies, presided over by half-educated professors, or professors of no education at all, often foreigners, who in their own country would get no hearing . . .' against whom Mrs. H. Coleman Davidson gave a warning in 1894.[1] There were, of course, many grades among the teaching profession, from the humble tyro giving lessons in a terrace-house drawing-room, to the exponent of some internationally famous 'method' running a London studio. But the majority of teachers then as now were men and women of average ability catering for average tastes and coaching pupils for examinations at all levels.

In her article Mrs. Davidson wrote: 'The musical profession is undoubtedly overstocked, and the increasing numbers of professional students threaten us, in years to come, with more teachers than learners.' According to the Census of 1881 the number of 'Musicians, Music Masters' was 25,546, representing an increase of 38 per cent on that recorded in 1871; in 1901 it was 43,249 and in 1911 47,116. The number of foreign musicians permanently employed in England showed a slight decline between the last two dates. But the great extension of the musical profession increased the need for amalgamation in order to maintain standards and to obtain satisfactory conditions of employment. Between 1870 and 1910 there were a number of associations among performers, though they were mostly local in origin and not many were of long duration: the nearest approach to a Musicians' Union was the Amalgamated Musicians' Union, founded in 1893, in which a leading spirit was the violinist John Tiplady Carrodus. Another organization known as the National Orchestral Union of Professional Musicians was set up in 1891 and the present Musicians' Union (1921) was formed out of a combination of these two groups. A National Union of

---

[1] Mrs. H. Coleman Davidson, *What our Daughters can Do for Themselves* (1894), pp. 197-8 (originally published in *Hearth and Home*).

Musical Instrument Makers was formed in 1879 and a Music Publishers' Association in 1881. But perhaps the most notable step taken to consolidate the musical profession as a whole in this period was the formation in 1882 of the Incorporated Society of Musicians (incorporated 1892). This aimed to put the musical profession on a footing enjoyed by the other professions, and among other things it sponsored the principle of registration for teachers of music. In 1887 Henry Fisher sent round to teachers a questionnaire asking 'Do you think the present methods of entering the musical profession are superior or the reverse to a regularly legalized plan such as is compulsory in the case of law and medicine?' The majority of the answers he obtained condemned the present *ad hoc* methods and spoke strongly in favour of registration, the main purpose of this, of course, being to put an end to the traffic in bogus qualifications and to ensure that on the teaching side of the profession the number of underqualified practitioners was reduced. This whole question was thoroughly investigated by Thomas Lea Southgate and as a result of his researches and the recommendations of the Society, a Teachers of Music Registration Bill was given its first reading in the House of Commons on 22 February 1901.

The Bill was withdrawn later in 1902. But the fact that it was introduced at all testifies to the seriousness with which music teachers believed that their professional interests must be protected. And they were joined by performers, instrument-makers and publishers, who also felt the need to assert their status. Ever since its foundation the Incorporated Society of Musicians has held an important place in the world of music. Another organization, the Music Teachers' Association (1908) was more specifically concerned with pedagogical questions. But at the same time its members turned their attention to larger problems. They saw early on that changing social conditions in the present century had already had a serious effect on the drift of musical taste. By 1914, in fact, mechanical reproduction of music presented a field for commercial exploitation which has turned out to be far wider than any we have yet discussed. This phenomenon and its bearing on the social history of our time will be the subject of the next chapter.

VII

$\diamond$

The Modern Age: Musical Culture and the Varying Pulse of the Machine

$\diamond$

I T would be difficult to think of a time when musicians were not engaged in the 'commercial exploitation' of music. In England, as in most European countries, performers who depended for a livelihood on the practice of their art constituted an identifiable social class long before the Reformation. By the seventeenth century large numbers of virtuosi commanded high salaries in opera and on the concert platform, and during the eighteenth and nineteenth centuries there was a manifold expansion of the musical profession as a whole. Over the last fifty years, however, developments in applied science have rendered musical activity a very lucrative source of profit in some quarters—though not necessarily among its 'primary producers'. Public music-making has always given employment to impresarios, concert agents and publicists. But in the past half-century the purely distributive aspect of the profession—involving great numbers of technicians as well as musicians themselves—has taken on a new significance. The means for disseminating music and for placing musical talent at the disposal of the public have altered considerably even since 1914: and, moreover, the public's attitude towards music itself has been seriously affected by changes outside the sphere of music proper. In discussing the social history of music during this period, therefore, we need to take into account technological advances and the effect of two major wars on cultural life in general.

I

On the outbreak of the First World War many people feared that there would be a total cessation of musical life in this country. Most of the larger provincial festivals were postponed indefinitely, and choral societies had great difficulty in deciding what was the morally right thing to do in the state of emergency. 'It is not only', wrote the *Musical Times*, 'that the sudden and alarming restriction of means on the part of practically every section of the community forces even hitherto well-to-do people to question expenditure, but that the intense obsession of the mind in following the evolution of stupendous events produces a sort of stupor and a feeling that the ordinary concerns of individual life are jejune and insignificant.'[1] After a time this feeling passed over, and though long-standing enthusiasms were inclined to abate, plans were eventually made for resuming normal musical activities as soon as possible. Yet almost from the outbreak of hostilities professional musicians were very despondent about their prospects. Teachers were not so badly affected, as the war had broken out in the middle of the summer holidays; but for full-time performers the position at first looked very grim.

On 13 October 1914 a meeting was held in the small Queen's Hall, London, to discuss the situation. Under the chairmanship of Sir Frederick Cowen, it was attended by leading composers, conductors and patrons of the musical world. Teachers, soloists and orchestral players gave evidence about the plight in which they believed themselves to be. From what was said it became clear that professional musicians everywhere had two main anxieties: they felt that engagements and teaching opportunities would slowly diminish, and they also contended that foreign musicians resident in this country would put English performers at a serious disadvantage. On this last point it was disclosed that for many years concert agents had persistently engaged foreign artists in preference to British singers and instrumentalists of equal standing. A considerable number of the so-called Hungarian and Viennese orchestras heard at society functions were, it appeared, largely made up of English players who had promised not to divulge their nationality. This did not greatly affect the question; but the position was aggravated by the

[1] *Musical Times*, 1 September 1914, p. 575.

arrival of refugees from Belgium, many of them excellent musicians, and public sympathy for the Belgians was not likely to help British musicians deprived of employment by the war. As a result of this meeting, however, a 'Music in Wartime' committee was set up, to decide what action could be taken against enemy aliens in the musical profession and to discover how suitable engagements might be found for English musicians. The General Secretary of the Amalgamated Musicians' Union pointed out that the problem here was a complicated one, because it involved more branches of the profession than teaching and performing. But in June 1915 representatives from a number of firms engaged in piano-making met at the Stanley Hall, Junction Road (North London), to protest against the fact that foreign manufacturers were still allowed to work freely in the musical trades. In the circumstances, it was held, an amendment was called for to Section 6 of the Trading with the Enemy Act.

War conditions affected musical activities in many subtle ways. Apart from the inevitable shortages which limited the number of new instruments that could be made (and also reduced the quantity of music printed), there was the fact that many large halls were taken over by the military authorities and were therefore not available for concerts. Although teachers of music were, on the whole, less adversely affected by war conditions than were performers, the number of entrants to the academies of music dropped, and local examinations had fewer candidates. During 1915 and 1916 there was a considerable falling-off in recitals and in private concert-giving, but orchestral activity was maintained by such bodies as the Royal Philharmonic Society and the London Symphony Orchestra, and the Promenade Concerts continued throughout the war. One obvious consequence of the conflict was the curtailment of foreign travel. As a result of this, tourists who normally went to the French, Austrian and Italian resorts during the summer had to be content with places like Bath, Cheltenham and Malvern or the south coast and North Wales. Harrogate, which had for years past enjoyed a fine musical tradition, soon felt the benefit of this: in February 1915 the Corporation empowered Julian Clifford, the conductor, to spend £3,500 on the orchestras in the Crescent Gardens and the Kursaal. And even in 1917 the Brighton Corporation found it possible to maintain an orchestra of thirty-two players. Brighton was one of the few places which managed to continue its choral festivals very much on the pre-war scale. At Sheffield, as elsewhere, the projected 1914 festival had to be abandoned, and in 1916 the festival secretary was still trying to dispose of the vocal scores which had been purchased for that occasion.

The strain of war conditions inevitably led many people to seek spiritual sustenance in great music, but at a time of crisis the notion of music as a social pursuit—the factor which had kept the larger choral organizations in being—lost much of its appeal. Some new choirs were formed, especially in localities where, as in towns engaged on munition-making, plenty of male voices were still available, but many of them were short-lived or had difficulty in keeping rehearsals up. The breakdown in international relations, which helped to disrupt concert promotion, had other curious results. For a long time a controversy raged as to whether or not 'enemy' music should be allowed in concert programmes. At the first season of Promenade Concerts after the outbreak of war it was decided to suspend the customary Wagner nights and perform Russian music instead. Later this decision was rescinded, and it was pointed out that a complete boycott of music originating in Germany would be impossible. Yet in the pages of the *Musical Standard* during 1917 Dr. Henry Coward contended fiercely that our conductors and choirmasters ought to have nothing whatever to do with any music written in Germany after 1870. This particular phobia continued even after the war. It deprived English audiences of much music by composers quite unaffected by nationalistic aims. At the same time it was largely responsible for the popularization of French and Russian music in this country from 1914 onwards, and it also gave some encouragement to younger British composers.

The introduction of conscription in 1916 drew younger men away from the theatre pits and from the concert platform. Women musicians, however, came forward to take their place. At several of the London theatres the orchestras began to be made up entirely of women, as also in the cinemas and cafés. Sir Edward Elgar spoke highly of the London Coliseum Orchestra, which had only one male performer (the tympanist). Drury Lane and the Aldwych also employed all-women orchestras. For the first time, in some cases, women were engaged in symphony orchestras, but it was in light music that they found the best outlet for their abilities. The war opened up a great number of opportunities for voluntary work, either in charity concerts at home or with concert parties sent out to entertain the troops stationed throughout England and along the Western Front. For a time there was an outcry against the abuse of talent (often inadequately remunerated) for purposes of charity, but in the absence of a comprehensive scheme for the entertainment of servicemen, a great deal was left to private initiative. With the help of the Y.M.C.A. and other bodies, a large number of projects were arranged, and small companies (usually consisting of three or four vocalists, an instrumentalist, an entertainer and an accompanist) toured the battle areas, giving musical and theatrical performances—frequently within range of enemy shellfire. As the war dragged on it became more and more difficult to find men who were still free to engage in this work, which was hardly suitable for those over military age. It was as a member of one of Lena Ashwell's concert parties, at Rouen in 1915, that Ivor Novello introduced the most famous of all the First World War songs, 'Keep the Home Fires Burning'.

Most of the music actually called into existence by the Great War may be divided into three classes: recruiting songs, communal songs, and more serious works composed for ceremonial or commemorative purposes. In the early days of the war the recruiting drive was often carried on with the help of army bands, which were intended to awaken patriotic responses in those who still hesitated about joining the colours. Recruiting songs were also sung in the music halls by such artists as Florrie Forde, Vesta Tilley and Alfred Lester. Alice Delysia sang 'We don't want to lose you, but we think you ought to go' (music by Paul Rubens), and Gwendolen Brogden 'On Sunday I walk out with a soldier', from the Palace Theatre revue, *The Passing Show*. The last-named song was already in circulation before the war broke out, and so was another First World War favourite, 'It's a long way to Tipperary'. This was ready for publication in 1911; it was sung on the halls by Jack Judge, and then revived in 1914. It might never have enjoyed the success it did but for the fact that a *Daily Mail* correspondent, hearing some British troops singing it in France, reported that 'Tipperary' was an approved marching song, and the publishers of the song seized on this as a means of boosting sales. Another First World War classic, 'Pack up your troubles in your old kit-bag', won a prize in a competition for marching songs. But the cheerful resolution of 'What's the use of worrying. . . ?' was not kept up in other songs of this time. There was, in fact, a good deal of simple fatalism in 'Tommy's Tunes', as well as an honest camaraderie. Some observers said that by comparision with that of the Russian and German soldiers, the singing of the British troops was puerile and unmusical, and there was certainly a temptation for men undergoing the rigours of trench warfare to indulge in nonsense and ribaldry. The Great War brought forth a mass of drinking songs, march tunes and satirical lyrics; the majority of these were parodies of well-known ballads (e.g. 'Our little wet trench in the West') and old-established national airs.

Conditions at the front were hardly conducive to subtlety and refinement. Some of the spiciest of the war songs were set to solemn hymn tunes, like 'Fred Karno's Army', which made use of 'The Church's One Foundation', and 'When this wretched war is over', which went to the tune of 'What a friend we have in Jesus'. Others were blatant vulgarizations of drawing-room songs, such as 'I wore a tunic', which appeared late in the war and remains one of the few war songs in English which display animosity against those who appear to have escaped military service. It begins:

> I wore a tunic,
>   A dirty khaki tunic,
> And you wore civilian clothes . . .

and was sung to the tune of 'I wore a tulip', a sentimental ballad of the royalty type. Many drawing-room songs of the time invited this treatment. W. J. Turner reported that at the soldiers' concerts he attended in France the most popular items were the ragtime duets. He added: 'This should be comforting to those who maintain, like myself, that the natural uncultivated taste in music is better than the large commercial product which the public is induced to consume—for there is no doubt whatever that most ragtimes, with their syncopation, vivid rhythms, and frequently attractive modulations, are the best music that many people hear, and far superior to what singers of ragtime would probably refer to as "high-class" songs, meaning the sort of unmusical twaddle you may see advertised any Saturday in the

Daily Telegraph.[1] But the 'oft-repeated assertion that "Tommy's" musical taste does not rise above ragtime or selections from musical comedy' was flatly denied by Arthur F. Milner, who pointed out the restorative value of good music when played to men whose nerves had been shattered by prolonged spells in the battle regions.[2] The serious music inspired by the war has not proved to be of durable quality. Of the innumerable hymns, anthems, cantatas and symphonic poems written expressly to voice feelings and aspirations suggested by wartime experience, only a few items such as Elgar's *Polonia* (1915) and *For the Fallen* (1916) still command respect. It might almost be argued that during the period from 1897 to 1911 English composers had already exhausted themselves in providing patriotic compositions, so that by the time the war came they had nothing original to say. An exception to this is Parry's 'Jerusalem', which was a contribution to the 'Fight for Right' movement,[3] but generally speaking the war ethos is more completely manifested in the light music of the day.

The reasons for this are fairly obvious. Both combatants and non-combatants were impelled, by the time war-weariness had set in, to seek the stimulus of gaiety. Light and easily assimilated amusement was given a tremendous boost by the fact that men and women felt the need to live intensely and with simulated abandon. 'In the early war-days', writes W. H. Berry, 'we quickly discovered that our *Tina* type of show was "the stuff to give the troops". A very large percentage of our audiences in those days were, of course, soldiers and sailors home on leave.'[4] But there were also the civilians—munition workers, Civil Servants and people in reserved occupations—for whom the sort of music that Paul Rubens composed was an ideal aid to relaxation. *Tina* (1915) was only one of his many successes. Like *Betty* (1915) and *The Happy Day* (1916) it is an inconsequential affair, but its melodies are just striking enough to dwell in the mind after the performance is over. During the war orchestral concerts and opera—particularly opera in English—drew reasonably good audiences, but the cinema and musical comedy also

[1] W. J. Turner, 'A Concert at the Front' in *Music and Life* (1921), p. 130.
[2] In a letter to the *Musical Times*, 1 December 1917, p. 549.
[3] See H. C. Colles, *Walford Davies: A Biography* (1942), pp. 108–9.
[4] W. H. Berry, *Forty Years in the Limelight* (1939), p. 183.

provided attractive antidotes to melancholy—though in rather different ways.

The war in Europe virtually cut off the supply of 'romantic' operetta. Before the war English theatrical managers had made a practice of going regularly to Vienna to engage artists and to confer with well-known composers; they now had to look elsewhere for new musical scores. So far as English musicians were concerned, this was all to the good. It was felt that central European composers had done well enough out of the reception given to their works in this country. It was now time for English and American musical plays to come into prominence. In 1916 an attempt was made by G. H. Clutsam and Basil Hood to revive the type of opera in which Sullivan had excelled; their *Young England* had a certain measure of success—though it is significant that Clutsam never tried to repeat it, his future stage productions being adaptations of other composers' music. But in popularity *Young England* fell far below such musical comedies as *Chu Chin Chow* (1916: 2,238 performances) and *The Maid of the Mountains* (1917: 1,352 performances). Clearly, the public for heavily sentimental musical comedy was still insatiable. But it was futile to imagine—as the *Musical Standard* did when *Young England* was put on—that 'syncopated melody from the New World' had had its day. On the contrary: revues and musical plays by American composers became all the rage. In his diary for October 1916 *The Times* correspondent, Michael Macdonagh, gives a vivid description of an evening at the Alhambra Theatre. 'The moon was at the full last night,' he writes, 'and as we have come to associate moonlit nights with recreation and amusement, free of the fear of a raid, I took the night off and went to the Alhambra to see the revue "The Bing Boys are Here".' He continues: 'The theatres, music-halls and cinemas are doing well. None of us, speaking generally, are pinched for money. We are being paid good wages or better salaries, both with war bonus additions, and so are ready to spend freely on relaxations from the tension of the War. . . . Matinées are held every day, and these are always well patronized. On dark nights, which are air raid nights, attendances are slack.'[1] Under such circumstances as these, shows like *Hanky Panky* (Max Darewski, 1917), *Houp-La!* (Nat D. Ayer, 1916) and *Bric-à-Brac* (Lionel

[1] Michael MacDonagh, *In London During the Great War* (1935), p. 143.

Monckton, 1915) exerted a special fascination. After the war, certainly, ruritanian musical comedy returned to favour and music by Lehar, Kalman and others—not to mention Ivor Novello, Montague Phillips and Vincent Youmans—was frequently heard on the English musical stage. But it had to face formidable competitors, and among the more important of these were jazz and the motion picture.

II

In 1914 the cinema, like the gramophone, was no new thing. But during the war it developed into a favourite form of entertainment, and its rapid progress had striking implications for the musical profession. Full-length silent films were incomplete without a fairly extensive musical accompaniment, and during the war the cinema provided a source of employment for pianists and organists who had fallen on hard times. It used to be said that in the early days of the cinema music was necessary to drown the noise made by the projector, but there is, of course, much more to it than that. In normal life practically all movement is associated with some kind of sound: to witness it in complete silence produces a false or comic effect. This principle was recognized in the theatre when melodrama still held the stage. Used in conjunction with 'straight' plays, indeed, music can produce many subtle effects: it can arouse feelings of anticipation, and it can create an 'atmosphere' with peculiar aptness. But since the subject-matter of films is wider in scope than that of stage drama, the cinema called for a more ambitious handling of musical material than was customary in the average theatre. The success of a film largely depended, in fact, on the attractiveness of its musical accompaniment: and if it were to be a box-office draw, the music could not be left to chance. Thus there arose a special kind of musical skill associated with the business of fitting suitable music to films. At first the standard classics were drawn upon to provide passages which would serve for 'romantic', 'agitated' or 'sinister' situations. But the great masters had not meant their work to accompany images of, say, 'tragic aftermath', hectic crowd scenes, big-game hunting or aeroplanes in flight; and since a question of exact timing arose, it became necessary for hack writers to produce mood-music that would

last for the right number of minutes or seconds. The film distributors accordingly issued 'cue sheets' informing musicians as to
how long particular films would run, and suggesting the music
that might be used. Before the film was actually shown in public
the cinema's musical director saw it through, and then compiled
his 'score' from the library of works available. Until sound films
changed the situation, leading British publishers such as Paxton,
Novello and Boosey and Hawkes issued innumerable series of
photo-play compositions, scored for almost any combination of
instruments.

'Were there no music within its walls,' wrote a contributor to
the *Birmingham Post* in 1927, 'the picture palace would be for
most of us a house of the dead, and we should be driven to any
other form of entertainment that might chance to be at hand.'
For this reason enterprising cinema managers were keen to
build up a good musical background: it was in their interest to
do so, since a poor musical setting could ruin a good film.
Cinema orchestras varied in size according to the seating capacity
of the cinema, but it was agreed that an ensemble made up of two
violins, cello, harmonium, piano and drums (with other percussive effects, such as rattles, whistles and gongs) was sufficient
for a moderately large picture palace. Yet even in the middle of
the 1914–18 War it was by no means uncommon to find orchestras of a dozen players performing in provincial cinemas, and
when ambitious films like D. W. Griffith's *Intolerance* or *The
Birth of a Nation* were shown additional players had to be engaged. At one time there was a vogue for films with full symphonic accompaniment, and in his book *Overture and Beginners*
Eugene Goossens describes how he conducted sixty-five players
from the London Symphony Orchestra in a lavish production of
the United Artists film *The Three Musketeers*, shown at Covent
Garden during 1922. Smaller cinemas had to make do with the
services of a pianist, though in some places cinema organs were
introduced, the first one in England being at the Palace Theatre,
Accrington, where it was played in 1913 by George Tootell.
Among the London cinemas a particularly good musical record
was established at the Stoll (formerly Oscar Hammerstein's
London Opera House). Here in 1917 an orchestra under George
Saker played for six hours daily, giving additional performances
on Sunday in aid of war charities.

But the cinema orchestra's duties were not confined to film accompaniment. It was occasionally called upon to perform music for which the audience had sent in requests. Indeed, the overture, interval music and finale amounted in many cases to a considerable concert, and it was not unknown for the audience to demand encores before the film itself could be given a showing. In 1929 Edwin Evans wrote: 'It is estimated, on the basis of union statistics, that picture theatres, great and small, are now providing between three-quarters and four-fifths of the paid musical employment in the country. It is further estimated . . . that the cinema is the sole, or at any rate the chief, avenue by which music reaches three-quarters of the potential audience in the population. For about fifty-nine hours weekly, music is being performed in upwards of three thousand cinemas, and for shorter periods in perhaps a thousand isolated halls. Setting aside all aesthetic considerations in favour of a purely objective view, one may say that the cinema is at present the most important musical institution in the country.'[1] This being so, it was inevitable that the quality of the music heard in cinemas should occasionally give music-lovers cause for concern. It was said, for instance, that cinema scores were frequently mere mosaics put together from passages out of well-known symphonies and sonatas; exception was taken to the manner in which favourite songs and *salon* pieces were garbled to suit the needs of the moment; and the leader-conductor's habit of 'showing off' was constantly denounced. But such strictures ignored the difficulties under which cinema musicians worked. In most picture palaces there was a mid-week change of programme; this meant that the musical director was expected to provide a large repertory of music, especially as the two or three films shown at each performance were all different in kind. In many cases photo-play music was distinctly inferior to the classical items with which the orchestra was familiar: so that a conductor could hardly be blamed for introducing items he had at his fingers' ends rather than the gallops, pensive interludes, oriental cameos and 'midnight terror' themes which were turned out by the hundred before the sound film made them obsolete.

Whether music in the silent cinema really debased public

[1] Edwin Evans, 'Music and the Cinema' in *Music and Letters*, January 1929, p. 65.

taste, as some claimed, is open to dispute. Occasionally, no doubt, cinema orchestras attempted to play music which was far too ambitious for them, with the result that pieces like 'Fingal's Cave' and the 'Traviata' preludes were shamelessly scrambled through. On the other hand, some cinema musicians did take care to select suitable music and to give it an adequate performance. Many cinema organists, for instance, had received a sound training as church musicians and were therefore adept at extemporization and rapid transposition, but dance-hall pianists who took up cinema work could not be relied upon to produce tasteful accompaniments so readily. Yet music for the silent films, in whatever form it was produced, gave rise to listening habits which the sound film later intensified. The most outstanding of these was unconscious assimilation.

To some extent this has always been a part of human experience, but the constant use of theme songs, and the frequent repetition of music that was highly 'atmospheric' in character induced the practice of hearing music without deliberately listening to it. This entails a psychological process which is different in kind from simply *mishearing* sounds; and film music is most successful when, in the words of a writer in the *Musical Times* for March 1922, 'So long as a picture is absorbing, we are hardly conscious of the music, though we miss it if it is absent.' Another habit encouraged by the cinema was that of associating certain kinds of movement with particular musical patterns. Having heard descending scale passages used to accompany the image of, say, a cascade of water, the spectator is inclined to conjure up that particular visual impression whenever such a passage is played again—that is, he concludes that such a musical sequence 'means' falling water, and so on. The cinema produced a wealth of type-situations all with corresponding musical background, and it was difficult for cinema musicians to avoid recurring musical clichés. Music teachers have been known to complain of the difficulty they experience in ridding their pupils of aural 'fallacies', to which film music has greatly contributed. But generally speaking, music in the silent cinema had a twofold effect; it made thousands of people who never went inside a concert hall familiar with simplified versions of ambitious classical works, and it gave rise to a form of effortless listening without an exact parallel in earlier phases of our musical history.

III

During the war the cinemas which sprang up everywhere provided a cheap means of allaying boredom: they were reasonably comfortable, and found favour with a clientele which did not normally frequent the theatres. Since the stringent demands for economy curtailed the production of films in Britain, distributors had to rely on importations from America. English audiences took readily to the image of life presented by trans-atlantic producers, and soon accustomed themselves to the conventions of feature-film acting. But by 1918 another form of diversion—namely Jazz—was well established in the United States, and American musicians were ready to introduce it into Europe in succession to the earlier ragtime which had caught on well before the war.

It was in the late summer of 1919 that the 'Original Dixieland Jazz Band' began a three months' season at the Hammersmith Palais de Danse. Playing entirely from memory (not one of them was in the habit of reading music), the Dixielanders performed such classics of jazz as 'Tiger Rag', 'Livery Stable Blues' and 'Sensation Rag'. The dancing craze, which had struck America in 1913, eventually spread to this country. After the war, jazz rhythms gave a certain spice to the night life which was becoming so popular in all the big cities. 'Every legitimate night-club proprietor', wrote W. W. Seabrook in 1924, '. . . knows that he might as well be out of business as to be without a saxophone performer. Players of this instrument are exceptionally rare.'[1] In pre-war days it was customary to engage a small string orchestra for dancing; but the fox-trot and the Charleston called for a less decorous accompaniment. 'The usual dance band', wrote Jack Hylton in 1926, 'consists of three saxophones, three brass instruments, and four rhythmic instruments, the latter acting as a background to all other effects. Thanks to the saxophones, the volume created by a small dance band of this type can equal that of a full "straight" orchestra comprising three or four times the number of players.'[2]

But jazz was not merely a background to dancing: it was a

---

[1] In Sydney A. Mosley, ed., *Brightest Spots in Brighter London* (1924), p. 139.

[2] Jack Hylton, 'Dance Music of To-day' in the *Musical Times*, 1 September 1926, p. 800.

musical entertainment in its own right. As such it gave rise to violent controversies, which continued throughout the 'twenties and 'thirties. One school of thought contended that this hectic and garish music was thoroughly decadent: another body of opinion applauded its verve and elemental power. At a conference of the Incorporated Society of Musicians in 1922, Sir Hugh Allen protested that 'Freak music is becoming more and more aggressive owing to commercialism and the desire for notoriety, and pleasure is being taken too easily in noises and barbaric rhythms, although, while listening, the public is usually primarily engaged in eating or dancing. Because musical taste is not sufficiently educated to appreciate good music, composers, to attract promiscuous and indiscriminate appetites, have adopted unsound procedures and make foul noises. Such pieces are written from a low motive and a bad impulse.' This represents a conventional academic view of the matter. In the estimation of many other serious musicians, however, the phenomenon of jazz was a welcome one, because it introduced elements of dash and brilliance which were missing from modern music as a whole. 'In the course of frequent visits to Hammersmith', writes the French composer Darius Milhaud à propos of Billy Arnold and his band when they were performing at the Palais, '. . . I tried to analyse and assimilate what I heard. What a long way we have travelled from the gypsies who before the war used to pour their insipid, mawkish strains intimately into one's ears.'[1] And a reporter on the *Musical Standard* in 1928 declared: 'Jazz with its brisk and grotesque rhythms has ousted our dismal ballads if it has done nothing else, and the waltz, declining into a state of Turkish delight has revived under this influence. Savagery in art is a tonic—when art is too tepid it is in danger of petering out.'[2] The jazz craze of the 1920s, when it was fashionable to talk about the desirability of releasing inhibitions, bears some resemblance to the waltz mania of a hundred years earlier. But jazz was more closely bound up with social and economic conditions peculiar to the time than was the 'spirit-stirring Waltz' of Byron's satirical poem.

One of these was the change in the status of women, and consequently in the relations between the sexes, which, beginning in the late Victorian era, had been noticeable since the early

---

[1] Darius Milhaud, *Notes Without Music* (New York, 1935), p. 118.
[2] See the *Musical Standard*, 30 June 1928, p. 212.

years of the present century. War conditions had shown that it was an insult to regard women—especially independent single women—as in need of constant protection. By 1918 the parental solicitude displayed by the imperious father in H. G. Wells's novel *Ann Veronica* (1909) was out of date; and whereas in the Victorian and Edwardian periods a chaperone was a *sine qua non* for most respectable young ladies, now in the 1920s the 'Bright Young Things' went to dances of her own accord and stayed out till the small hours. At an earlier stage it was in doubtful taste for a lady to reveal a craving for ballroom dancing, though in 1893 the author of *Etiquette of Good Society* had written that 'young blood always enjoys being in motion; and dancing on the green turf at the close of a summer picnic, after an afternoon's hard work on the lawn-tennis ground, or a carpet waltz impromptu on an autumn evening—each and all are acceptable, and enjoyed with as much zest as the Twelfth-night ball is in cold January; at no season is dancing considered unseasonable'. Despite their considerable formality, balls and dances before the war were arranged for purposes of discreet match-making as much as anything else. After 1918 there was less pretence about this, and with the vogue of the tea-dance and the dinner-dance in the 1920s dancing began to play an important part in the lives of young people anxious to meet members of the opposite sex without the intervention of their elders. The erotic strain in jazz music proved obnoxious to those who regarded dancing as merely a vigorous exercise, but the institution of public dances at regular intervals provided the younger generation with an agreeable prelude to serious courtship.

'Jazz', wrote R. W. S. Mendl in 1927, 'is the product of a restless age: an age in which the fever of war is only now beginning to abate its fury; when men and women, after their efforts in the great struggle, are still too much disturbed to be content with a tranquil existence . . . when America is turning out her merchandise at an unprecedented speed and motor cars are racing along the roads . . . when the extremes of Bolshevism and Fascismo are pursuing their own ways simultaneously, and the whole world is rushing helter-skelter in unknown directions.'[1] The ever-increasing appeal of jazz music in the 'twenties and 'thirties gave it a high market value; it was a consumer good

[1] R. W. S. Mendl, *The Appeal of Jazz* (1927), p. 186.

for which the demand was constantly being stimulated by various assaults upon the public's susceptibilities. Dance music was made as attractive as possible by the use of stunt orchestrations, perpetually changing styles of performance, and novel instrumental feats. And from the outset jazz addressed itself to the young and adventurous. Its proponents scoffed at the sedateness of wisdom and experience. In their publicity they tried to create the impression that jazz-lovers were smart and up-to-the-minute and therefore socially admirable. The characteristic irreverence of the jazz-minded was expressed in the procedure known as 'jazzing the classics', which was defended by some dance musicians on the grounds that it brought serious music down to the level of the man in the street. 'The "highbrows" disdain jazz music,' wrote the *Musical Standard* in 1927, 'but no one can deny there is money in it.' Within ten years, indeed, English jazz musicians had mastered the business of high-pressure salesmanship; their managers, agents, publishers and arrangers quickly responded to the opportunities held open to them. So insidious, for example, was the practice of 'song-plugging' in the early 1930s that dance bands broadcasting from restaurants and hotels had to submit to the B.B.C. full details of their programmes in order to ensure that particular numbers were not repeated too frequently.

A typical professional career of the period was that of Jack Payne, who was for decades one of the best known of British dance-band leaders. In his autobiography, *Signature Tune* (1947), Payne describes how, on his return from war service with the Royal Flying Corps, he got together a small dance band in the Midlands with the intention of cashing in on the fact that 'Everyone was going dance-crazy'. After a period in which he provided music for various hotels and dance halls in the Birmingham area, Jack Payne was inspired by the example of Paul Whiteman, the principal American exponent of 'symphonic jazz', to form a show band and tour the variety theatres. He felt, as he puts it, that there was 'big money on the stage', and he was not the only leading dance musician of the time who saw that substantial fortunes were to be made in organization and agency work rather than executive musicianship itself. Jack Payne's association with the Hotel Cecil's orchestras is particularly interesting. For while he was under contract with the Hotel Cecil,

Payne was also building up a connection in the theatre world. This became necessary because the Hotel Cecil, instead of moving with the times, was then slowly losing ground to rival establishments run on more up-to-date lines. In due course Jack Payne managed to break the monopoly which the Savoy Hotel seemed to hold over broadcast dance music, and his first broadcast from the Hotel Cecil took place on Boxing Day 1925. This was only one of many such rivalries, for the advent of radio stiffened competition among all grades of dance musicians.

IV

In the period 1920 to 1925 a number of new firms sprang up to meet the demand for dance numbers printed in sheet-music form, and the Charing Cross Road area of London became the accepted home of the light-music industry. This found powerful allies in the disc gramophone and radio. During the First World War portable gramophones were in great demand and did much to break the monotony of existence in dug-outs and prison camps. 'Popular patriotic songs were recorded and distributed in thousands', writes Fred Gaisberg; 'the gramophone was encouraged by the military authorities of both sides, who looked upon it as a vital necessity. . . . The vast quantities of cheap gramophones available to the Tommies were later to be found in thousands of humble homes, and so paved the way for the wonderful post-war boom. Estimated sales of songs like "Keep the Home Fires Burning", "Pack up your troubles", "Mademoiselle from Armentières" and "Tipperary" amounted to anything up to half a million discs each.'[1] Before the war gramophone motors had been imported from Germany and Switzerland, but British firms now took up the manufacture of mechanical components for the gramophone trade, and soon over seventy firms were making gramophones, records, needles and other accessories. Fortunately, the gramophone industry remained comparatively free from labour troubles in the period after the Armistice, and advertisements in various musical journals reveal that the companies were making great efforts to improve on pre-war standards of reproduction. As a result the musical profession gradually dropped its prejudices against the gramophone: the

[1] Fred Gaisberg, *Music on Records* (1946), pp. 76–77.

'talking machine' was at length taken with full seriousness. Even before 1920 there had been periodicals devoted to it, but the inception of *The Gramophone* in 1923 shows that the contrivance which ten years earlier had been regarded by music-lovers as almost a toy now enjoyed a moderate critical acclaim.

In his essay on the pianola C. E. M. Joad recalls that during the 1920s the catalogues of available music rolls began to include more and more non-serious items. The gramophone likewise aided the dissemination of light music. In any case it had a number of advantages over the player-piano, the most important being that it required less physical exertion on the part of the person using it. Moreover, it introduced a simulacrum of orchestral tone into the drawing-room, and gave a passable representation of opera. But like other machines it had its drawbacks. For one thing, the necessity of having to change the record every few minutes meant that the listener was inclined to anticipate the conclusion of each side. There was also the problem of finding a suitable sound box and needles. Improved models came on the market every season, and many ingenious devices were thought of to overcome these inconveniences; but so long as 78 r.p.m. remained the standard playing speed for disc gramophone recordings such disabilities necessarily limited the listener's enjoyment. Where long works were concerned the practice of automatic coupling proved a great advantage. It was the advent of reasonably inexpensive radio-gramophone units, however, which made 'high fidelity' reproduction something more than a lucky speculation.

Wireless telephony had been undertaken successfully some years before the First World War, but it was not until the 1920s that regular broadcasts were carried on in this country. Sir Henry Hadow recalls how 'One afternoon in February 1920 a Committee, assembled in the rooms of the Royal Society, was adjourned by its Chairman in order that the members might witness "a rather interesting experiment" which was to be tried in an adjoining lecture theatre. There they heard from two small bits of apparatus a programme of songs, pianoforte pieces, addresses and bursts of applause, emanating as it appeared from a studio in Chelmsford, thirty miles away.'[1] At first, broadcast

---

[1] Henry Hadow, Preface to *New Ventures in Broadcasting: A Study in Adult Education* (1928).

programmes were of an amateurish nature and somewhat parochial in style, but the possibilities of radio were such as to
warrant the formation of companies equipped to send out ambitious and prolonged transmissions. The public for radio in
Britain grew rapidly. 'By the autumn of 1922,' writes Asa
Briggs, 'when the B.B.C. was formed and took over the station,
2 LO had a "public" of about 30,000 licensed "listeners-in" and
a total audience of about 50,000 people, including wireless enthusiasts as far away as the Shetland Islands.'[1] Before the end of
1926 well over two million licences had been issued, and public
interest in the potentialities of radio was greatly increasing. By
June 1939 more than nine million people held licences in this
country. The inauguration of the present British Broadcasting
Corporation was intended to prevent the practice—already common in America—of commercial sponsorship. This may seem to
be of little relevance to music, but it does mean that in this
country manufacturers have had less power than is available to
them in the United States for determining the contents of radio
programmes.

The immediate effect which developments in radio had on
professional musicians was an unfortunate one. Performers in
orchestras and theatre bands concluded that the success of wireless would mean the virtual extinction of public concert-giving
and possibly a serious reduction in dramatic and variety performances. The failure of several concert organizations in the early
days of British broadcasting seemed to confirm these anticipations. The British Women's Symphony Orchestra, for instance,
did not manage to survive, and even the British National Opera
Company, which did excellent work from 1923 to 1929, had
eventually to go into voluntary liquidation. Most musical concerns in this period experienced considerable financial difficulties, and the possibility that the B.B.C. might take advantage of
its position to run concerts at uneconomical rates filled many
interested parties with apprehension. At the time there was a
certain amount of justifiable criticism about the menace of broadcasting, but much more serious was the loss sustained by rank-
and-file musicians when, in 1928, sound films began to replace
silent pictures. This made cinema orchestras redundant, and

[1] Asa Briggs, *The History of Broadcasting in the United Kingdom*, I. *The Birth of Broadcasting* (1961), p. 75.

although the cinema organ still held its own, hundreds of violinists and 'cellists found themselves out of work and with poor prospects of alternative musical employment.

'Broadcasting has indeed disintegrated the musical profession,' said a writer in *The Stage* in 1933, 'and brought widespread distress upon it and upon the music-publishing trade, too.'[1] But this has to be considered in the context of the general economic situation and with reference to competition from sound films and the gramophone. In the period under discussion mechanized reproduction of music had two main consequences: it gradually reduced the sale of sheet music (which only brought in £284,691 in 1933 as against £566,459 in 1925) and it depressed the position of rank-and-file musicians in favour of first-class virtuosi. But though the advent of radio caused a certain amount of contraction in the musical profession generally, it also had beneficial effects which were not fully appreciated at the time. It is certain, for example, that the B.B.C. saved the Queen's Hall Promenade Concerts from disaster. After more than thirty years of reasonable success, the Proms seemed to be threatened during the 1920s with financial collapse: the B.B.C.'s offer to take on responsibility for them thus prevented the break-up of a valuable musical tradition. It is also clear that in the long run broadcasting stimulates concert-going in unexpected ways. This was suggested by the editor of the *Musical Times* in February 1928. He believed that the B.B.C.'s own winter season concerts at Queen's Hall had 'clearly tapped a fresh public. At each concert I have found myself surrounded by refreshingly unsophisticated folk. Evidently they had heard orchestras at home, and had decided to go and see one—for they took in almost as much pleasure through the eye as through the ear. At first one thought these hearers were Promenaders who had stolen back to their old haunt, but clearly they were quite new hands.'[2] Time has shown that the desire to watch favourite performers in the flesh is a constant factor in contemporary musical life, and one which even television has not greatly reduced.

Before the construction of Broadcasting House the B.B.C. did not have at its disposal enough studio space for continuous broadcasting from London. Regional stations were therefore set

---

[1] Quoted in the *Musical Times*, September 1933, p. 806.

[2] *Musical Times*, February 1928, p. 123.

up, and a good deal of use was made of outside broadcasts. In the 1930s at least a dozen London hotels and restaurants were contributing programmes regularly, and light orchestras from seaside resorts were a prominent feature during the summer months. This kind of activity created a 'hidden' audience for many types of music and gave listeners the illusion that they were participating vicariously in a communal experience taking place many miles away. By the time the loudspeaker had superseded earphones in private houses the radio had given birth to a fair number of regular feature programmes, of which Christopher Stone's gramophone record reviews may be quoted as one favourite example. Broadcasting also provoked a series of controversies similar to those which had occurred earlier in connection with the gramophone. How serious, for example, was the element of distortion when music was being broadcast? Is a broadcast somehow *more* faithful to the music than a live performance? Is an audience necessary for a concert to be really successful? These questions and others related to them were frequently thrashed out. They are not susceptible of a final answer, because even when the height of mechanical perfection is reached, tastes differ. On the question of the audience, confusion is caused by statements made by performers themselves: some confess to a degree of nervousness in front of the microphone which they do not feel in the concert hall, while others regard studio conditions as ideal for concentrated and meaningful performances.

It has been said that in the musical sphere broadcasting has finally broken down the class barriers which at an earlier stage kept all but the wealthy from hearing the best music. Radio (and, still more, television) has given the listener a box at Covent Garden and placed him in the best position for hearing the finest orchestras and soloists. Far more important is the fact that radio has at last enabled all listeners to hear great music in its original form. 'My first introduction to the Beethoven Symphonies', wrote a London schoolmistress in 1927, 'was in the form of pianoforte duets; my pupils are learning to appreciate their orchestral colour as well as their form and principal themes by hearing excellent gramophone records.'[1] This sounds plausible until we recall that the early recordings of orchestral works were made

---

[1] Joyce Herman, 'Music in Girls' Schools' in *The Sackbut*, May 1927, p. 293.

possible only by re-scoring them so as to compensate for the deficiencies of acoustical reproduction. Radio has eventually eliminated this necessity; and in modern gramophone recordings also it is no longer necessary to fake the instrumental balance. Another great virtue of broadcasting is that it can present large-scale works with full choral and instrumental forces—something that is quite impossible in the thousand and one churches and chapels throughout the country at which performances of *The Messiah* take place once or twice a year. For generations the great majority of music-lovers have had to be content with 'arrangements' of major classical masterpieces. Now, thanks to the resources on which the B.B.C. is able to draw, faithful renderings of operas, oratorios, ambitious chamber works and experimental compositions are relatively frequent. It would be just as true, of course, to say that radio has helped to popularize the various arrangements of 'The Arrival of the Queen of Sheba', 'Jesu, Joy of Man's Desiring' and 'Jamaican Rumba', but there is no longer any justification for the complaint that the original versions of these pieces are never heard.

Radio has unquestionably made listeners more critical, at least so far as technique goes. It is hardly likely that a man who has listened to accomplished pianists such as Solomon, Myra Hess or Clifford Curzon will be impressed by the playing of less competent performers: and this kind of criterion applies even more sharply where singers are concerned. It could be argued, perhaps, that a ruthless insistence on the first-rate smacks of pedantry, yet one can hardly deny that some branches of musical composition have maintained their hold on the musically literate public simply because the latter were kept in ignorance of anything better. The royalty ballad is one obvious example. There were many admirable compositions in this genre by composers such as John Ireland and Roger Quilter, but the majority of them reached a level of abject sentimentality which seems quite absurd when they are compared with even the simplest songs of Fauré and Tschaikovski. It would be untrue to say that broadcasting has killed the royalty ballad—indeed, the B.B.C. ran its own Ballad Concerts for a number of years and 'song orchestrations' are used regularly in such programmes as 'Grand Hotel'. What radio did, however, was give the royalty-ballad public a chance to revise its preferences. In a different sphere, Hilda Jennings and

Winifred Gill assure us that 'Accustomed to the high standard of execution, and of rhythm in particular, of broadcast music, dancers will not tolerate second-rate playing, even from their friends.'[1]

This question of *tolerance* arises when we come to consider some of the disadvantages of radio—in its cultural aspects, that is. The compulsive appeal of radio has tended, among other things, to make listeners suspect the abilities of artists who have not appeared in front of the microphone. Radio performances have certainly evoked the concert-hall atmosphere within the family circle, but at the same time radio has encouraged a certain superficiality among those who have come to take it for granted that the world's finest singers and players can be heard daily at little cost. And, as Thomas Armstrong pointed out in 1926, 'Mere desire to get perfect mechanical results holds many who have no real enthusiasm for the art'[2]—a feature which has become much more noticeable since 1945. In the concert hall a listener, even if he cannot read music, does gain some impression of the contribution which the various sections of the orchestra are making to the progress of the musical composition being played; over the radio subtleties of scoring are quite likely to pass unnoticed if attention has not been drawn to them beforehand. Music critics and others have tried to forestall this difficulty, and reference will be made to it later. But there is a decided irony in the fact that even those who are quite dogmatic on questions of 'taste' occasionally have a very inadequate knowledge of how musical sounds are produced and how the various parts of symphonies and concertos are held together. Moreover, hundreds of listeners are perfectly content to accept the 'Clock' Symphony on exactly the same terms as 'The Rite of Spring'. The very fact that the B.B.C. (and latterly the Independent Television companies) may command the best talent available is enough to ensure that a good many listeners will never feel strongly the need for *active* participation in musical performances. 'If we are listeners,' it has been said, 'we are only receiving, we are creating nothing, we are giving nothing.'[3] It

[1] Jennings and Gill, *Broadcasting in Everyday Life. A Survey of the Social Effects of the Coming of Broadcasting* (1939), p. 20.

[2] Thomas Armstrong, 'Wireless and the Concert-Goer' in the *Musical Times*, 1 December 1926, p. 1079.

[3] *Music and the Community. The Cambridgeshire Report on the Teaching of Music* (1933), p. 15.

would be ridiculous, of course, to imply that every amateur musician is, in the exactest sense of the word, a 'creative' artist: but there is some virtue (the supporters of the competitive festival movement would say a *supreme* virtue) in wanting to get closer to the music than the merely passive recipient is able to do. Radio—and the gramophone as well—has created a new kind of dilettante whose love of music may be intense, but whose knowledge of the art is severely (and voluntarily) circumscribed.

Yet the effect of broadcasting on amateur music has not been as deplorable as might be imagined. A conference on 'The Future of Amateur Music' arranged jointly by the B.B.C. and the National Federation of Music Festivals and held at Broadcasting House in June 1933 was taken by many people as signifying an implicit recognition on the B.B.C.'s part that broadcasting had to a large extent demoted the amateur. But as F. H. Shera remarked in 1939, 'it would be foolish to ascribe the decline in amateur music-making entirely to the advent of mechanical music. The attractions of the open air, the light car, and the cinema, all consume time once given to the practice of music.'[1] It is also worth remembering that since 1918 a change has taken place in the relationship between parents and children: the *lien* which fathers and mothers formerly held on their sons and daughters is now much weaker than it was in Victorian and Edwardian times. In those days young people learned music largely out of deference to the wishes of their elders, but this incentive has become less powerful (or has been replaced by something else), and advantage is taken of the fact that 'When we can get the best on the wireless, we're not going to put up with the children strumming "The Blue Bells of Scotland".'[2] It is perhaps impossible to measure accurately the loss and gain occasioned by the popularity of radio. Choral societies, certainly, are less numerous today than they were in 1900, but in certain cities amateur orchestras and operatic companies make a very good showing. The brass-band world has not been seriously affected by broadcasting, and many of its long-standing traditions are maintained. Of recent years, guitar playing (thanks largely to the influence of radio) has enjoyed a popularity unheard of before

[1] F. H. Shera, *The Amateur in Music* (1939), p. 67.
[2] Jennings and Gill, *op. cit.*, p. 36.

the Second World War: this has much to commend it, because the guitar is a very suitable instrument for adults who have missed the chance of learning some other instrument at an earlier stage. What is incontestable, however, is the fact that radio has caused thousands of people to regard music simply as an additional or background amenity, a public utility to be switched on and off as unceremoniously as the electricity or water supply. The advocates of musical appreciation—who have held an important place in English education since 1918—regard this as a deplorable attitude. In the words of one report: 'The growing habit of turning on the wireless set or the gramophone as an accompaniment to conversation or on other sociable occasions seems wholly bad: it is bad for the social intercourse, worse for the nervous constitution and worst of all for the musical growth of those present. Real listening demands intense concentration.'[1] The implications of these remarks must now be considered.

V

The musical-appreciation movement has a long history, which may be traced in Percy Scholes's *Music, the Child and the Masterpiece* (1935). A reference to its later phases is necessary here because it takes its place among the countless schemes of reconstruction which were drawn up at the end of the First World War. Recalling the steps which led to the passing of the Education Act of 1918, H. A. L. Fisher wrote: 'The vast expenditure and harrowing anxieties of the time, so far from extinguishing the needs of social progress, helped to promote a widespread feeling for improvement in the general lot of the people . . . The country was in a spending mood and eager to compensate the wastage of war by some contribution to the arts of peace.'[2] In consequence, many schemes were started for the purpose of enabling younger people to enjoy the national heritage in the arts as well as other branches of life. Efforts were made to put new spirit into the provincial festivals and to give fresh encouragement to the competitive festival movement, which had continued on a reduced scale throughout the war years. The Community Singing movement, which was in a sense a rival to

[1] *Music and the Community, ed. cit.*, p. 14.
[2] H. A. L. Fisher, *An Unfinished Autobiography* (1940), p. 94.

the competitive festivals, was set on foot in the mid-'twenties by the *Daily Express* and other newspapers; mass meetings were held in the Albert Hall, London, and in other cities. At one time Lord Beaverbrook and his colleagues were enthusiastic about the possibilities of community singing, though the musical Press was sceptical. As the *Musical Times* commented in April 1927: 'Its musical and artistic value is necessarily limited, but it will have an immense influence on the musical future of the country if a large proportion of those who take part in it will follow Sir Richard Terry's unreported advice and join regularly constituted choral bodies.' The *Music Teacher* regarded the community-singing craze as merely a stunt, and R. H. Hull wrote it off in the *Musical Times* for August 1929 as 'advertisment pure and simple'. Frequent reference is made in literary histories and elsewhere to the post-war disillusionment of the 1920s, but equally characteristic of the time was the idealism which led to the formation of the Arts League of Service, the League of Arts for Civic and National Ceremony, and similar bodies.

Comparable with the Community Singing movement was the campaign to brighten religion, which achieved some prominence in the 1920s. The war had done very little to arrest the decline in church-going, and leading members of the Anglican communion feared that in its lust after trivial diversions the nation had finally forgotten God. The Church had in any case lost touch with the mass of the people, and several attempts were made—among them a revival of religious drama—to regain public confidence. It was suggested that one reason for the empty pews might lie in the fact that so much of the music used in church services was stale and out of date, and there was talk of worshippers staying away from church rather than listen to the 'debased' sacred music of Victorian and Edwardian composers. A revival of English hymnody had started with Robert Bridges's *Yattendon Hymnal* (1899) and the *English Hymnal* (1906): but *Songs of Praise* (1926)—described by Erik Routley as 'breezy, zestful, youthful and fresh in its approach'—was a direct contribution to the religious recovery for which the Church of England hoped. In 1923 a report on *Music in Worship* was issued by the Archbishops' Committee, and this recommended many reforms in the organization of church music. Perhaps the most important outcome of it was the foundation in 1927 of the School of English Church

Music, which has for its main aim the proper training of choristers and the affiliation of choirmasters throughout the Anglican Church. At the time this school was opened not much improvement was called for in the case of cathedrals and collegiate churches: it was in the parish churches that conditions for rendering liturgical music were less than satisfactory. As the *Musical Times* for May 1928 put it: 'There are today many parish churches at which, for various reasons, the musical direction is in the hands of amateurs and semi-professionals.' In a number of smaller towns, indeed, organists gave up ecclesiastical work when the cinema offered more lucrative employment, and it was becoming more and more difficult to maintain choirs capable of revivifying the musical side of church life. All denominations were affected by the increasing secularity of the time. 'I know the greatness of Christianity,' wrote D. H. Lawrence in 1924; 'it is a past greatness. . . . The adventure is gone out of Christianity. We must start on a new venture towards God.' This attitude is reflected even in church music. For though new hymns, anthems and other choral pieces were plentiful, the practice of 'Community Hymn Singing' anywhere but in church became for many people a substitute for religious services themselves.

In the post-war period a considerable effort was made to assert what may be called the 'Englishness' of English music—as can be seen to some extent in *Songs of Praise*. The British Music Society (founded in 1918) aimed to promote interest in the work of such composers as Peter Warlock, Cyril Scott, Frank Bridge and Ivor Gurney, and in the 'twenties Arnold Bax, John Ireland and Vaughan Williams produced some of their most ambitious compositions. Their efforts were in a way a response to happenings in the musical world abroad, but at the same time several composers tried to advance the cause espoused before the war by the folk-song enthusiasts. Instrumental arrangements of folk tunes appeared in considerable numbers, and the adaptations made by Percy Grainger and others represent an attempt to popularize homespun melodies outside the circles in which Cecil Sharp's disciples moved. It is safe to say, however, that few of the academically trained composers—with the exception of those who, like Eric Coates, remained respectably conventional—made any significant contact with the 'folk'. Surreptitiously, as it were, William Walton and Constant Lambert adopted the jazz idiom, but the works in which they exploited it were intended for a 'concert' public: they were powerless to make any impression on the vast audiences which throve on *Hit the Deck* (Vincent Youmans, 1927), *Bitter Sweet* (Noel Coward, 1929) and the C. B. Cochran productions.

Music and musical education were very much affected by the aspirations which encouraged the spread of the folk-dance movement, the provision of children's concerts, the establishment of musical summer schools and the publication of such journals as *The Music Teacher* (1922–37) and *Music and Youth* (1921–32). The inter-war period witnessed a great deal of innovation in school music-making, such as the organization of classes in recorder playing, the formation of percussion bands among younger children, and the establishment of school orchestras (though some local authorities had made it possible for these to be started before the First World War). And it is clear that the apostles of musical appreciation were actuated by a common desire—to resist the worst effects consequent upon the commercialization of music. In the words of Stewart Macpherson, 'the true appreciation of music by the community at large can only come about by means of some kind of systematic endeavour, on the part of musicians, to present the best examples of their art in such a way as to make clear to all and sundry that in such things there is really some element of greatness and truth which it is *worth while troubling about*'.[1] The italics are Macpherson's own; and it is evident from this passage and from the rest of his theorizing that, in common with many others, he believed that the public at large was being subjected to musical experiences which were emphatically *not* worth troubling about.

The value of musical appreciation had been frequently discussed before the war. To many teachers and examiners it was apparent that the musical instruction given in most schools still left much to be desired. (An exception must, of course, be made in respect of the public schools and many of the larger grammar schools.) Excellent though the Tonic Sol-Fa régime was, it tended to harden into a stereotyped system for drumming a small selection of songs into classes of children whose fundamental musical sensibility was not necessarily being exercised by the

[1] Stewart Macpherson, *The Appreciation Class* (1923), p. 3.

ability to sing 'by note'. As a pleasant form of drill the Tonic Sol-Fa system was admirable, but it did not go very far towards making the children perceive structural relationships in musical composition. In any case Tonic Sol-Fa was originally intended to assist the learning of vocal music, but now instrumental music was gaining in popularity, which meant that students had of necessity to learn the staff notation if they were going to get anywhere at all. A Tonic Sol-Fa training, admittedly, led thousands of people to discover that a good deal of satisfaction could be derived from cultivating an intellectual skill in association with others, but it failed, by and large, to suggest the depth of enjoyment which lies in the development of individual taste and awareness. 'It is really surprising', wrote Charles T. Smith in 1918, 'how many members of choirs, orchestral and choral societies there are who perform their allotted tasks and have little or no interest in music, comprehensively speaking.'[1] These were the professed music-lovers; but the great majority of people, it must be remembered, received no musical instruction of any kind except at elementary schools and to a less degree at Sunday schools. Educationalists now needed to be persuaded that the time was ripe for a big drive in favour of general musical education—but on a much broader basis than that of the simple singing class. In some respects, conventional private teaching was also at fault: the local examination system on which so much importance was placed tended to encourage technical dexterity at the expense of critical insight. But in any case the rising generation must be put on its guard against the enticements of the innumerable hucksters now crowding the musical marketplace.

In the decades after 1918 musical appreciation was taken up energetically by great numbers of music teachers. In practice it entailed a certain amount of straightforward analysis of musical form backed up by factual information about conditions of performance, instrumentation, musical conventions, and so forth. All this needed to be set out in such a way as to diminish the apparent initial difficulties. Enthusiasts for musical appreciation were guided by a variety of aspirations, but at the back of their minds was the conviction that if the layman were induced to understand and appreciate music of first-rate quality he would

[1] Charles T. Smith, *The Music of Life* (1919), p. 12.

ipso facto be inclined to eschew whatever was inferior. There may have been a certain naïvety about some of these assumptions. But the amount of music now disseminated publicly was so large and so disparate in its nature that the ordinary listener needed some elementary guidance as to what really was worth while. The harmful effects of the 'mass media' could best be counteracted by recourse to the mass media themselves: and in this way the gramophone became the first major ally of the musical appreciation movement, since it had so many obvious advantages over the classroom piano. Soon after the First World War the Gramophone Company began to develop the possibility of using gramophones extensively in schools and colleges. Special records were issued and informative leaflets made available, and among the commentators engaged to write explanatory notes were such men as Walter Yeomans, Alec Robertson and Percy Scholes (1877–1958).

Scholes's position as a popularizer of knowledge is comparable with that of Charles Knight, the editor of *The Penny Magazine.* He began his career as an assistant librarian at the Yorkshire College (now Leeds University) and cultivated a passion for collecting and classifying detailed information. He had some excellent teaching experience at Kent College, Canterbury, Kingswood College (South Africa) and the Leeds School of Music; he also engaged in adult education and was the founder of the Home Music Study Union, on the lines of the National Home Reading Union. Scholes's musical abilities were made known to the editor of *The Times* by Dr. Herbert Thompson, then music critic of the *Yorkshire Post,* and he eventually worked for several London papers. During the Great War he was in charge of the 'Music for the Troops' section of the Y.M.C.A., and continued this activity into the demobilization period. Scholes was a very popular lecturer and a voluminous author. His various Listener's Guides and other expository writings display an extraordinary capacity for handling complicated subjects in a lively and unpretentious manner. Unlike some musicologists, Scholes was very much alive to developments in non-serious music, and in common with another great musical educator of this period, Sir Walford Davies, he addressed himself with a kind of missionary fervour to the questions likely to be asked him by the Plain Man. But though Scholes was certainly an enthusiast for broadcasting as a channel for popular instruction, it was Walford Davies whose later career was more completely identified with the art of explaining the 'Foundations of Music' over the microphone.

Henry Walford Davies (1869–1941) was a fine all-round musician who had had experience of almost every kind of serious musical activity to be found in England from the 1890s onwards. He was trained as an organist, and his main appointments were at the Temple Church and later at St. George's Chapel, Windsor. After the war, in which he took part in the 'Music in Wartime' movement and acted as director of music for the R.A.F., Davies became Professor of Music at Aberystwyth and was invited to co-ordinate musical affairs throughout Wales. In this capacity he developed the individual style of lecturing which served him so well when in 1924 he was called upon to present music courses on the radio. His 'Music and the Ordinary Listener' series for adults began in 1926 and ran for four years. He was a familiar figure in educational circles, and A. E. F. Dickinson has written of him: 'Sir Walford Davies's musical sincerity, illustrative charm and early appearance in the field, entitle him to a high place among the friends of the new and vast listening-in public.'[1] It would be out of place to examine here the charge—made with particular vehemence by Kaikhosru Sorabji—that musical appreciation is something which cannot be taught (least of all *en masse*), and that the whole musical-appreciation movement was a prolonged imposture. At this stage we may simply recapitulate that throughout the 1920s and 1930s a triple combination of cinema, radio and gramophone was making available for public consumption an enormous amount of music, good, bad and indifferent. Our concern now is to examine the cumulative effect of this on taste in general—particularly as revealed during the Second World War.

VI

When the war broke out in September 1939 there was an immediate cancellation of public musical activities. The general fear of attack from the air made the Government decide that theatres and concert halls must be closed by 6 p.m. The Promenade Concerts terminated abruptly on September 1st, and for a

[1] A. E. F. Dickinson, *Musical Experience* (1932), p. 69.

time home broadcasting was confined to one wavelength, the various departments of the B.B.C. being evacuated to remote parts of the kingdom. The restrictions imposed by blackout regulations threatened to dislocate professional entertainments altogether. But in due course the situation became less tense, and things went on much as usual until the really serious air raids started in the summer of 1940. Recalling the situation in the First World War, Sir Henry Wood in a letter to *The Times* on 7 September 1939 asked: 'Are all our British artists, vocal and instrumental and dramatic, who have devoted their lives to their art, to be turned down to face, in many cases, I fear, dreadful poverty just because their vocation, and particular training, is not of technical service in wartime?' But although some musicians and actors did suffer hardship for this reason, the situation as it existed in the early days of the 1914–18 War was not repeated.

This time the position as regards foreign musicians was completely different. For some years many victims of Nazi persecution had fled to England and America, and all sections of the English musical profession benefited by the presence of players and teachers who had been denied the chance of making a career in Germany. During the first years of the war the larger orchestras and opera companies faced a difficult period, but they were able to meet it by going on tour. In time, the various army commands set up choral and orchestral groups, and organizations were got together for the entertainment of troops and civilians alike. These worked with great efficiency. There was, in fact, a phenomenal demand for all kinds of musical enterprise. This was catered for by the Entertainments National Service Association on the one hand and the Council for the Encouragement of Music and the Arts on the other—the former representing (roughly) variety, and the latter 'the arts' (of music, ballet, drama and painting).

These two organizations were not mutually exclusive, and though C.E.M.A. did not present variety performances, E.N.S.A. concerts were frequently of an entirely serious nature. Here it may be worth recalling that the work of C.E.M.A. had to some extent been anticipated a few years before the war by a body called the League of Audiences, of which the Vice-Presidents included Lady Howard de Walden, B. Seebohm Rowntree and

R. H. Tawney. The League of Audiences had as one of its main objects the preservation of personal as distinct from mechanized interpretations of music and drama. It was not hostile to mechanization as such, but it maintained that this must not be allowed to supplant personal interpretation. The League had wider aspirations, however. In the words of its organizing secretary (in 1936), 'Many influential people share with thoughtful legislators a growing concern about the problem of leisure. Enforced unemployment has already made it serious, and with the shorter working day, which is a certainty of the future, it will become more so. Cultural recreation needs stimulus and direction.' Similarly in 1931 an organization known as The Leisure Society issued a proclamation to the effect that it intended 'to preach a wider and richer use of leisure; and to this end to encourage all art, research, scholarship, travel, crafts and sport'. But so far as music was concerned the League of Audiences did not mean to rely on the good effects of the musical appreciation movement: it proposed 'to organize in every constituency a demand from the electors that the Government shall give to Music and Drama the practical recognition which it already gives to Libraries, Museums and Picture Galleries'. To this end it framed a Music and Drama Bill under which eight Commissioners would be appointed to encourage musical and dramatic art and to awaken in audiences a sense of their powers and responsibilities. The League of Audiences' good intentions were largely frustrated by the onset of the war, but many of its principles were acted on by C.E.M.A. in the years that followed.

The sudden wartime demand for music has been much discussed and can be easily misunderstood. In the letter quoted above, Sir Henry Wood wrote: 'In the last Great War, I received thousands of letters from the trenches begging us to keep the 'Proms' going, and the Sunday Afternoon Concerts, as they (the correspondents) were longing for "leave" and wanted to come and hear and see the real thing.' A similar situation arose in the Second World War, and in a great number of cases the uncertainty of life quickened the demand for serious music. Yet at the same time there was also a considerable boom in light entertainment. Once longer hours of opening were permitted, dance halls and night clubs were crowded, and 'fashionable West-End resorts like the Dorchester, Quaglino's and the Café de Paris reported tremendous business'.[1] The inauguration of the Forces' Programme in February 1940 gave scope for variety artists who could appease homesickness and induce a cheerful outlook. It was important that singers and instrumentalists should make a strong personal appeal to servicemen—hence the popularity of artists like Ann Shelton and Vera Lynn. 'If you don't happen to approve of the Forces Programme,' wrote Antonia White in 1941, 'remember that it was based on the express wishes of the soldiers, sailors and airmen for whom it was planned. Remember, too, the conditions in which it is usually heard. A man sitting quietly by his own fireside can concentrate on a Beethoven string quartet or a Shaw play. No soldier, however intelligent, can listen in the same concentrated way in a crowded canteen.'[2] As before, men in the armed forces sang their own songs, on and off duty. But by comparison with those of the First World War, the Second World War songs—the product, for the most part, of Tin Pan Alley or its English equivalent—are negligible. 'There'll always be an England' and 'We're going to hang out the washing on the Siegfried Line' had enormous sales, it is true: but no one can pretend that the years 1939 to 1945 brought forth anything comparable musically with 'Keep the Home Fires Burning'.

The apparently unquenchable thirst for music can be attributed in part to the fact that from the autumn of 1939 onwards military preparations caused a continual shifting about of personnel and sudden concentrations of population in unexpected places. Navy, Army and Air Force stations could provide audiences at almost any hour of the day, and men and women were only too glad to break the routine of wartime existence. As members of a group, ordinary people tend to follow inclinations they would not pursue individually. When, therefore, concerts and dramatic entertainments were provided as part of the campaign to boost morale, many people found themselves attending symphony concerts and chamber-music recitals almost as a matter of course. At the height of the blitz variety artists put on musical entertainments in the disused tube stations where Londoners were sheltering, and George Stratton describes how after the air-raid sirens had sounded at the end of a Promenade Con-

---

[1] Tom Harrisson and Charles Madge, eds., *War Begins at Home* (1940), p. 225.
[2] Antonia White, *BBC At War* (1941), p. 8.

cert he and his colleagues would continue with an impromptu chamber recital until the all-clear made it safe for the audience to leave the hall.[1]

A typical instance of the transformation brought about by the war in comparatively uneventful places—though it could be paralleled by many more impressive examples—is the case of a small south-Midlands town, Bletchley. Before the war, Bletchley was known to travellers on the Euston-Crewe line as an undistinguished railway junction. Roughly equidistant from Oxford and Cambridge, it housed a few small factories and had a slowly rising population. Soon after the war began, an important Government Department was moved to Bletchley Park; this brought hundreds of 'billetees' into the district, among them a high proportion of intellectuals who happened in many cases to be professional or semi-professional musicians. During the same period the B.B.C. Symphony Orchestra was resident at Bedford, and the Corn Exchange was invariably crowded when broadcast concerts were thrown open to the public. A great many Bletchley Park personnel lodged at Bedford, and from a musical point of view Bedford also was a thriving place during the 1940s. It declined in this respect after the war, and when in the early 1960s the B.B.C. Symphony Orchestra returned to give a Sunday-afternoon concert under Rudolf Schwartz the Corn Exchange was almost half empty.

For thousands of people not actually in the fighting services the period from 1940 to 1945 was full of novelty and interest. One typical development was the formation of music clubs, many of them supported by C.E.M.A. The Council's report for 1944, for instance, spoke of one such group in a North Western town which grew out of a single C.E.M.A. concert. This club managed to enrol 350 subscribers, and the kind of progress it made is representative of the enterprise which prevailed almost everywhere. During the war itself—and afterwards—it was only natural that a seemingly propitious situation should be spoken of with pride. Such ventures as the National Gallery Concerts, the Royal Exchange Concerts, the provincial tours of the London orchestras, and the increasing popularity of ballet and opera all seemed to indicate that there need be no further discussion about

[1] See Hubert Foss and Noel Goodwin, eds., *London Symphony: Portrait of an Orchestra* (1954), p. 203.

the necessity for elementary musical-appreciation classes. Gramophone records (despite the imposition of purchase tax) sold by the hundred thousand, and new musical journals started up to meet the demand for *rapportage* and critical comment. All this was taken as a sign that ordinary people were anxious to educate themselves in the art of responding sensitively to the world's musical masterpieces.

Up to a point the available evidence supports this kind of interpretation—though there is also another side to the question. 'Despite the absence of hundreds of professionals and amateurs on service,' wrote R. J. Manning in 1947, 'despite the blackout and general war-weariness, music has had in this country an extraordinary flowering. This increased activity, however, raises certain problems. It will be very easy for the growth to decay as quickly as it came, and for this disorganized, almost hectic music-making to have a deleterious effect in the long run upon standards of musical taste.'[1] Wartime music-making did act as a truly enlightening force, and it brought to notice talent that would otherwise have remained uncultivated. At the same time it revealed the existence of a large and relatively unadventurous 'middlebrow' audience of catholic rather than discriminating taste. This was reflected time and again in the programmes presented by the leading concert organizations. As a writer in the *Annual Register* for 1943 put it, 'This sudden propagation of the masterpieces was no bad thing in itself: nobody wished to complain that Beethoven was being listened to by more people than ever before. It was the misdirection of the new industry that aroused misgivings. The new audience was being taught to believe that the highest musical ideal lay in the colourful, emotional, and impressive effect produced only by a large and varied body of instruments. Moreover, this one-sided view was being further narrowed by a limited choice of music. Travelling orchestras and their impresarios were more concerned with box-office returns than with the spread of appreciation; so they fell into the easy habit of repeating the works that drew the biggest crowds, and the crowds fell into the easy habit of assembling for the works that were most often repeated.'[2]

[1] R. J. Manning, 'The Future of the Amateur' in the *Music Review*, VIII (1947), p. 140.
[2] M. Epstein, ed., *The Annual Register* 1943 (1944), pp. 346–7.

Symphony orchestras, like other business concerns, are obliged to balance their books, and we shall see presently some of the difficulties this entails. But they can hardly be blamed for trying to attract large audiences. The effect of the procedure noted by the *Annual Register* was to distend the scope of ostensibly 'serious' musical programmes by the inclusion of works from the repertoire of lighter music, so that an evening which began with the 'Egmont' Overture, followed by a concerto or symphony, might conclude with some miscellaneous operatic pieces, the 'Merry Widow' waltz and 'The Stars and Stripes'. This pattern is familiar from the promenade concerts of an earlier day, but the strength of 'middlebrow' taste in the 1940s was admirably demonstrated by the case of the 'Warsaw Concerto'.

In its original setting the 'Warsaw Concerto' formed part of the sound track for the film *Dangerous Moonlight*. As a rule only a very small percentage of the music written for films makes its way into the concert programmes, but Richard Addinsell's *Dangerous Moonlight* score is an exception. The 'Warsaw Concerto' itself is a short movement for piano and orchestra; it would more properly be described as a rhapsody rather than a concerto, but the title is appropriate because Addinsell's music bears a strong resemblance to that of Rachmaninov, whose Second Piano Concerto was also extremely popular during the war years. Heavily romantic in style and technically brilliant, the 'Warsaw Concerto' is comparable from a musical point of view with Gershwin's *Rhapsody in Blue*, but its significance—quite apart from its association with the cinema—lies in the fact that it was received with rapturous applause by audiences who were convinced that in responding to it they were enjoying authentic 'classical' music. In the estimation of thousands the 'Warsaw Concerto' was placed on the same level as the Grieg and Tschaikovski concertos, and was indeed frequently played along with them in the same programme. At the height of its popularity much fine music was being written for film productions by British composers such as Walton, Bax and Vaughan Williams, yet none of this enjoyed the vogue of the 'Warsaw Concerto', which was published in several arrangements, issued on records and broadcast at least once or twice a week. Its triumphant success was due to the skill with which the composer managed to arouse the susceptibilities of the middlebrow audience—which is, in the last analysis, a product of the commercialism by which the present century of musical history is distinguished.

But the 'Warsaw Concerto' is, after all, only one item in a very large repertoire, and compositions which resemble it in mode of appeal have existed in one form or another for a long time. It is, of course, easy to sneer at the middlebrow public; if the musical appreciation movement had really been effective, we might submit, the kind of music represented by the 'Warsaw Concerto' would not have thrilled huge crowds, for the majority of listeners would have spurned such obvious pastiche. But the position is not quite as simple as that, and the association of Richard Addinsell's name with that of Liszt and Rachmaninov is very much to the point. For if only the professors of musical appreciation had done their work more thoroughly they would have been in honour bound to make quite clear that a great deal of the music written over the past hundred years or so by well-known composers falls decisively, when submitted to close examination, within the middlebrow range. This fact is given tacit recognition by conductors of light music such as Kostelanetz and Mantovani, who are in the habit of including 'light classics' —'Finlandia', 'Invitation to the Waltz', the Hungarian Rhapsodies, and so on—in their programmes along with selections from *Rose Marie* and *South Pacific*. This practice may well antagonize the *précieuses* of our time. Yet the middlebrow audience, whatever its detractors may say, has an important function in current musical life: it helps materially, by the purchase of gramophone records, wireless licences and electrical equipment, to subsidize the production of music which appeals to the tastes it does not happen to share.

VII

'What, with all this affluence and opportunity', asked Robert Bell in 1933, 'will the position be in thirty years? . . . Will the rising generation continue to provide an eager audience for Bach and Beethoven and Mozart as they seem to do for the Savoy operas?'[1] At this stage—though taking a somewhat broader view than Robert Bell, who confined himself to radio—we can

[1] Robert Bell, 'The BBC and the Family' in *Music and Letters*, January 1933, p. 50.

attempt an answer to these questions. In music, as in other aspects of social life, the post-war period has certainly been one of affluence and opportunity. There are even signs that in one respect the glut of music has had a deleterious effect on general musical sensibility: it has made the average man more disposed to endure a constant stream of sound for hours on end. How much this is a legacy of the Forces Programme it would be hard to say, because such conditions were observable in the 1930s. Yet the number of people who keep the radio on for most of the day, irrespective of programme, is surprisingly large. The virtues of 'Music While you Work' as an 'organized reintroduction into social life of one of the most elemental effects of music on man' being acknowledged,[1] it is now customary to find wireless sets operating continuously in factories, workshops, and even on building sites, the strains of light music intermingling with the hum of flywheels, grindstones and automatic drills. In other surroundings, thanks to the transistor set and tape-recordings, it is possible for some kind of music to accompany all human activities, and the juke box has now become such a common feature of coffee bars and snack counters that no one nowadays need fear the agony of complete silence.

But while it cannot be denied that as a commodity music is now extremely cheap, it must also be admitted that the range of opportunities open to those who want to make music themselves or to listen to it purposefully is unusually varied. Here it is worth our while to notice that during the Second World War several new types of musical-appreciation movements arose in connection with adult education. The most popular of these were the lecture courses given by Walter Dobson and Walter Young to civilians and members of the Forces. Dobson and Young evolved a highly successful technique for making serious music entertaining. They first teamed up in 1941, and for some years were employed by the Central Advisory Council for Education in H.M. Forces, their method consisting of an informal talk by Dobson illustrated by musical extracts played on the gramophone which Young operated. By some critics Dobson and Young were spurned as cheapjacks who were smart enough at raising a laugh, but not to be taken seriously. Others regarded their procedure as

[1] See Richard Freymann, 'Music While You Work' in the *Musical Times*, November 1941, p. 397.

legitimate, since they had 'published the banns of marriage between Education and Enjoyment'.[1] In the 1940s they were constantly in demand at youth clubs, community centres and
gramophone circles; they broadcast frequently in the 'Music
with a Smile' series, and after the war appeared on television.

Very different from Dobson and Young were lecturers like
Michael Tippett and Wilfrid Mellers, who worked with more
advanced adult groups. They were notable for, among other
things, their anxiety to foster a respect for pre-classical music at
a time when, as we have seen, the standard works of a small
number of composers—Beethoven, Brahms, Tschaikovski, Sibelius—were being repeated over and over again in the concert
halls of Britain. In 1939, it would be safe to say, a taste for the
music of Byrd, Gibbons, Gesualdo and Monteverdi was just as
much a 'minority' taste as a *penchant* for Bartok, Hindemith or
Stravinski. A number of contemporary composers, of whom
Mellers and Tippett were only two, propounded the theory that
musical appreciation of the conventional kind must be informed
by a sharp sense of historical perspective brought to bear on 'this
modern stuff' as well as on music written before the time of
Handel. This was one of the best ways of utilizing musical knowledge acquired by men like Arnold Dolmetsch, Safford Cape,
Edmund Fellowes and other editors. These wartime efforts to
give currency to music hitherto supposed to be of merely antiquarian interest are important because they helped to strengthen
the case for an additional radio programme devoted entirely to
'cultural' transmissions. The Third Programme, established in
1946, was a significant item in the social history of our music,
because it at once sharpened the distinctions between highbrow,
middlebrow and lowbrow; it also further increased the scope of
broadcasting in this country by making timetables more flexible
and by broadening the repertoire of works performed.

The Third Programme is one of a number of agencies serving
the interests of two groups in particular—musical 'connoisseurs'
and non-executant amateurs. Over the past twenty years or so
there have been many developments in musical education—the
growth of the Rural Music Schools, the establishment of week-
end courses at adult colleges, the great success of the National

[1] 'An Observer with the Forces', 'Dobson and Young' in *Adult Education*, XVI
(June 1944), p. 156.

Youth Orchestra, etc. Yet in spite of these, the number of amateur musicians who actively engage in music-making is still greatly exceeded by those who, while professing an enlightened interest in music, have no inclination to play or sing. Whether or not it is advisable to weed out the unpromising would-be performers and convert them into intelligent listeners is difficult to decide. It may be, indeed, that many unmusical devotees are voluntarily suppressing the urge to become 'passengers' in choirs and orchestras. But the fact is that the *typical* amateur musician these days is not a pianist, a violinist, a 'cellist or a choir member: he is an ardent enthusiast for the long-playing record or the tape-recorder. And the range of music now available on disc records and tape is so vast that a young person's reluctance to embark on an exacting course of music study can be understood.

It would take too long to enumerate those musical phenomena of the post-war period which have become standing invitations to connoisseurship: the establishment of 'celebrity' festivals at Edinburgh, Cheltenham, Aldeburgh, Bath and elsewhere; the reconstitution of C.E.M.A. as the Arts Council; the Bryanston, Dartington Hall and Canford Summer Schools; the resumption of the Glyndebourne opera seasons; the B.B.C. Invitation Concerts, and so on. These events naturally give prominence to personalities, of whom perhaps the most interesting to the social historian is the composer Benjamin Britten. Britten first came to public notice in the 1930s when he produced large quantities of music for plays and for films such as the G.P.O. Film Unit's *Night Mail* and *Coal Face*; he allied himself with the 'intellectual Left' and wrote music for W. H. Auden's *Our Hunting Fathers*, Louis Macneice's *Out of the Picture* and Randall Swingler's *Ballad for Heroes*. By 1940 Britten had revealed himself as competent in practically all forms of musical composition. But it was in the post-war period that his full stature became evident; his *Peter Grimes* (1945) has been called 'the first great English opera of the century'.[1]

'The special significance of Britten as a composer', writes Eric Walter White, 'is that in an age when there is a perilous tendency for the artist to become divorced from society, he has succeeded to a unique extent in bridging that gap. The best of

[1] Eric Blom, *Music in England* (revised ed., 1947), p. 249.

his music meets with the approval, not only of the connoisseur, but also of the general public. This can be seen most clearly in his operas and in many of his choral and vocal works'.[1] This pronouncement must not be accepted without qualification, however. We have heard a great deal in the past thirty or forty years about the necessity of bringing the artist and his audience together again, and we have a right to know precisely how this can be done. In this connection Britten's record is illuminating. It is necessary to stress that he began his career as a composer of incidental music, though unlike many other composers of our time he is not committed to any particular type of writing. He is a distinguished practical musician, however, with a concert 'presence' and a brilliant keyboard technique which tells in his favour: and Paul Beard has testified that of all the well-known composers under whose baton he performed in the course of a long career as orchestral leader, none (and the names include Kodaly, Strauss, Sibelius, Hindemith and many others) had such a sure command of conducting as did Benjamin Britten. By now such works as *The Young Person's Guide to the Orchestra* and the *Serenade* for tenor, horn and strings have become favourites with the 'general' public, and Britten's operas, certainly, have won him a European reputation. We may sum up their importance as follows: first, Britten shows in his choice of subject a strong disposition towards social realism rather than a fondness for heavily romantic situations; secondly, he has broken with many of the accepted conventions of presentation in order to develop his own individual style; and thirdly, he has been able to make articulate an attitude towards the audience which is rather uncommon. This can best be expressed by saying that Britten does all he can to implicate the listener—to draw him into the music, so to speak, and make him a participant rather than a mere spectator. This tendency was overtly demonstrated in *Let's Make an Opera*.

This work represents an attempt to solve the problem of how to create music-drama with only limited resources. It was originally performed by the English Opera Group, of which Britten was the founder. The *dramatis personae* include six adult singers and seven children's voices, with an accompaniment of strings, percussion and piano. In the first part the miniature opera 'The Little Sweep' is conceived and then put into rehearsal, the audi-

---

[1] Eric Walter White, *Benjamin Britten* (2nd ed., 1954), p. vii.

ence being issued with song sheets and invited to join in some of the items; after the interval 'The Little Sweep' is performed by the full company. In other hands than those of Britten, *Let's Make an Opera*—which is billed as a musical 'entertainment'— might have turned out to be a novel musical freak. But in actual fact the opera itself is thoroughly convincing, because the characters really come to life and enact a theme which can be taken seriously.

Let's Make an Opera, although small in scope when compared with *Peter Grimes*, cannot succeed unless there is a total *rapprochement* between the actors and the audience. Many people who attended performances of it without having previous knowledge of its structure found that Britten's music was quite as meaningful to them as, say, Sullivan's—and far more moving than anything in the 'musicals' which were then coming on to the English stage in something of a spate. By reason of its unconventional melodic shapes and unorthodox procedures, *Let's Make an Opera* may never achieve the acclaim that greeted *My Fair Lady* or *West Side Story*. But the very fact that it made some impression on a public which is inclined to be hostile towards opera (especially by a modern composer) is instructive. It indicates that one first-rate composer can, without condescension or loss of prestige, communicate directly with an audience for whom the symphonies of Walton and Vaughan Williams are too difficult. Britten is incapable of 'writing down' to a wide public; but this is not the only work (the *St. Nicholas* Cantata is another) which suggests that a musician of integrity may succeed—given the right conditions—in *educating* his listeners while providing them with music which is meant for their immediate enjoyment.

Opinions differ as to the merits of Britten's operas other than *Peter Grimes*. But there can be no doubt that his success with that work aroused the hopes of those who foresaw a promising future for operas by English composers. Yet the large-scale works by Tippett, Walton, Goossens and others have not caught on with the public which enjoys an occasional Sadler's Wells or Carl Rosa performance of *Madam Butterfly* or *Il Trovatore* sung in English. The presence of versatile musicians is not enough, it seems, to make the English people as opera-conscious as music-lovers in other European countries are said to be. Opera has its devotees, of course; but it is not an integral part of our social life in the same way that the orchestral concert—within limits—and the gramophone industry are. Something must now be said about recent developments in these spheres of musical activity.

By 1947 there were signs that the great wartime boom in music-making was slackening. Most of the metropolitan musical organizations continued to flourish, but the major national orchestras (with the exception of those employed by the B.B.C.) foresaw a dangerous period ahead. Despite the great popularity of orchestral music, it became apparent that permanent orchestras cannot now maintain their existence without heavy subsidies. This does not apply so much to smaller ensembles and chamber groups of which the members are not full-time salaried players. But at rates insisted on by the Musicians' Union, the cost of a single orchestral concert may be anything up to £500. Thus in order to remain solvent a large orchestra will need to undertake four or five concerts a week, which entails extensive travelling and a consequent diminution of time available for rehearsals. Broadcasting and recording fees may account for some part of the total income, but if a satisfactory profit margin is to be ensured, audiences will need to be consistently large week in and week out. Since the war, however, the public for miscellaneous orchestral concerts (outside the larger cities, that is) has dropped off considerably—though even now certain types of programme (*The Messiah* at Christmastime, for example) will prove a sell-out. In the provinces there are not many concert halls as large as the Albert Hall and the Royal Festival Hall, and it is not too much to say that a modern symphony orchestra needs a capacity audience of Royal Festival Hall size for *every* concert if its finances are to remain intact. Such support can hardly be hoped for now (things were bad enough, as the record of the London Symphony Orchestra shows, after the *First* World War). So orchestras like the Hallé, the Royal Liverpool Philharmonic and the Birmingham Symphony have had to fall back on guarantees supplied from public funds. Yet even with an annual grant from the Leeds City Council the Yorkshire Symphony Orchestra failed to survive. In some cases regional orchestras, as at Newcastle and Bournemouth, have succeeded in persuading the public to subscribe, and supporters' clubs have been organized: yet nothing can disguise the fact that, as compared with thirty or forty years ago, and taking the country as a whole, the public orchestral concert, considered as a straight-forward business proposition, is in decline.

Its place has, to a large extent, been taken by the radio and the gramophone, but especially the latter. So far as the average listener is concerned, it can be argued that it is preferable to employ a small number of first-rate organizations producing high-class records and regular broadcasts than to solicit the public's support for concerts given by provincial artists whose standards of performance are less than satisfactory. Better one Philharmonia Orchestra making half a dozen records each year, it might be said, than half a dozen orchestras in the provinces struggling to secure an audience on grounds of local patriotism. Against this argument is the unquestionable fact that the concert-hall atmosphere has attractions which are peculiar to itself. The element of sociability does have some influence in persuading the public to patronize 'live' performances—for which reason the public concert will not vanish altogether. Yet there is no denying the overwhelming importance of the record-player in current musical life. The reports issued by such companies as Decca and E.M.I. reveal a huge annual turnover from the marketing of discs, and the introduction of the long-playing record in the 1950s pushed the sales of gramophone equipment far above the wartime average. The generation which was coming to maturity in the 1950s finds it difficult to believe that not so many years ago a quartet or symphony usually took up five or six separate records; but now that two symphonies can be contained on one disc a small cabinet is sufficient to hold a veritable record library. And the once-prized 'Society' volumes which seemed such luxuries are now completely outmoded, since the items of which they were made up have in most cases been recorded anew several times. Not only are long-playing records better value from a purely technical point of view than 78 r.p.m. discs: they will also endure a greater number of playings before showing signs of fatigue. What is more, the fact that gramophone records are an expendable commodity causes very little concern to present-day discophiles. The main purchasers of popular recordings—young people in the 16 to 25 age group—are now earning high wages at an earlier age than was the case in 1939, and the existence of a large 'teenage' public for extended-play records partly explains why so many 'hit' songs of the post-war period are (by comparison with the best of Gershwin, Cole Porter and Jerome Kern) trite and ephemeral. In the 1920s the audience addressed by the jazz composer was at least supposed to be adult, but, as Peter Stadlen points out, 'In the "pop" song youth prevails.'[1] This may account for the cult of 'classical' jazz among distinguished intellectuals such as Kingsley Amis and Philip Larkin; jazz, as they see it, is an art form which must not be allowed to lose its primitive purity of texture just because its inferior derivatives happen to have become a strong selling line.

VIII

During the last war the subject of music in the post-war world was frequently discussed along with other aspects of planning for the future. In January 1941 the *Musical Times* opened a series of articles on 'Music after the War' with these words: 'For a variety of reasons the public concert has for some years past been losing ground. The greatly increased number of more accessible and less expensive counter-attractions; changes in social customs (e.g. the growth of the week-end habit, which has considerably reduced the Saturday and Sunday concert-going public); the development of broadcasting and the beginning of television; against any one of these factors the concert might have held its own, but together they are steadily becoming too much for it.' Now that television has proved, since its reintroduction after the war, to be the most congenial form of mass communication, it is natural to ask what effect its coming had on musical culture. Allowance must, of course, be made for the transitional period up to about 1950; but in general the answer is: surprisingly little of a radical nature. Television makes use, like the cinema, of a great deal of music, but up to now its tendency has been to reduce concert audiences rather than to empty the concert halls completely. Despite its obvious advantages over sound radio so far as 'immediacy' is concerned, it seems unlikely that television can ever be an adequate substitute for concert conditions, some of which do, after all, come through to the listener on sound radio. The fact that television is a family entertainment imposes restrictions on the permissible length of programmes; but even

[1] Peter Stadlen, 'The Aesthetics of Popular Music' in the *British Journal of Aesthetics*, II (October 1962), p. 361.

if this were not the case, there would be no point in televising long recitals because eventually the purely visual element would give out. Admittedly, the audience in the Wigmore Hall or the Royal Festival Hall is *watching* the artists as they perform; but it is not watching with the same intensity as that called into play by television. From this point of view ballet is a more attractive proposition than abstract music. Even in the best musical pro- grammes the viewer can hardly fail to notice that the producer is constantly forced to create what he considers to be visual signifi- cances (the pianist's rapid finger-work, the calculated move- ments of the tympanist, the leader's bracing up to a solo entry, and so on), but these are not always relevant to our enjoyment of the music. A conductorless orchestra, a one-armed pianist or a bizarre group of soloists may have the charm of novelty: but the fact is that the majority of serious musical compositions are long works that have simply got to be listened to without distraction. Unfortunately for those whose business it is to arrange television programmes, every opera cannot be a gala performance at Covent Garden, and every orchestral concert cannot be a last night at the 'Proms'.

Television would seem, on the face of it, to be the ideal medium for the presentation of opera. In the *B.B.C. Annual* for 1935 Ernest Newman wrote: 'A ten years' evolution of tele- vision of the same character and scope as a ten years' evolution we have witnessed in wireless may well render unnecessary all the new devices of opera construction that were designed to overcome our inability to see the scene and to follow the action.' On sound radio, of course, most of the standard operas broadcast have been abridged and adapted for studio presentation—or, alternatively, a commentator at the opera house has supplied *sotto voce* a discreet account of the stage action. But television gives rise to another problem, that of the close-up. In the case of spoken drama it may well be an advantage if the audience can be given frequent glimpses of the leading actors from only two or three feet away, but this is not necessarily an asset in opera. The operatic music of Mozart, Beethoven and Bellini (to say nothing of Wagner) imposes severe strain on the singers; and it is hardly fair to fix the camera on their vocal organs for long stretches of time. The classical composers all envisaged a situa- tion in which the spectator kept his distance from the stage and, by remaining in his seat throughout the performance, placed the singers—whether as soloists or as members of the chorus—in a constant frame of vision. But on the television screen the viewer is shown images which vary in magnitude, with the result that large ensembles are diminished in size, even though the body of sound may remain full. This is an incongruity which tells against the transmission of operas not specially written for television. Chamber operas such as Haydn's *Apothecary* might well be televised without much alteration, but the crowd scenes in *Tannhäuser* or *Boris Godounov* would seem oddly miniaturized if presented in the normal way. For some viewers, at least, television is hardly likely to prove a suitable medium for the presentation of 'grand' opera, except in selections: this does not preclude, of course, the possibility of a special kind of televised music-drama that would not succeed on the stage.

Yet it would be wrong to suppose that television has nothing of value to offer the serious music-lover. Performances of master works by fine musicians such as Menuhin and Oistrakh are a pronounced success, and small orchestras like the various festival ensembles and the Philomusica of London reveal their special characteristics very well on the television screen. The camera can also provide fascinating insights into unfamiliar aspects of music—instrument-making, the design of automata, the manufacture of gramophone records, etc.—which require visual explanation. Television is at least as effective as sound radio in providing elementary musical instruction, particularly when a first-rate speaker is in charge of the connecting discourse. But musicians themselves are less happy about some of the musical feature programmes given on television. Like many of the musical films, these have tended to play up the emotional lives of certain famous composers or to use music rather ineptly. There is, for example, a great deal of second-rate music which lends itself quite inoffensively to 'background' purposes; but to put on a performance of some established masterpiece and then fill the screen with 'period' photography or travel pictures is surely an abuse of the medium. Television is capable of great disservice to music if it tends—as the cinema frequently does—to persuade viewers that every serious musical composition is programmatic in intention.

On the whole, the case for a large allocation of concert music in the television programmes—even if a greater number of channels were available—is no stronger now than it was in the earliest days of British television. The very limitations of the medium may have strengthened the position of sound radio where chamber and orchestral music are concerned, but as yet there are no indications that television has awakened in large numbers of people a desire to perform their own music or to develop their latent powers of appreciation. This may seem relatively unimportant in view of some other topics discussed in this chapter; but it will perhaps explain why television is of less general consequence to the social historian of music than to students of twentieth-century *mores* in their non-artistic aspects.

Conclusion

THE main intention of this volume has been to suggest the
nature of the non-musical forces (and the aspirations of the individuals caught up in them) which determine why at certain
periods specific kinds of musical activities come into prominence
and others do not. Having surveyed some of the more notable
features of our musical past, we may now ask whether it is possible to discern a significant pattern in the social history of
English music.

Not in the fullest sense, perhaps, until we reach modern times.
But this does not mean that the Middle Ages are of no account in
our scheme of things. It was then, after all, that archetypal forms
and conventions originated, and a body of musical material
evolved which was passed on for later use. Yet before 1500 the
rate of fundamental change was exceedingly slow, and for this
reason the sense of historical perspective is difficult to attain. It
is the rise to maturity of the musical public—together, of course,
with its subsequent fragmentation—which largely determines
the pattern after the Reformation. And this is closely bound up
with the opportunities available for hearing music and for learning to read and perform it. That is why so much of our discussion
has been devoted to musical education; for no one can make
music a part of social life until he or she has been given a chance
to form some kind of 'taste'—which in a complicated society
such as ours will not develop of its own accord.

But in this particular development a special importance
attaches to the eighteenth century, when a large-scale diffusion
of musical knowledge began. In the nineteenth century the
musical instruction of the masses became something of a *cause*

célèbre and as such was affected by the conflicts, sectarian and otherwise, which were associated with the provision of general education. Throughout the Victorian era we find musicians contending with the ingrained Puritanism which lay at the back of middle-class prosperity; and during the subsequent periods music has provided one means of emancipation from this, thanks to events which have been responsible for diminishing Britain's insularity. In the present century it has been said that the performers of popular music are deliberately appealing to the 'lowest common denominator' of public taste. But is this habit, we may ask, a peculiarity of our own time? Could not the same thing be said of the ballad-makers of the eighteenth century, or of the song-writers who supplied the music halls with lachrymose effusions at so much a time? To some extent, certainly. But a great feature of popular music today is the poverty of invention displayed by those who compose it. Some of the most successful 'pop' song writers have been men without any basic feeling for music, apart from the mechanical ability to spin out catchy tunes: and of the countless hit melodies disseminated in the course of a year, not one in a hundred has the character (now seen as 'period charm') of 'Tea for Two' or 'Sonny Boy'. Of late the popular music trade has come to depend on the services of arrangers and ghost-writers of a kind whose powers of fabrication were not required when there were large numbers of traditional melodies to draw on. And this is only another way of saying that as a result of cultural and social changes the old-established practice of handing on received tunes—retained in the memory generation after generation on the strength of their distinctive quality —is falling into abeyance.

Another aspect of our general pattern concerns the relationship which has existed at different times between English musicians and their counterparts in other countries—and this, of course, is bound up with the 'commercial' aspects of composition and performance. Ever since the early Renaissance this question has occupied some part of the musical public's attention: but its effect has differed from one period to another. Here again the eighteenth century is a key period. For without the genius and personal influence of Handel—and to a lesser degree of other composers from Italy, France and Germany—the social history of English music would have been very different. Handelian oratorio appeared at a time when the spiritual condition of England was ready for it, and Handel's idiom was congenial to the understanding both of the *virtuosi* and of an enlightened proletariat. At other periods the presence in our midst of foreign musicians has aroused misgivings, but the contributions made by Mendelssohn, Jullien, Johann Strauss and Gounod have eventually been incorporated into our national musical life. Since the French Revolution *émigrés* of all kinds have found asylum in Britain, and this has had important effects on our musical history —particularly after 1848, 1870, 1914 and 1933. During the Second World War music aided the establishment of cultural relations with the Soviet Union, and since those days it has been a subsidiary means for helping to create solidarity with the United States.

The dangers of foreign competition have been less acute since the autonomy of the musical profession achieved general recognition in England: and it is now true to say that the position of British musicians, music publishers and musical instrument manufacturers is a strong one on the world market. Musical culture, however, has had to accommodate itself to the extraordinary technological achievements which have taken place in the present century. And no social history of music would be complete without some consideration of the developments which have made it possible for every individual to hear some kind of music for a large part of each day in the year.

What, however, of the present situation and possible future developments? This study began with some account of a period in which music was largely functional, and when the personal inclinations of the composer—as expressed in his music—had little significance. Over the last two or three hundred years musicians have been jealously asserting their artistic status, and as music in general has become increasingly complex so the composer and performer have been obliged to adopt a 'specialist' approach to their work. This is partly a result of the wide range of opportunities for professional training now open to musicians and partly a consequence of changes in the habits of day-to-day life in a mechanized society. But in recent years functional music has taken on a new significance. There will always be a demand for 'concert' music (using the term in a sense broad enough to include opera and oratorio): but some of the developments we have already discussed have ensured that no modern composer of calibre can afford to turn up his nose at the purely utilitarian openings confronting him. These may now be considered with reference to the headings used in our first chapter—though in a different order.

Ballroom dancing was never more popular than it is today. But it is unlikely that serious musicians will ever find dance music a suitable outlet for creative talent. It is not that they are unable to produce fox-trots, tangos and quick-steps: but when they do, their efforts turn to parody because the very material from which such music is made does not lend itself to variation and development. To modern dance musicians styles of presentation and executive skill are of greater consequence than melodic originality. Indeed, the standard of ensemble and attack attained by the instrumentalists who work for dance-band leaders such as Victor Sylvester and Geraldo would have astounded rank-and-file musicians of forty years ago—even though the music they are called upon to play is sometimes inferior in quality to the 'Old Tyme' numbers lately resuscitated for the enjoyment of those who have passed their first youth.

The production and distribution of dance music is now an important industry. The same is to some extent true of religious music, since there is a steady demand for hymn books, anthems and voluntaries. But this is a consequence of denominational observance rather than of a widespread appreciation of good hymnody, for in many churches and chapels a small number of tried favourites continues to do duty all the year round. This is not to deny, of course, that an enterprising choirmaster may even now create a situation in which

> some to church repair,
> Not for the doctrine, but the music there,

but in some denominations the musical part of the service is characterized by a peculiar staleness and routine. Recent attempts to render devotional words in the 'pop' song style music must (in spite of clerical sanction) be pronounced a failure. The quip about the devil appropriating all the good tunes may have been fair enough in John Wesley's time, but the associations of 'pop' music are worldly and cynical and so out of place in a setting devoted to serenity and genuflection. Yet despite the fact that

287

religion is no longer at the centre of most people's lives, many modern composers of distinction have produced convincing devotional works, conscious that current modes of worship do not call for the heavy and ostentatious scoring that was in vogue sixty or seventy years ago. But the sacred compositions of men like Rubbra, Britten and Berkeley make their appeal to a somewhat specialized 'concert' audience, rather than to the larger public which has learned to take *Elijah*, Verdi's *Requiem* and *The Dream of Gerontius* in its stride. All the same, the love of 'choralism' still remains a strong trait of the English musical character, and the traditions maintained in the cathedrals and collegiate churches ensure that this will continue to be so.

There remains dramatic or incidental music. And here some important developments have taken place over the last few decades. Writing about the early years of the present century, Sir Adrian Boult asserted that 'The life and the livelihood of every orchestral player was based on the fact that in those days no decent theatre could exist without an orchestra of at least twenty.'[1] Today very few theatres employ orchestras of anything like that size, and most productions of 'straight' plays use canned music exclusively. On the other hand, the cinema, radio and television have created a heavy demand for scores to accompany dramatic action or documentary programmes. In most cases this must of necessity be entirely new music. And here the sound film has been of the first importance: it has shown that under modern conditions acceptable incidental music demands the services of composers who are in full command of their resources and are adept at matching the producer's expertise with a corresponding freshness of musical ideas. Exactly the same thing applies to sound radio and television, and so long as the public supports these two media musical talent of a high order will be needed to supply the musical background.

It would be absurd, of course, to pretend that all the music written for radio productions and televised features is of equal merit. But enough incidental music of high quality comes on the air each week to permit at least one modest speculation. A very high percentage of the listening and viewing public is never likely to see the inside of a concert hall or to gain first-hand experience of music-making. At the same time it is perforce

[1] Foss and Goodwin, eds., *London Symphony: Portrait of an Orchestra*, p. 2.

hearing—along with much else, obviously—musical textures of considerable subtlety: and this fact is something to set against the more disagreeable features of radio mentioned in our last chapter. For although the matter could never be put to an adequate test, it is conceivable that a new 'musical-appreciation' movement is being brought about by means which were undreamt of at an earlier stage. The 'complicated apparatus of amusement' has, as it were, placed in the composer's hands an instrument for influencing taste *from within*: and it may not be too rash to surmise that as a result of social situations which we have witnessed over the last twenty-five years the musical consciousness of the English people is slowly being broadened and intensified. If this *should* happen to be the case, it may well restore the confidence of those who fear a decline in the standards of English musical culture—even though, as is probable, another Golden Age is not now in prospect.

Bibliographical Note

THE following brief reference guide gives some account of the source material drawn upon generally in this study. Such works as Henry Davey's *History of English Music* (1921 ed.), the *Oxford Companion to Music* and Percy Scholes's *List of Books about Music* are, of course, indispensable; but in some ways the earlier editions of Grove's *Dictionary of Music and Musicians* are more valuable to the social historian than is the latest one.

INTRODUCTORY. Of the many recent encyclopedic works which incorporate a good deal of social history, Paul H. Lang's *Music in Western Civilization* (1942) is notable. See also the writings of Rutland Boughton—in particular his *Reality of Music* (1934)—Cyril Scott, Herbert Antcliffe and Frank Howes. The work of Reginald Nettel (*The Englishman Makes Music*, 1952: *Seven Centuries of Popular Song*, 1956) has broken new ground in this field; see also John D. Standen, 'The Place of Music in the History Syllabus' in *History*, XLVIII (October, 1963), pp. 317–31.

I. MUSIC AND SOCIETY IN THE MIDDLE AGES. Special aspects of Anglo-Saxon music are taken up in L. M. Larson, *The King's Household before the Norman Conquest* (Wisconsin, 1904): H. H. Carter, *A Dictionary of Middle English Musical Terms* (Bloomington, Indiana, 1961) draws on the literature of several centuries. Pre-Reformation religious custom is studied in William Maskell, *A Dissertation upon the Ancient Service Books of the Church of England* (1846) and in W. H. Frere's edition of the *Winchester Troper* (1894). R. R. Terry's *Catholic Church Music* (1907) provides a fair introductory survey which can be followed up in the relevant sections of the *New Oxford History of Music*. The musical aspects of the craft plays are discussed by John Stevens in 'Music in Mediaeval Drama' (*Proc. Mus. Ass.*, 1957/8), and minstrelsy is treated in J. J. Jusserand, *English Wayfaring Life in the Middle Ages* (1889). Matthew Hodgart discusses music as well as words in *The Ballads* (1950) and in *The Traditional Games of England . . .* (2 vols., 1894–9) Alice Bertha Gomme traces back many of the older dances which have survived as children's games. Representations of mediaeval instruments occur in F. W. Galpin, *Old*

English Instruments of Music (1910) and Edith K. Prideaux, *The Carvings of Musical Instruments in Exeter Cathedral* (Exeter, 1915).

II. RENAISSANCE, REFORMATION AND THE MUSICAL PUBLIC. Among 'background' studies, A. L. Rowse's *The England of Elizabeth* (1950) and G. R. Elton's *England under the Tudors* (1955) supplement the works already noted. For education see Foster Watson, *The English Grammar Schools to 1660* (1908): Nan Cooke Carpenter, *Music in the Mediaeval and Renaissance Universities* (1958): and M. C. Boyd, *Elizabethan Music and Music Criticism* (new edition, 1962), which is a useful introduction to the whole period. Developments in religious life are covered in Philip Hughes's *The Reformation in England* (3 vols., 1950–4): Charles Wheatly's *Rational Illustration of the Book of Common Prayer* (Cambridge, 1858) and the *New History of the Book of Common Prayer* (1901) by W. H. Frere (after F. Procter). The role of music in Elizabethan drama is discussed in T. W. Baldwin, *The Organisation and Personnel of the Shakespearean Company* (1927): M. C. Bradbrook, *The Rise of the Common Player* (1962): and H. Macaulay Fitzgibbon, 'Instruments and their Music in the Elizabethan Drama' (*Musical Quarterly*, July, 1931). Mid-seventeenth-century musical custom is the subject of 'Music as a Social Force during the English Commonwealth and Restoration (1649–1700)' (*Musical Quarterly*, October, 1929). On the post-Restoration period see W. C. Sydney, *Social Life in England from the Restoration to the Revolution* (1892): Robert Elkin, *The Old Concert Rooms of London* (1955) and Emmett L. Avery, *The London Stage 1660–1800* (1960).

III. THE EIGHTEENTH CENTURY. W. C. Sydney's *England . . . in the Eighteenth Century* (2 vols., 1892) is a fertile source of information, while *Johnson's England* (ed. A. S. Turberville, 1926) is more carefully organized. Opera is the subject of important passages in Charles Gildon's *Life of Betterton* (1710) and Colley Cibber's *Apology for his Life* (1740). On ballad opera in general see E. M. Cagey, *Ballad Opera* (1937): Frank Kidson's *The Beggar's Opera . . .* (1922) and A. V. Berger, 'The Beggar's Opera, the Burlesque, and Italian Opera' (*Music and Letters*, April, 1936). The early pleasure gardens are described in W. B. Boulton, *The Amusements of Old London* (2 vols., 1901) and Mollie Sands, *Invitation to Ranelagh* (1946), the musical side of charity concerns being referred to in Sampson Low, *Charities of London* (1850) and Betsy Rodgers, *Cloak of Charity* (1949). The provincial festivals receive attention in John Crosse, *An Account of the Grand Musical Festival at York* (1825): Joseph Cox Bridge, *A Short Sketch of the Chester Music Festivals* (Chester, n.d.) and J. Sutcliffe Smith, *The Story of Music in Birmingham* (1945). Eighteenth century church music is well characterized by L. E. Elliott-Binns in *The Early Evangelicals* (1953). S. C. Carpenter's work on *Eighteenth Century Church and People* (1959) is also useful for an Anglican point of view, and the Weslyan contribution is discussed in J. T. Lightwood, *Methodist Music in the Eighteenth Century* (1927). One of the best books on English hymnody is Louis F. Benson, *The English Hymn* (1915).

IV. INDUSTRIAL SOCIETY AND THE PEOPLE'S MUSIC. For general discussion see J. H. Whiteley's *Wesley's England* (1938): Neil Smelser, *Social Change in the Industrial Revolution* (1959) and such specialized studies as W. G. Rimmer, *Marshalls of Leeds* (1960) and Frances Collier, 'Samuel Greg and Styal Mill' (*Proc. Manchester Lit. and Phil. Soc.*, 1941/3). A lively account of the popular ballad is given in Leslie Sheppard, *The Broadside Ballad* (1962); John Ashton, *Modern Street Ballads* (1888) also contains useful material. The evolution of the English music-hall is traced by C. D. Stuart and A. J. Park in *The Variety Stage* (1895). Light is thrown on other kinds of working class recreation by J. M. Ludlow and Lloyd Jones, *The Progress of the Working Class* (1867) and Matthew Browne, *Views and Opinions* (1866).

V. THE VICTORIAN ERA: NATIONAL EDUCATION AND MUSICAL PROGRESS. The 'progress' of music in this period is the subject of Thomas Oliphant, *A Short Account of Madrigals* (1836): John Hullah, 'Popular Songs of the Last Half Century' in *Macmillan's Magazine* (XXI, 1869/70): the anonymous 'Victorian Music' (*Musical Times*, June-August 1887): Sir Walter Parratt, 'Music' in T. H. Ward, *The Reign of Queen Victoria* (1887). John Hullah's professional career is discussed in Frank Smith, *The Life and Work of Sir James Kay-Shuttleworth* (1923); the work of John Curwen is shrewdly assessed by J. A. Fuller-Maitland in 'Tonic Sol Fa: Pro and Con' (*Musical Quarterly*, 1921). Choral association is the subject of *United Praise* by F. G. Edwards: the best modern study of the brass band movement is by J. F. Russell and J. H. Boulton (*The Brass Band Movement*, 1936). An account of the musical tradition established at the Crystal Palace is given in Joseph Bennett, *Forty Years of Music* (1908). *British Manufacturing Industries* (ed. G. Phillips Bevan, 1876/77) sums up recent inventions, and *Phases of Musical England* by F. J. Crowest (1881) does justice to the vogue of the pianoforte. This volume also gives an excellent sketch of the 'Gregorian' movement of the period, which is traced in greater detail by Frederick Helmore in his *Memoir of the Rev. T. Helmore* (1891). The autobiographical writings of men like Sir George Grove, John Ella, H. R. Haweis, William Pole, J. W.

Davison and H. F. Chorley are all important. Some idea of the extent of musical journalism can be gathered from *Poole's Index to Periodical Literature*.

VI. FIN DE SIÈCLE: THE ETHOS OF COMPETITIVE ENTERPRISE. An excellent short conspectus of the Edwardian period in music occurs in a review by George Sampson of A. L. Bacharach's *British Music of our Time* (*Music and Letters*, July, 1946). See also R. H. Gretton, *A Modern History of the English People, 1880–1922* (1930): *Fifty Years: Memories and Contrasts* (articles from *The Times*, 1932): *Musical England* by W. J. Galloway (1910) and C. L. Graves, *Post-Victorian Music* (1911). On the subject of German competition see Philip Magnus, *Educational Aims and Efforts* (1910): H. Saxe Wyndham, *August Manns and the Saturday Concerts* (1909), and the reminiscences of Ethel Smyth (in particular *Impressions that Remained*, 1919). The provincial festivals were well reported in the musical Press: but see especially an article on 'The Question of Festivals: A Plea for Continuance' in the *Musical Times* for February, 1919. The musical stage is featured in H. S. Wyndham, *Annals of Covent Garden* (1906): Malcolm Sterling Mackinlay, *Light Opera* (1926) and W. Macqueen-Pope, *Nights of Gladness* (1956). There is an account of the royalty song composers in Percy Scholes's *The Mirror of Music* (I.293): the workings of the pianola are described by G. C. Ashton Jonson (in *Proc. Mus. Ass.*, 1915/16): and the early history of the gramophone is outlined in Roland Gelatt, *The Fabulous Phonograph* (1954).

VII. THE MODERN AGE: MUSICAL CULTURE AND THE VARYING PULSE OF THE MACHINE. For the First World War period see H. C. Colles, 'Music in War-time' (*Proc. Mus. Ass.* 1914/15) and the monthly accounts of professional and non-professional activities in the *Musical Times*. First World War songs are given in F. T. Nettleinghame, *Tommy's Tunes* (1917) and in *Songs and Slang of the British Soldier* (1930) by John Brophy and Eric Partridge. The post-war situation is evoked with particular effectiveness in the short-lived *Musical Mirror*, as also in the *Musical Standard, Musical Opinion* and the writings of W. J. Turner. On the cinema see Kurt London, *Film Music* (1936): Louis Levy, *Music for the Movies* (1936) and Roger Manvell, *The Film and the Public* (1955). Ursula Greville's 'Radio in Britain' (*Musical Quarterly*, April, 1925) and the symposium on 'Broadcasting and the Future of Music' (*Proc. Mus. Ass.* 1926/7) reflect responsible opinion on the development of radio. Sir Compton Mackenzie's paper on 'The Gramophone: Its Past, its Present, its Future' (*Proc. Mus. Ass.*, 1924/5) outlines the position of disc recording up to the time *The Gramophone* first appeared. A comprehensive study of musical appreciation as it relates to the changing school curriculum is to be found in the chapter called 'The End of a Golden String' in R. D. Bramwell, *Elementary School Work 1900–1925* (Institute of Education, University of Durham, 1961). This traces the musical appreciation movement back to its earliest days.

For the 1939–45 period there is excellent material in the *Annual Register* and in the various numbers of *Hinrichsen's Music Year Book*, as well as in more ephemeral publications. In 1947 *The Economist* published (January 11 and 18) two articles on 'The Music Boom'. There is a well-balanced essay on music by Desmond Shawe-Taylor in *The Third Programme. A Symposium of Opinions and Plans* (1946).

CONCLUSION. Ostensibly this study concludes about the year 1950. But *Britain. An Official Handbook* (H.M.S.O., 1962) gives a fair idea of tastes and opinions which had prevailed for some years beforehand. The Penguin book *Music 1950* (ed. Ralph Hill) provides some indication of what serious musicians have been doing since the end of the Second World War. For the light music field, recourse may be had to Peter Gammond and Peter Clayton, *A Guide to Popular Music* (1960). Reports issued by the Arts Council, the National Council for Social Service, the B.B.C. and the television companies make reference to many other aspects of the national musical life.

Index

Abel, K. F., 117
Academy of Ancient Music, 114
Addinsell, Richard, 271–2
Addison, Joseph, 95
Aelred of Rievaulx, 23–24
Agincourt Carol, 46
Albinoni, Tommaso, 107
Albion and Albanius (Grabu), 82
Aldeburgh Festival, 275
Alexandra Palace, 184, 195, 196
Alison, Richard, 68
Allen, Sir Hugh, 248
All the Year Round, 179
Althorpe Park (Northamptonshire), 70
Amalgamated Musicians' Union, 233, 237
Amateur musicians, 10, 89, 258
American competition, 222–8
American organ, 224
Amis, Kingsley, 280
Anatomie of Abuses (Stubbes), 78
Ann Veronica (H. G. Wells), 249
Anthem, 60
Arbeau, Thoinot (pseud. of Jehan Tabourot), 42
Arkwright, G. E. P., 72
Arne, Thomas Augustine, 83, 104, 105, 106, 108, 117, 124, 125
Arnold, Matthew, 12, 43
Arnold, Samuel, 104
'Arrival of the Queen of Sheba, The', 256
Arsinoë (Thomas Clayton), 94
Arts League, 260
Ascham, Roger, 50
Ashwell, Lena, 239
Associated Board, 232
Athenaeum, The, 179
Atlas, The, 179

Augusta Triumphans (Defoe), 101, 110
Avison, Charles, 125

'Bach Bow', 8
Bach, J. C., 7, 89, 117
Bach, J. S., 6, 8
Bacon, Francis, 71
Bacon, Richard Mackenzie, 179
Bacon, Roger, 24
Baines, Edward, 186
Baldwin, William, 53
Balfe, Michael, 189
Balkan Princess, The (Paul Rubens), 228
Ballad (sixteenth century), 76–77
Ballad (late eighteenth and early nineteenth), 133–41
Ballad concerts, 177, 256
Ballad opera, 100
Band of the Garde Republicaine, 214
Banister, John, 83
Barclay, Alexander, 43
Baring-Gould, Sabine, 216, 217
Barnett, Canon Samuel A., 201
Barrow Shipyard Band, 206
Baskervill, C. R., 76
Bates, Joah, 113, 128, 165
Bath (Somerset), 10, 106, 197, 207, 237, 275
B.B.C. Invitation Concerts, 275
Beard, Paul, 276
Beaverbrook, William Maxwell Aitken, Lord, 260
Bede, Venerable, 14
Beethoven, Ludwig van, 6, 215, 226, 255, 274
Bedford, Arthur, 101
Beggar's Opera, The, 99–102
Belgian refugees (First World War), 237